CORVETTE
1984-1987
SHOP MANUAL

ALAN AHLSTRAND
Editor

JEFF ROBINSON
Publisher

CLYMER PUBLICATIONS

World's largest publisher of books
devoted exclusively to automobiles and motorcycles

12860 MUSCATINE STREET • P.O. BOX 4520 • ARLETA, CALIFORNIA 91333-4520

589416
96 7810

FIRST EDITION
First Printing June, 1987

Printed in U.S.A.
ISBN: 0-89287-407-4

Production Coordinators, Janet Long and Dianne Gordon

COVER: Photographed by Michael Brown Photographic Productions, Los Angeles, California.

CONTENTS

CORVETTE
1984-1987
SHOP MANUAL

QUICK REFERENCE DATA

MAINTENANCE SCHEDULE

Every 7,500 miles or 12 months	• **Engine oil** [1] • **Chassis lubrication** • **Check brake system** • **Check exhaust system** • **Check rear axle and manual transmission fluid levels** • **Check/adjust drive belts** • **Check suspension and steering** • **Check throttle linkage**
At 7,500 miles	• **Check throttle body mounting torque (1984)**
At first 7,500 miles, then every 15,000 miles	• **Replace oil filter** • **Check and rotate tires**
At first 7,500 miles, then every 30,000 miles	• **Check throttle body hoses**
Every 15,000 miles	• **Check automatic transmission fluid** [1] • **Check cooling system** [2] • **Replace fuel filter**
Every 30,000 miles	• **Replace spark plugs** • **Change overdrive unit fluid and filter** • **Check ignition timing** • **Check ignition wiring** • **Check PCV system**
Every 30,000 miles or 24 months	• **Drain, flush and refill cooling system**
Every 30,000 miles or 36 months	• **Check air cleaner system operation** • **Replace air cleaner filter** • **Replace crankcase ventilation filter** • **Check EGR system operation**
Every 100,000 miles	• **Change automatic transmission fluid and filter** [1]

1. **SEVERE SERVICE OPERATION: If the vehicle is operated under any of the following conditions, change engine oil @ 3,000 miles or 3 month intervals and oil filter @ alternate oil changes. Clean and regap spark plugs every 6,000 miles. Change automatic transmission fluid and filter every 100,000 miles.**
   a. **Extended idle or low-speed operation (short trips, stop-and-go driving).**
   b. **Trailer towing.**
   c. **Operation @ temperatures below 10° F for 60 days or more with most trips under 10 miles.**
   d. **Very dusty or muddy conditions.**
2. **Check coolant protection and condition once a year.**

APPROXIMATE REFILL CAPACITIES

	qt.	pt.
Engine crankcase*		
With filter change		6.0
Without filter change		5.0
Automatic transmission		
After rebuild		10.0
Fluid change		7.0
Manual transmission		2.0
Overdrive unit		4.0
Differential		4.0
Cooling system	14.5	

***Includes one qt. for oil cooler.**

OIL VISCOSITIES

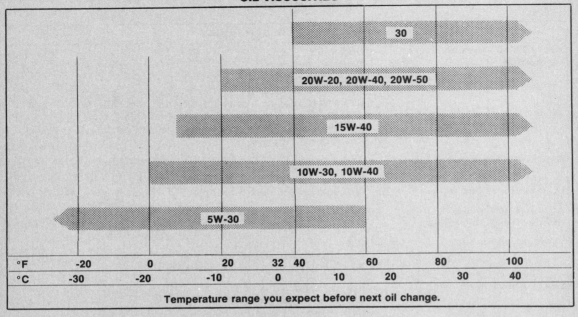

Temperature range you expect before next oil change.

ENGINE SPECIFICATIONS

Type	90° V8
Displacement	350 cid (5.7 liter)
Bore	4.000 in
Stroke	3.480 in
Cylinder arrangement	
Left bank	1-3-5-7
Right bank	2-4-6-8
Firing order	1-8-4-3-6-5-7-2
Cylinder bore	
Maximum out-of-round	0.0020 in.
Maximum taper	
Thrust side	0.0005 in.
Relief side	0.0010 in.
Piston	
Clearance	0.0025-0.0035 in.
Piston rings	
Clearance	
Top	0.0012-0.0032 in.
Bottom	0.0012-0.0032 in.
Oil	0.002-0.007 in.

(continued)

Piston rings (cont.)
  Gap
    Top   0.010-0.020 in.
    Bottom   0.010-0.025 in.
    Oil   0.015-0.055 in.

Piston pin
  Diameter   0.9270-0.9273 in.
  Clearance   0.001 in. max.
  Fit in rod   0.0008-0.0016 in. interference

Crankshaft
  Main journal diameter
    Front   2.4484-2.4493 in.
    Intermediate   2.4481-2.4490 in.
    Rear   2.4479-2.4488 in.
  Main journal taper   0.0010 in. max.
  Main journal out-of-
    round   0.0010 in. max.
  Main bearing clearance
    Front   0.0008-0.0020 in.
    Intermediate   0.0011-0.0023 in.
    Rear   0.0017-0.0032 in.
  End play   0.002-0.006 in.
  Crankpin diameter   2.0986-2.0998 in.
  Crankpin taper   0.001 in. max.
  Crankpin out-of-round   0.001 in. max.
  Rod bearing clearance   0.0013-0.0035 in.
  Rod side clearance   0.008-0.014 in.

Camshaft
  Journal diameter   1.8682-1.8692 in.
  End play   0.004-0.012 in.
  Lobe lift
    Intake   0.2733 in.
    Exhaust   0.2820 in.

Valve system
  Lifter   Hydraulic
  Rocker arm ratio   1.50:1
  Valve lash   One turn down from zero lash
  Face angle
    Intake and exhaust   45°
  Seat angle
    Intake and exhaust   46°
  Seat runout   0.002 in.
  Seat width
    Intake   1/32-1/16 in.
    Exhaust   1/16-1/32 in.
  Stem clearance   0.0010-0.0027 in.
  Valve spring free length   2.03 in.
  Valve spring load
    Intake
      Closed   76-84 lb. @ 1.70 in.
      Open   194-206 lb. @ 1.25 in.
    Exhaust
      Closed   76-84 lb. @ 1.61 in.
      Open   194-206 lb. @ 1.16 in.
    Damper
      Free length   1.86 in.
      Approximate number of coils   4

TIGHTENING TORQUES

Fastener	in.-lb.	ft.-lb.
Camshaft sprocket		20
Clutch pressure plate		30
Connecting rod cap		45
Crankcase front cover	80	
Crankshaft pulley		26-37
Cylinder head bolts		65
Distributor hold-down clamp		25
Engine mount		
To engine		30-44
To mount bracket		21-25
Exhaust manifold		15-24
Flywheel		60
Flywheel housing		30
Flywheel housing cover	80	
Intake manifold		30-35
Intake manifold cover		11-18
Main bearing cap		70-85
Oil filter		25
Oil filter bypass valve	80	
Oil pan		
Attaching bolts		
1/4-20	80	
5/16-18	165	
Drain plug		20
Oil pump		65
Rocker arm stud		50
Spark plug		17-27
Temperature sending unit		20
Thermostat housing		30
Torsional damper		59-81
Valve cover	50	
Water outlet		20
Water pump		30

RECOMMENDED LUBRICANTS

Engine crankcase	API service SF, SF/CC or SF/CD oil
Engine coolant	Ethylene glycol antifreeze meeting GM specification 1825M (part No. 1052753) or equivalent
Brake fluid	Delco Supreme II or other DOT 3 fluid
Power steering pump	GM power steering fluid or equivalent
Manual transmission	SAE 80W or SAE 80W-90 GL-5 gear lubricant
Overdrive unit	DEXRON II or equivalent
Automatic transmission fluid	DEXRON II or equivalent
Rear axle	GM part No. 1052271 and 4 ounces of GM part No. 1052358 or equivalent
Chassis and parking brake cables	Chassis grease meeting GM specification 6031M or equivalent
Shift linkage, hood latch, all hinges	Engine oil
Key lock cylinders	WD-40 or equivalent
Windshield washer	GM Optikleen solvent (part No. 1051515) or equivalent

INTRODUCTION

This detailed, comprehensive manual covers the 1984-1987 Chevrolet Corvette. The expert text gives complete information on maintenance, repair and overhaul. Hundreds of photos and drawings guide you through every step. The book includes all you need to know to keep your Corvette running right.

Where repairs are practical for the owner/mechanic, complete procedures are given. Equally important, difficult jobs are pointed out. Such operations are usually more economically performed by a dealer or independent garage.

Where special tools are required or recommended, the tool numbers are provided. These tools can sometimes be rented from rental dealers, but they can always be purchased from Kent-Moore Tool Division, 28635 Mound Road, Warren, MI 48092.

A shop manual is a reference. You want to be able to find information fast. As in all Clymer books, this one is designed with such in mind. All chapters are thumb-tabbed. Important items are indexed at the rear of the book. All the most frequently used specifications and capacities are summarized on the *Quick Reference Data* pages at the front of the book.

Keep the book handy. Carry it in your glove box. It will help you to better understand your car, lower repair and maintenance costs and generally improve your satisfaction with your Corvette.

CHAPTER ONE

GENERAL INFORMATION

The troubleshooting, tune-up, maintenance, and step-by-step repair procedures in this book are written for the owner and home mechanic. The text is accompanied by useful photos and diagrams to make the job as clear and correct as possible.

Troubleshooting, tune-up, maintenance, and repair are not difficult if you know what tools and equipment to use and what to do. Anyone not afraid to get their hands dirty, of average intelligence, and with some mechanical ability can perform most of the procedures in this book.

In some cases, a repair job may require tools or skills not reasonably expected of the home mechanic. These procedures are noted in each chapter and it is recommended that you take the job to your dealer, a competent mechanic, or machine shop.

MANUAL ORGANIZATION

This chapter provides general information and safety and service hints. Also included are lists of recommended shop and emergency tools as well as a brief description of troubleshooting and tune-up equipment.

Chapter Two provides methods and suggestions for quick and accurate diagnosis and repair of problems. Troubleshooting procedures discuss typical symptoms and logical methods to pinpoint the trouble.

Chapter Three explains all periodic lubrication and routine maintenance necessary to keep your vehicle running well. Chapter Three also includes recommended tune-up procedures, eliminating the need to constantly consult chapters on the various subassemblies.

Subsequent chapters cover specific systems such as the engine, transmission, and electrical systems. Each of these chapters provides disassembly, repair, and assembly procedures in a simple step-by-step format. If a repair requires special skills or tools, or is otherwise impractical for the home mechanic, it is so indicated. In these cases it is usually faster and less expensive to have the repairs made by a dealer or competent repair shop. Necessary specifications concerning a particular system are included at the end of the appropriate chapter.

When special tools are required to perform a procedure included in this manual, the tool is illustrated either in actual use or alone. It may be possible to rent or borrow these tools. The inventive mechanic may also be able to find a suitable substitute in his tool box, or to fabricate one.

The terms NOTE, CAUTION, and WARNING have specific meanings in this manual. A NOTE provides additional or explanatory information. A CAUTION is used to emphasize areas where equipment damage could result if proper precautions are not taken. A WARNING is used to stress those areas where personal injury or death could result from negligence, in addition to possible mechanical damage.

SERVICE HINTS

Observing the following practices will save time, effort, and frustration, as well as prevent possible injury.

Throughout this manual keep in mind two conventions. "Front" refers to the front of the vehicle. The front of any component, such as the transmission, is that end which faces toward the front of the vehicle. The "left" and "right" sides of the vehicle refer to the orientation of a person sitting in the vehicle facing forward. For example, the steering wheel is on the left side. These rules are simple, but even experienced mechanics occasionally become disoriented.

Most of the service procedures covered are straightforward and can be performed by anyone reasonably handy with tools. It is suggested, however, that you consider your own capabilities carefully before attempting any operation involving major disassembly of the engine.

Some operations, for example, require the use of a press. It would be wiser to have these performed by a shop equipped for such work, rather than to try to do the job yourself with makeshift equipment. Other procedures require precision measurements. Unless you have the skills and equipment required, it would be better to have a qualified repair shop make the measurements for you.

Repairs go much faster and easier if the parts that will be worked on are clean before you begin. There are special cleaners for washing the engine and related parts. Brush or spray on the cleaning solution, let it stand, then rinse it away with a garden hose. Clean all oily or greasy parts with cleaning solvent as you remove them.

WARNING
Never use gasoline as a cleaning agent. It presents an extreme fire hazard. Be sure to work in a well-ventilated area when using cleaning solvent. Keep a fire extinguisher, rated for gasoline fires, handy in any case.

Much of the labor charge for repairs made by dealers is for the removal and disassembly of other parts to reach the defective unit. It is frequently possible to perform the preliminary operations yourself and then take the defective unit in to the dealer for repair, at considerable savings.

Once you have decided to tackle the job yourself, make sure you locate the appropriate section in this manual, and read it entirely. Study the illustrations and text until you have a good idea of what is involved in completing the job satisfactorily. If special tools are required, make arrangements to get them before you start. Also, purchase any known defective parts prior to starting on the procedure. It is frustrating and time-consuming to get partially into a job and then be unable to complete it.

Simple wiring checks can be easily made at home, but knowledge of electronics is almost a necessity for performing tests with complicated electronic testing gear.

During disassembly of parts keep a few general cautions in mind. Force is rarely needed to get things apart. If parts are a tight fit, like a bearing in a case, there is usually a tool designed to separate them. Never use a screwdriver to pry apart parts with machined surfaces such as cylinder head and valve cover. You will mar the surfaces and end up with leaks.

Make diagrams wherever similar-appearing parts are found. You may think you can remember where everything came from — but mistakes are costly. There is also the possibility you may get sidetracked and not return to work for days or even weeks — in which interval, carefully laid out parts may have become disturbed.

Tag all similar internal parts for location, and mark all mating parts for position. Record number and thickness of any shims as they are removed. Small parts such as bolts can be identified by placing them in plastic sandwich bags that are sealed and labeled with masking tape.

Wiring should be tagged with masking tape and marked as each wire is removed. Again, do not rely on memory alone.

When working under the vehicle, do not trust a hydraulic or mechanical jack to hold the vehicle up by itself. Always use jackstands. See **Figure 1**.

Disconnect battery ground cable before working near electrical connections and before disconnecting wires. Never run the engine with the battery disconnected; the alternator could be seriously damaged.

Protect finished surfaces from physical damage or corrosion. Keep gasoline and brake fluid off painted surfaces.

Frozen or very tight bolts and screws can often be loosened by soaking with penetrating oil like Liquid Wrench or WD-40, then sharply striking the bolt head a few times with a hammer and punch (or screwdriver for screws). Avoid heat unless absolutely necessary, since it may melt, warp, or remove the temper from many parts.

Avoid flames or sparks when working near a charging battery or flammable liquids, such as brake fluid or gasoline.

No parts, except those assembled with a press fit, require unusual force during assembly. If a part is hard to remove or install, find out why before proceeding.

Cover all openings after removing parts to keep dirt, small tools, etc., from falling in.

When assembling two parts, start all fasteners, then tighten evenly.

The clutch plate, wiring connections, brake shoes, drums, pads, and discs should be kept clean and free of grease and oil.

When assembling parts, be sure all shims and washers are replaced exactly as they came out.

Whenever a rotating part butts against a stationary part, look for a shim or washer. Use new gaskets if there is any doubt about the condition of old ones. Generally, you should apply gasket cement to one mating surface only, so the parts may be easily disassembled in the future. A thin coat of oil on gaskets helps them seal effectively.

Heavy grease can be used to hold small parts in place if they tend to fall out during assembly. However, keep grease and oil away from electrical, clutch, and brake components.

High spots may be sanded off a piston with sandpaper, but emery cloth and oil do a much more professional job.

Carburetors are best cleaned by disassembling them and soaking the parts in a commercial carburetor cleaner. Never soak gaskets and rubber parts in these cleaners. Never use wire to clean out jets and air passages; they are easily damaged. Use compressed air to blow out the carburetor, but only if the float has been removed first.

Take your time and do the job right. Do not forget that a newly rebuilt engine must be broken in the same as a new one. Refer to your owner's manual for the proper break-in procedures.

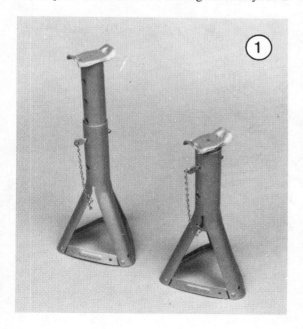

SAFETY FIRST

Professional mechanics can work for years and never sustain a serious injury. If you observe a few rules of common sense and safety, you can enjoy many safe hours servicing your vehicle. You could hurt yourself or damage the vehicle if you ignore these rules.

1. Never use gasoline as a cleaning solvent.

2. Never smoke or use a torch in the vicinity of flammable liquids such as cleaning solvent in open containers.

3. Never smoke or use a torch in an area where batteries are being charged. Highly explosive hydrogen gas is formed during the charging process.

4. Use the proper sized wrenches to avoid damage to nuts and injury to yourself.

5. When loosening a tight or stuck nut, be guided by what would happen if the wrench should slip. Protect yourself accordingly.

6. Keep your work area clean and uncluttered.

7. Wear safety goggles during all operations involving drilling, grinding, or use of a cold chisel.

8. Never use worn tools.

9. Keep a fire extinguisher handy and be sure it is rated for gasoline (Class B) and electrical (Class C) fires.

EXPENDABLE SUPPLIES

Certain expendable supplies are necessary. These include grease, oil, gasket cement, wiping rags, cleaning solvent, and distilled water.

Also, special locking compounds, silicone lubricants, and engine cleaners may be useful. Cleaning solvent is available at most service stations and distilled water for the battery is available at most supermarkets.

SHOP TOOLS

For proper servicing, you will need an assortment of ordinary hand tools (**Figure 2**).

As a minimum, these include:

a. Combination wrenches
b. Sockets
c. Plastic mallet
d. Small hammer
e. Snap ring pliers
f. Gas pliers
g. Phillips screwdrivers
h. Slot (common) screwdrivers
i. Feeler gauges
j. Spark plug gauge
k. Spark plug wrench

Special tools necessary are shown in the chapters covering the particular repair in which they are used.

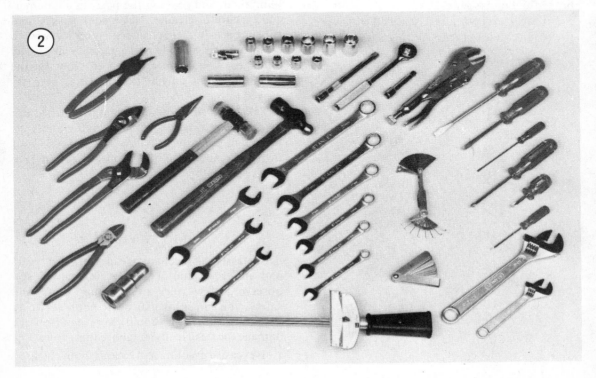

Engine tune-up and troubleshooting procedures require other special tools and equipment. These are described in detail in the following sections.

EMERGENCY TOOL KIT

A small emergency tool kit kept in the trunk is handy for road emergencies which otherwise could leave you stranded. The tools listed below and shown in **Figure 3** will let you handle most roadside repairs.

a. Combination wrenches

b. Crescent (adjustable) wrench

c. Screwdrivers — common and Phillips

d. Pliers — conventional (gas) and needle nose

e. Vise Grips

f. Hammer — plastic and metal

g. Small container of waterless hand cleaner

h. Rags for clean up

i. Silver waterproof sealing tape (duct tape)

j. Flashlight

k. Emergency road flares — at least four

l. Spare drive belts (water pump, alternator, etc.)

TROUBLESHOOTING AND TUNE-UP EQUIPMENT

Voltmeter, Ohmmeter, and Ammeter

For testing the ignition or electrical system, a good voltmeter is required. For automotive use, an instrument covering 0-20 volts is satisfac-

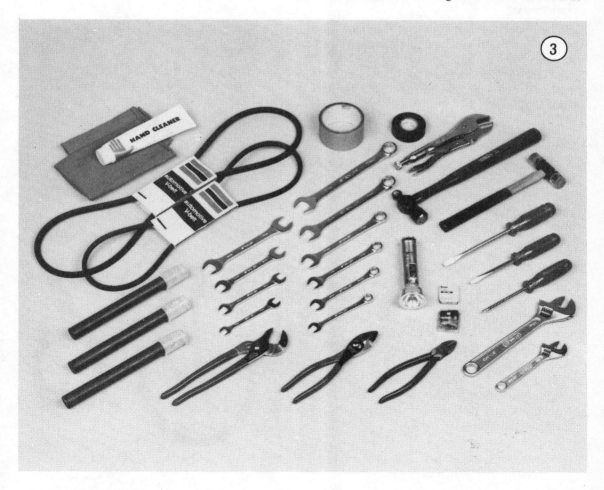

tory. One which also has a 0-2 volt scale is necessary for testing relays, points, or individual contacts where voltage drops are much smaller. Accuracy should be ± ½ volt.

An ohmmeter measures electrical resistance. This instrument is useful for checking continuity (open and short circuits), and testing fuses and lights.

The ammeter measures electrical current. Ammeters for automotive use should cover 0-50 amperes and 0-250 amperes. These are useful for checking battery charging and starting current.

Several inexpensive VOM's (volt-ohm-milliammeter) combine all three instruments into one which fits easily in any tool box. See **Figure 4**. However, the ammeter ranges are usually too small for automotive work.

Hydrometer

The hydrometer gives a useful indication of battery condition and charge by measuring the specific gravity of the electrolyte in each cell. See **Figure 5**. Complete details on use and interpretation of readings are provided in the electrical chapter.

Compression Tester

The compression tester measures the compression pressure built up in each cylinder. The results, when properly interpreted, can indicate general cylinder and valve condition. See **Figure 6**.

Vacuum Gauge

The vacuum gauge (**Figure 7**) is one of the easiest instruments to use, but one of the most difficult for the inexperienced mechanic to interpret. The results, when interpreted with other findings, can provide valuable clues to possible trouble.

To use the vacuum gauge, connect it to a vacuum hose that goes to the intake manifold. Attach it either directly to the hose or to a T-fitting installed into the hose.

NOTE: *Subtract one inch from the reading for every 1,000 ft. elevation.*

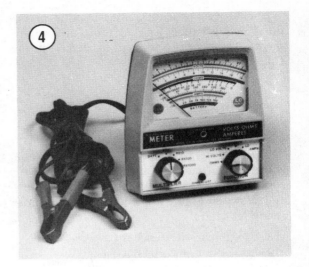

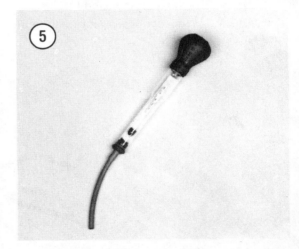

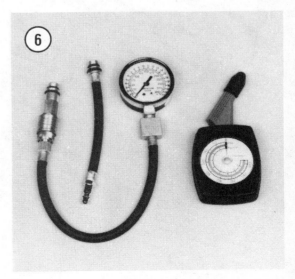

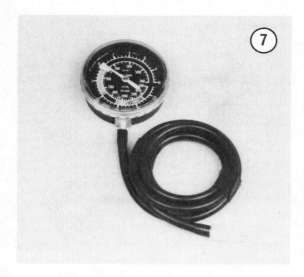

Fuel Pressure Gauge

This instrument is invaluable for evaluating fuel pump performance. Fuel system troubleshooting procedures in this manual use a fuel pressure gauge. Usually a vacuum gauge and fuel pressure gauge are combined.

Dwell Meter (Contact Breaker Point Ignition Only)

A dwell meter measures the distance in degrees of cam rotation that the breaker points remain closed while the engine is running. Since this angle is determined by breaker point gap, dwell angle is an accurate indication of breaker point gap.

Many tachometers intended for tuning and testing incorporate a dwell meter as well. See **Figure 8**. Follow the manufacturer's instructions to measure dwell.

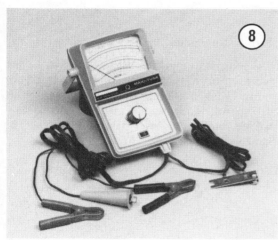

Tachometer

A tachometer is necessary for tuning. See **Figure 8**. Ignition timing and carburetor adjustments must be performed at the specified idle speed. The best instrument for this purpose is one with a low range of 0-1,000 or 0-2,000 rpm for setting idle, and a high range of 0-4,000 or more for setting ignition timing at 3,000 rpm. Extended range (0-6,000 or 0-8,000 rpm) instruments lack accuracy at lower speeds. The instrument should be capable of detecting changes of 25 rpm on the low range.

Strobe Timing Light

This instrument is necessary for tuning, as it permits very accurate ignition timing. The light flashes at precisely the same instant that No. 1 cylinder fires, at which time the timing marks on the engine should align. Refer to Chapter Three for exact location of the timing marks for your engine.

Suitable lights range from inexpensive neon bulb types ($2-3) to powerful xenon strobe lights ($20-40). See **Figure 9**. Neon timing lights are difficult to see and must be used in dimly lit areas. Xenon strobe timing lights can be used outside in bright sunlight. Both types work on this vehicle; use according to the manufacturer's instructions.

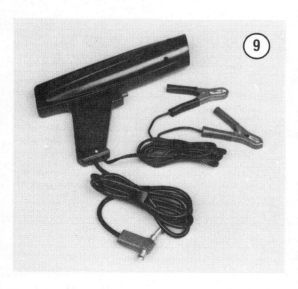

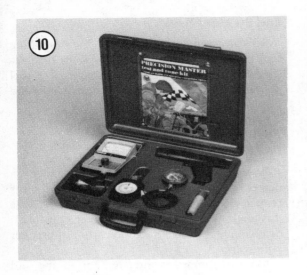

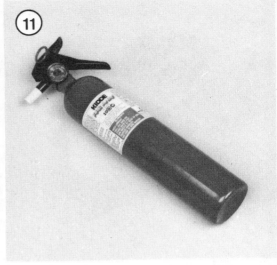

Tune-up Kits

Many manufacturer's offer kits that combine several useful instruments. Some come in a convenient carry case and are usally less expensive than purchasing one instrument at a time. **Figure 10** shows one of the kits that is available. The prices vary with the number of instruments included in the kit.

Fire Extinguisher

A fire extinguisher is a necessity when working on a vehicle. It should be rated for both *Class B* (flammable liquids—gasoline, oil, paint, etc.) and *Class C* (electrical—wiring, etc.) type fires. It should always be kept within reach. See **Figure 11**.

CHAPTER TWO

TROUBLESHOOTING

Troubleshooting can be a relatively simple matter if it is done logically. The first step in any troubleshooting procedure must be defining the symptoms as closely as possible. Subsequent steps involve testing and analyzing areas which could cause the symptoms. A haphazard approach may eventually find the trouble, but in terms of wasted time and unnecessary parts replacement, it can be very costly.

The troubleshooting procedures in this chapter analyze typical symptoms and show logical methods of isolation. These are not the only methods. There may be several approaches to a problem, but all methods must have one thing in common — a logical, systematic approach.

STARTING SYSTEM

The starting system consists of the starter motor and the starter solenoid. The ignition key controls the starter solenoid, which mechanically engages the starter with the engine flywheel, and supplies electrical current to turn the starter motor.

Starting system troubles are relatively easy to find. In most cases, the trouble is a loose or dirty electrical connection. **Figures 1 and 2** provide routines for finding the trouble.

CHARGING SYSTEM

The charging system consists of the alternator (or generator on older vehicles), voltage regulator, and battery. A drive belt driven by the engine crankshaft turns the alternator which produces electrical energy to charge the battery. As engine speed varies, the voltage from the alternator varies. A voltage regulator controls the charging current to the battery and maintains the voltage to the vehicle's electrical system at safe levels. A warning light or gauge on the instrument panel signals the driver when charging is not taking place. Refer to **Figure 3** for a typical charging system.

Complete troubleshooting of the charging system requires test equipment and skills which the average home mechanic does not possess. However, there are a few tests which can be done to pinpoint most troubles.

Charging system trouble may stem from a defective alternator (or generator), voltage regulator, battery, or drive belt. It may also be caused by something as simple as incorrect drive belt tension. The following are symptoms of typical problems you may encounter.

1. *Battery dies frequently, even though the warning lamp indicates no discharge* — This can be caused by a drive belt that is slightly too

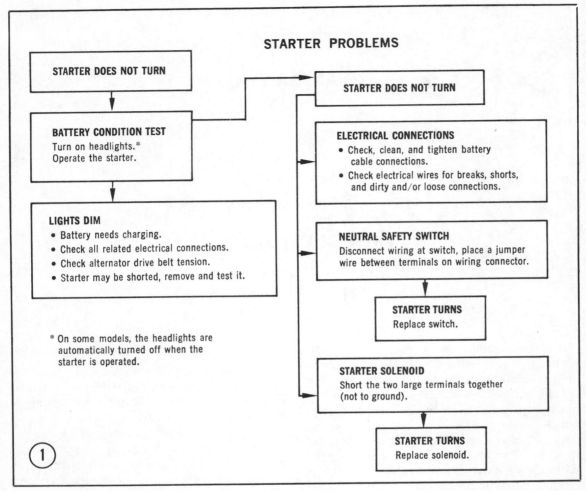

STARTER PROBLEMS

STARTER DOES NOT TURN

BATTERY CONDITION TEST
Turn on headlights.*
Operate the starter.

LIGHTS DIM
- Battery needs charging.
- Check all related electrical connections.
- Check alternator drive belt tension.
- Starter may be shorted, remove and test it.

* On some models, the headlights are
automatically turned off when the
starter is operated.

STARTER DOES NOT TURN

ELECTRICAL CONNECTIONS
- Check, clean, and tighten battery
  cable connections.
- Check electrical wires for breaks, shorts,
  and dirty and/or loose connections.

NEUTRAL SAFETY SWITCH
Disconnect wiring at switch, place a jumper
wire between terminals on wiring connector.

STARTER TURNS
Replace switch.

STARTER SOLENOID
Short the two large terminals together
(not to ground).

STARTER TURNS
Replace solenoid.

①

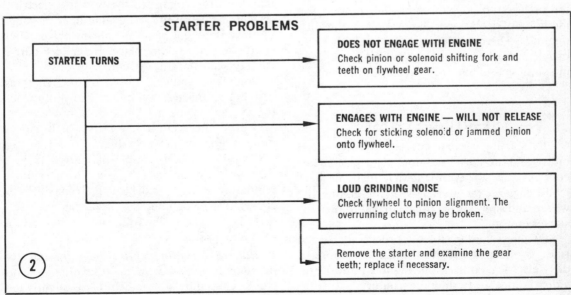

STARTER PROBLEMS

STARTER TURNS

DOES NOT ENGAGE WITH ENGINE
Check pinion or solenoid shifting fork and
teeth on flywheel gear.

ENGAGES WITH ENGINE — WILL NOT RELEASE
Check for sticking solenoid or jammed pinion
onto flywheel.

LOUD GRINDING NOISE
Check flywheel to pinion alignment. The
overrunning clutch may be broken.

Remove the starter and examine the gear
teeth; replace if necessary.

②

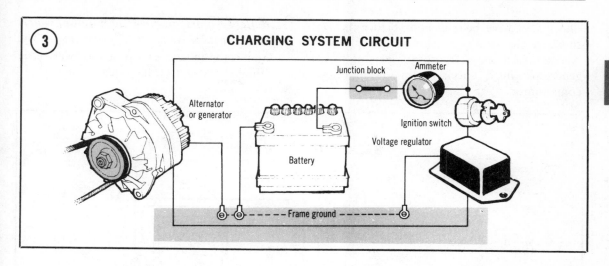

③ CHARGING SYSTEM CIRCUIT

Junction block · Ammeter · Alternator or generator · Ignition switch · Voltage regulator · Battery · Frame ground

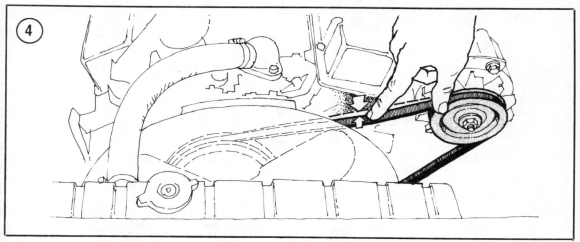

④

loose. Grasp the alternator (or generator) pulley and try to turn it. If the pulley can be turned without moving the belt, the drive belt is too loose. As a rule, keep the belt tight enough that it can be deflected about ½ in. under moderate thumb pressure between the pulleys (**Figure 4**). The battery may also be at fault; test the battery condition.

2. *Charging system warning lamp does not come on when ignition switch is turned on* — This may indicate a defective ignition switch, battery, voltage regulator, or lamp. First try to start the vehicle. If it doesn't start, check the ignition switch and battery. If the car starts, remove the warning lamp; test it for continuity with an ohmmeter or substitute a new lamp. If the lamp is good, locate the voltage regulator

and make sure it is properly grounded (try tightening the mounting screws). Also the alternator (or generator) brushes may not be making contact. Test the alternator (or generator) and voltage regulator.

3. *Alternator (or generator) warning lamp comes on and stays on* — This usually indicates that no charging is taking place. First check drive belt tension (**Figure 4**). Then check battery condition, and check all wiring connections in the charging system. If this does not locate the trouble, check the alternator (or generator) and voltage regulator.

4. *Charging system warning lamp flashes on and off intermittently* — This usually indicates the charging system is working intermittently.

Check the drive belt tension (**Figure 4**), and check all electrical connections in the charging system. Check the alternator (or generator). *On generators only*, check the condition of the commutator.

5. *Battery requires frequent additions of water, or lamps require frequent replacement* — The alternator (or generator) is probably overcharging the battery. The voltage regulator is probably at fault.

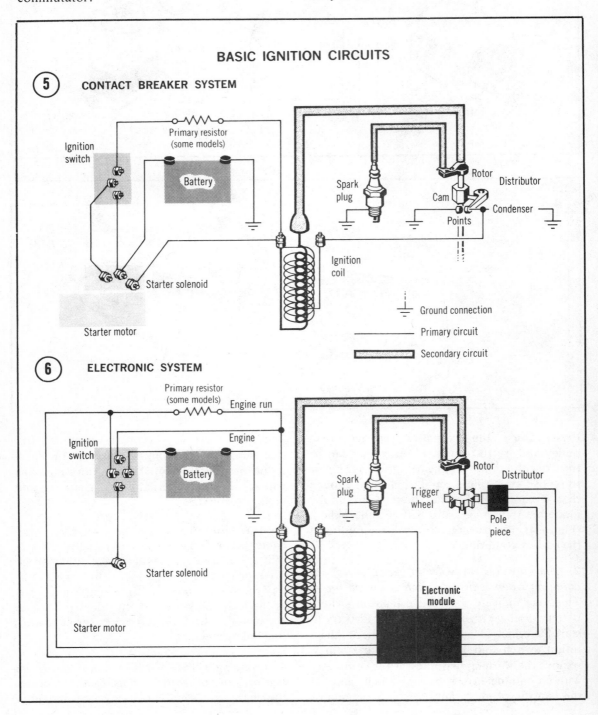

BASIC IGNITION CIRCUITS

5 CONTACT BREAKER SYSTEM

Ignition switch

Primary resistor (some models)

Battery

Starter solenoid

Starter motor

Spark plug

Cam

Points

Rotor

Distributor

Condenser

Ignition coil

Ground connection
Primary circuit
Secondary circuit

6 ELECTRONIC SYSTEM

Primary resistor (some models)

Engine run

Engine

Ignition switch

Battery

Starter solenoid

Starter motor

Spark plug

Trigger wheel

Rotor

Distributor

Pole piece

Electronic module

6. *Excessive noise from the alternator (or generator)* — Check for loose mounting brackets and bolts. The problem may also be worn bearings or the need of lubrication in some cases. If an alternator whines, a shorted diode may be indicated.

IGNITION SYSTEM

The ignition system may be either a conventional contact breaker type or an electronic ignition. See electrical chapter to determine which type you have. **Figures 5 and 6** show simplified diagrams of each type.

Most problems involving failure to start, poor performance, or rough running stem from trouble in the ignition system, particularly in contact breaker systems. Many novice troubleshooters get into trouble when they assume that these symptoms point to tne fuel system instead of the ignition system.

Ignition system troubles may be roughly divided between those affecting only one cylinder and those affecting all cylinders. If the trouble affects only one cylinder, it can only be in the spark plug, spark plug wire, or portion of the distributor associated with that cylinder. If the trouble affects all cylinders (weak spark or no spark), then the trouble is in the ignition coil, rotor, distributor, or associated wiring.

The troubleshooting procedures outlined in **Figure 7** (breaker point ignition) or **Figure 8**

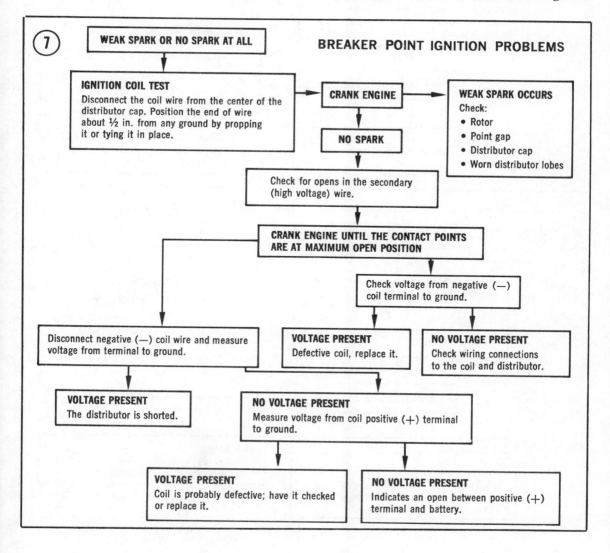

(electronic ignition) will help you isolate ignition problems fast. Of course, they assume that the battery is in good enough condition to crank the engine over at its normal rate.

ENGINE PERFORMANCE

A number of factors can make the engine difficult or impossible to start, or cause rough running, poor performance and so on. The majority of novice troubleshooters immediately suspect the carburetor or fuel injection system. In the majority of cases, though, the trouble exists in the ignition system.

The troubleshooting procedures outlined in **Figures 9 through 14** will help you solve the majority of engine starting troubles in a systematic manner.

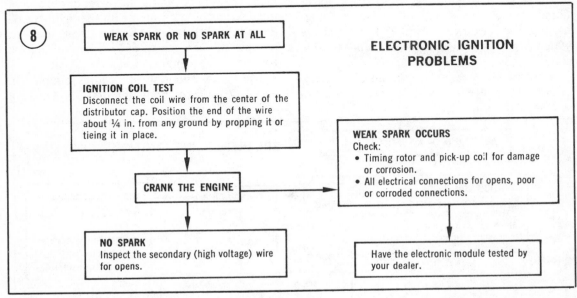

(8) **WEAK SPARK OR NO SPARK AT ALL**

ELECTRONIC IGNITION PROBLEMS

IGNITION COIL TEST
Disconnect the coil wire from the center of the distributor cap. Position the end of the wire about ¼ in. from any ground by propping it or tieing it in place.

CRANK THE ENGINE

WEAK SPARK OCCURS
Check:
• Timing rotor and pick-up coil for damage or corrosion.
• All electrical connections for opens, poor or corroded connections.

NO SPARK
Inspect the secondary (high voltage) wire for opens.

Have the electronic module tested by your dealer.

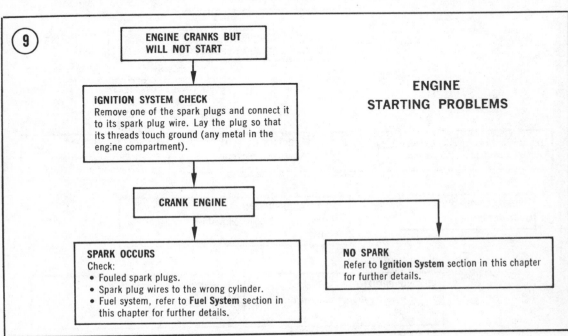

(9) **ENGINE CRANKS BUT WILL NOT START**

ENGINE STARTING PROBLEMS

IGNITION SYSTEM CHECK
Remove one of the spark plugs and connect it to its spark plug wire. Lay the plug so that its threads touch ground (any metal in the engine compartment).

CRANK ENGINE

SPARK OCCURS
Check:
• Fouled spark plugs.
• Spark plug wires to the wrong cylinder.
• Fuel system, refer to **Fuel System** section in this chapter for further details.

NO SPARK
Refer to **Ignition System** section in this chapter for further details.

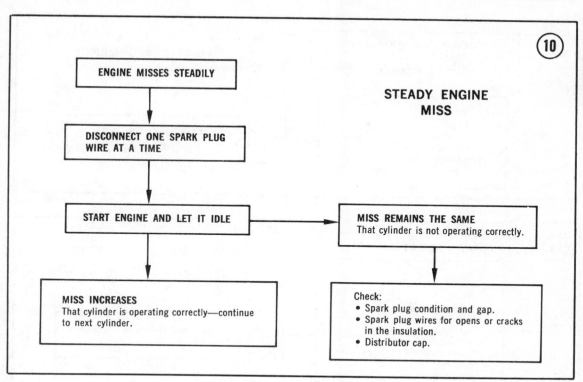

⑩

ENGINE MISSES STEADILY

STEADY ENGINE
MISS

DISCONNECT ONE SPARK PLUG
WIRE AT A TIME

START ENGINE AND LET IT IDLE → MISS REMAINS THE SAME
That cylinder is not operating correctly.

MISS INCREASES
That cylinder is operating correctly—continue
to next cylinder.

Check:
• Spark plug condition and gap.
• Spark plug wires for opens or cracks
  in the insulation.
• Distributor cap.

2

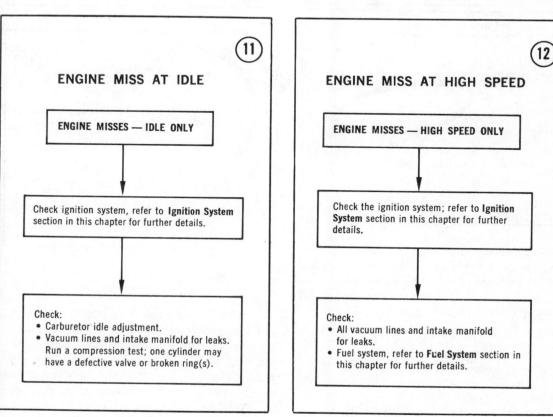

⑪

ENGINE MISS AT IDLE

ENGINE MISSES — IDLE ONLY

Check ignition system, refer to **Ignition System**
section in this chapter for further details.

Check:
• Carburetor idle adjustment.
• Vacuum lines and intake manifold for leaks.
  Run a compression test; one cylinder may
  have a defective valve or broken ring(s).

⑫

ENGINE MISS AT HIGH SPEED

ENGINE MISSES — HIGH SPEED ONLY

Check the ignition system; refer to **Ignition
System** section in this chapter for further
details.

Check:
• All vacuum lines and intake manifold
  for leaks.
• Fuel system, refer to **Fuel System** section in
  this chapter for further details.

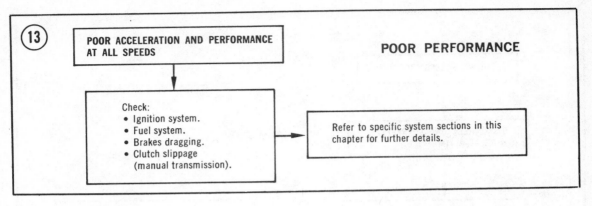

⑬ POOR ACCELERATION AND PERFORMANCE AT ALL SPEEDS

POOR PERFORMANCE

Check:
• Ignition system.
• Fuel system.
• Brakes dragging.
• Clutch slippage (manual transmission).

Refer to specific system sections in this chapter for further details.

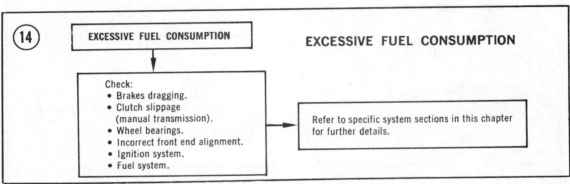

⑭ EXCESSIVE FUEL CONSUMPTION

EXCESSIVE FUEL CONSUMPTION

Check:
• Brakes dragging.
• Clutch slippage (manual transmission).
• Wheel bearings.
• Incorrect front end alignment.
• Ignition system.
• Fuel system.

Refer to specific system sections in this chapter for further details.

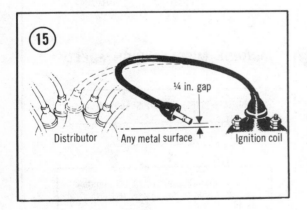

⑮ ¼ in. gap

Distributor   Any metal surface   Ignition coil

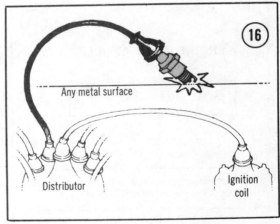

⑯ Any metal surface

Distributor   Ignition coil

Some tests of the ignition system require running the engine with a spark plug or ignition coil wire disconnected. The safest way to do this is to disconnect the wire with the engine stopped, then prop the end of the wire next to a metal surface as shown in **Figures 15 and 16.**

WARNING
Never disconnect a spark plug or ignition coil wire while the engine is running. The high voltage in an ignition system, particularly the newer high- *energy electronic ignition systems could cause serious injury or even death.*

Spark plug condition is an important indication of engine performance. Spark plugs in a properly operating engine will have slightly pitted electrodes, and a light tan insulator tip. **Figure 17** shows a normal plug, and a number of others which indicate trouble in their respective cylinders.

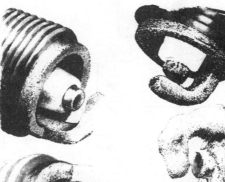

- Appearance—Firing tip has deposits of light gray to light tan.
- Can be cleaned, regapped and reused.

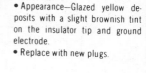

- Appearance—Glazed yellow deposits with a slight brownish tint on the insulator tip and ground electrode.
- Replace with new plugs.

- Appearance—Dull, dry black with fluffy carbon deposits on the insulator tip, electrode and exposed shell.
- Caused by—Fuel/air mixture too rich, plug heat range too cold, weak ignition system, dirty air cleaner, faulty automatic choke or excessive idling.
- Can be cleaned, regapped and reused.

- Appearance — Brown colored hardened ash deposits on the insulator tip and ground electrode.
- Caused by—Fuel and/or oil additives.
- Replace with new plugs.

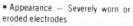

- Appearance—Wet black deposits on insulator and exposed shell.
- Caused by—Excessive oil entering the combustion chamber through worn rings, pistons, valve guides or bearings.
- Replace with new plugs (use a hotter plug if engine is not repaired).

- Appearance — Severely worn or eroded electrodes.
- Caused by—Normal wear or unusual oil and/or fuel additives.
- Replace with new plugs.

- Appearance — Melted ground electrode.
- Caused by—Overadvanced ignition timing, inoperative ignition advance mechanism, too low of a fuel octane rating, lean fuel/air mixture or carbon deposits in combustion chamber.

- Appearance — Yellow insulator deposits (may sometimes be dark gray, black or tan in color) on the insulator tip.
- Caused by—Highly leaded gasoline.
- Replace with new plugs.

- Appearance—Melted center electrode.
- Caused by—Abnormal combustion due to overadvanced ignition timing or incorrect advance, too low of a fuel octane rating, lean fuel/air mixture, or carbon deposits in combustion chamber.
- Correct engine problem and replace with new plugs.

- Appearance—Yellow glazed deposits indicating melted lead deposits due to hard acceleration.
- Caused by—Highly leaded gasoline.
- Replace with new plugs.

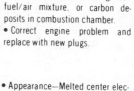

- Appearance—Melted center electrode and white blistered insulator tip.
- Caused by—Incorrect plug heat range selection.
- Replace with new plugs

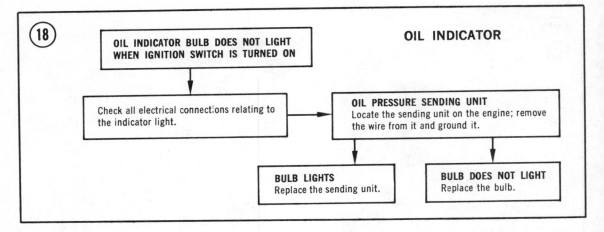

ENGINE OIL
PRESSURE LIGHT

Proper oil pressure to the engine is vital. If oil pressure is insufficient, the engine can destroy itself in a comparatively short time.

The oil pressure warning circuit monitors oil pressure constantly. If pressure drops below a predetermined level, the light comes on.

Obviously, it is vital for the warning circuit to be working to signal low oil pressure. Each time you turn on the ignition, but before you start the car, the warning light should come on. If it doesn't, there is trouble in the warning circuit, not the oil pressure system. See **Figure 18** to troubleshoot the warning circuit.

Once the engine is running, the warning light should stay off. If the warning light comes on or acts erratically while the engine is running there is trouble with the engine oil pressure system. *Stop the engine immediately.* Refer to **Figure 19** for possible causes of the problem.

FUEL SYSTEM
(CARBURETTED)

Fuel system problems must be isolated to the fuel pump (mechanical or electric), fuel lines, fuel filter, or carburetor. These procedures assume the ignition system is working properly and is correctly adjusted.

1. *Engine will not start* — First make sure that fuel is being delivered to the carburetor. Remove the air cleaner, look into the carburetor throat, and operate the accelerator

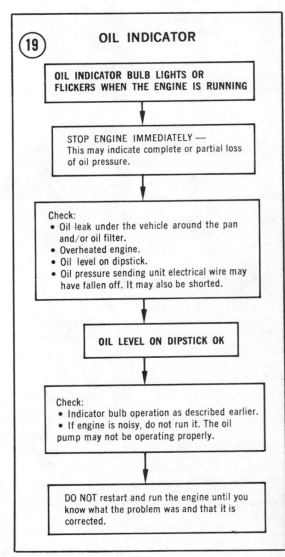

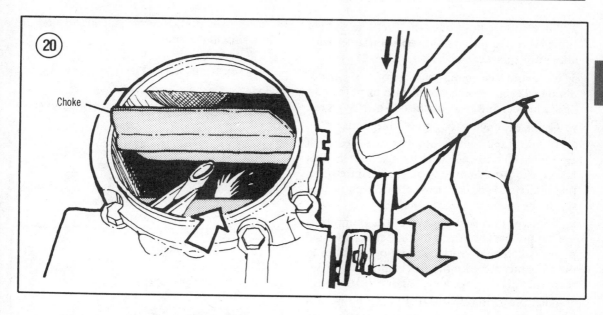

linkage several times. There should be a stream of fuel from the accelerator pump discharge tube each time the accelerator linkage is depressed (**Figure 20**). If not, check fuel pump delivery (described later), float valve, and float adjustment. If the engine will not start, check the automatic choke parts for sticking or damage. If necessary, rebuild or replace the carburetor.

2. *Engine runs at fast idle* — Check the choke setting. Check the idle speed, idle mixture, and decel valve (if equipped) adjustment.

3. *Rough idle or engine miss with frequent stalling* — Check idle mixture and idle speed adjustments.

4. *Engine "diesels" (continues to run) when ignition is switched off* — Check idle mixture (probably too rich), ignition timing, and idle speed (probably too fast). Check the throttle solenoid (if equipped) for proper operation. Check for overheated engine.

5. *Stumbling when accelerating from idle* — Check the idle speed and mixture adjustments. Check the accelerator pump.

6. *Engine misses at high speed or lacks power* — This indicates possible fuel starvation. Check fuel pump pressure and capacity as described in this chapter. Check float needle valves. Check for a clogged fuel filter or air cleaner.

7. *Black exhaust smoke* — This indicates a badly overrich mixture. Check idle mixture and idle speed adjustment. Check choke setting. Check for excessive fuel pump pressure, leaky floats, or worn needle valves.

8. *Excessive fuel consumption* — Check for overrich mixture. Make sure choke mechanism works properly. Check idle mixture and idle speed. Check for excessive fuel pump pressure, leaky floats, or worn float needle valves.

FUEL SYSTEM (FUEL INJECTED)

Troubleshooting a fuel injection system requires more thought, experience, and know-how than any other part of the vehicle. A logical approach and proper test equipment are essential in order to successfully find and fix these troubles.

It is best to leave fuel injection troubles to your dealer. In order to isolate a problem to the injection system make sure that the fuel pump is operating properly. Check its performance as described later in this section. Also make sure that fuel filter and air cleaner are not clogged.

FUEL PUMP TEST (MECHANICAL AND ELECTRIC)

1. Disconnect the fuel inlet line where it enters the carburetor or fuel injection system.

2. Fit a rubber hose over the fuel line so fuel can be directed into a graduated container with about one quart capacity. See **Figure 21**.

3. To avoid accidental starting of the engine, disconnect the secondary coil wire from the coil or disconnect and insulate the coil primary wire.

4. Crank the engine for about 30 seconds.

5. If the fuel pump supplies the specified amount (refer to the fuel chapter later in this book), the trouble may be in the carburetor or fuel injection system. The fuel injection system should be tested by your dealer.

6. If there is no fuel present or the pump cannot supply the specified amount, either the fuel pump is defective or there is an obstruction in the fuel line. Replace the fuel pump and/or inspect the fuel lines for air leaks or obstructions.

7. Also pressure test the fuel pump by installing a T-fitting in the fuel line between the fuel pump and the carburetor. Connect a fuel pressure gauge to the fitting with a short tube (**Figure 22**).

8. Reconnect the coil wire, start the engine, and record the pressure. Refer to the fuel chapter later in this book for the correct pressure. If the pressure varies from that specified, the pump should be replaced.

9. Stop the engine. The pressure should drop off very slowly. If it drops off rapidly, the outlet valve in the pump is leaking and the pump should be replaced.

EMISSION CONTROL SYSTEMS

Major emission control systems used on nearly all U.S. models include the following:

a. Positive crankcase ventilation (PCV)

b. Thermostatic air cleaner

c. Air injection reaction (AIR)

d. Fuel evaporation control

e. Exhaust gas recirculation (EGR)

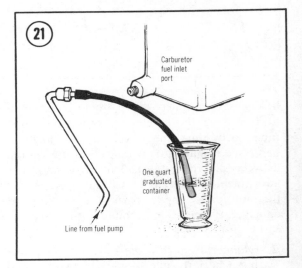

Carburetor fuel inlet port

One quart graduated container

Line from fuel pump

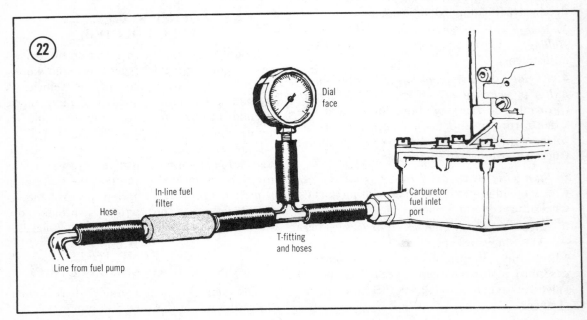

Dial face

In-line fuel filter

Hose

Carburetor fuel inlet port

T-fitting and hoses

Line from fuel pump

Emission control systems vary considerably from model to model. Individual models contain variations of the four systems described here. In addition, they may include other special systems. Use the index to find specific emission control components in other chapters.

Many of the systems and components are factory set and sealed. Without special expensive test equipment, it is impossible to adjust the systems to meet state and federal requirements.

Troubleshooting can also be difficult without special equipment. The procedures described below will help you find emission control parts which have failed, but repairs may have to be entrusted to a dealer or other properly equipped repair shop.

With the proper equipment, you can test the carbon monoxide and hydrocarbon levels.

Figure 23 provides some sources of trouble if the readings are not correct.

Positive Crankcase Ventilation

Fresh air drawn from the air cleaner housing scavenges emissions (e.g., piston blow-by) from the crankcase, then the intake manifold vacuum draws emissions into the intake manifold. They can then be reburned in the normal combustion process. **Figure 24** shows a typical system. **Figure 25** provides a testing procedure.

Thermostatic Air Cleaner

The thermostatically controlled air cleaner maintains incoming air to the engine at a predetermined level, usually about 100°F or higher. It mixes cold air with heated air from the exhaust manifold region. The air cleaner in-

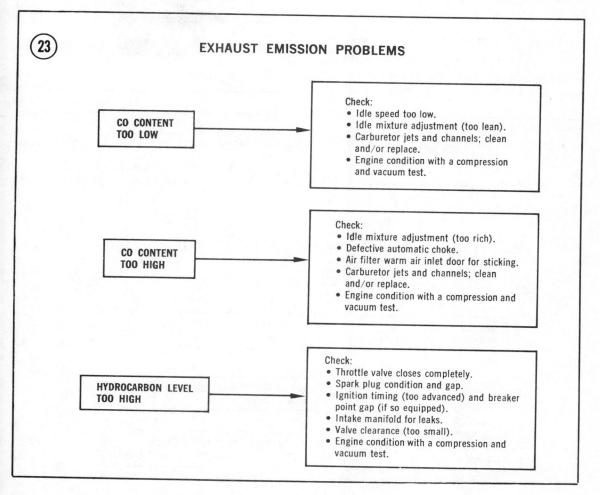

(23) **EXHAUST EMISSION PROBLEMS**

CO CONTENT TOO LOW →
Check:
• Idle speed too low.
• Idle mixture adjustment (too lean).
• Carburetor jets and channels; clean and/or replace.
• Engine condition with a compression and vacuum test.

CO CONTENT TOO HIGH →
Check:
• Idle mixture adjustment (too rich).
• Defective automatic choke.
• Air filter warm air inlet door for sticking.
• Carburetor jets and channels; clean and/or replace.
• Engine condition with a compression and vacuum test.

HYDROCARBON LEVEL TOO HIGH →
Check:
• Throttle valve closes completely.
• Spark plug condition and gap.
• Ignition timing (too advanced) and breaker point gap (if so equipped).
• Intake manifold for leaks.
• Valve clearance (too small).
• Engine condition with a compression and vacuum test.

cludes a temperature sensor, vacuum motor, and a hinged door. See **Figure 26**.

The system is comparatively easy to test. See **Figure 27** for the procedure.

Air Injection Reaction System

The air injection reaction system reduces air pollution by oxidizing hydrocarbons and carbon monoxide as they leave the combustion chamber. See **Figure 28**.

The air injection pump, driven by the engine, compresses filtered air and injects it at the exhaust port of each cylinder. The fresh air mixes with the unburned gases in the exhaust and promotes further burning. A check valve prevents exhaust gases from entering and damaging the air pump if the pump becomes inoperative, e.g., from a fan belt failure.

Figure 29 explains the testing procedure for this system.

Fuel Evaporation Control

Fuel vapor from the fuel tank passes through the liquid/vapor separator to the carbon canister. See **Figure 30**. The carbon absorbs and

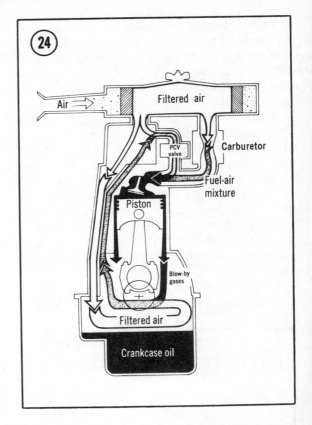

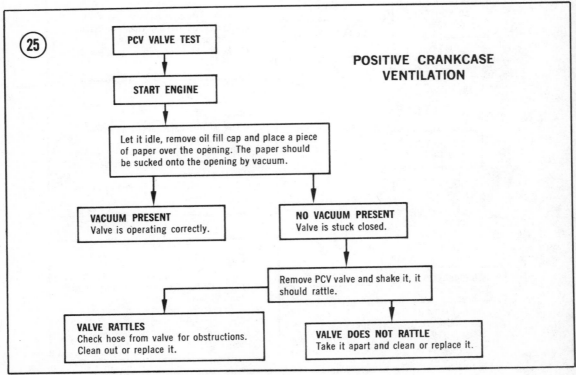

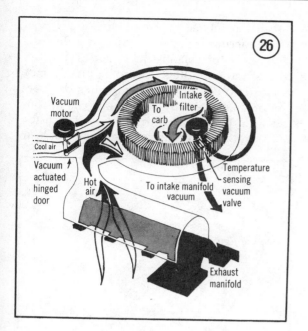

(26)

Vacuum motor

To carb

Intake filter

Cool air

Vacuum actuated hinged door

Hot air

Temperature sensing vacuum valve

To intake manifold vacuum

Exhaust manifold

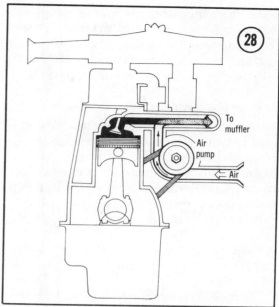

(28)

To muffler

Air pump

Air

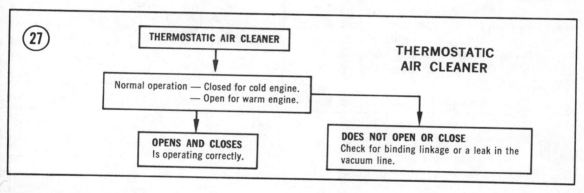

(27)

THERMOSTATIC AIR CLEANER

Normal operation — Closed for cold engine.
— Open for warm engine.

OPENS AND CLOSES
Is operating correctly.

DOES NOT OPEN OR CLOSE
Check for binding linkage or a leak in the vacuum line.

THERMOSTATIC AIR CLEANER

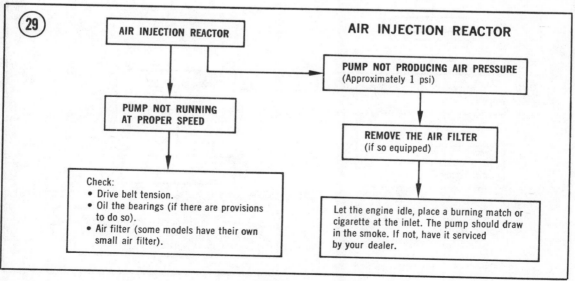

(29)

AIR INJECTION REACTOR

PUMP NOT RUNNING AT PROPER SPEED

Check:
• Drive belt tension.
• Oil the bearings (if there are provisions to do so).
• Air filter (some models have their own small air filter).

AIR INJECTION REACTOR

PUMP NOT PRODUCING AIR PRESSURE
(Approximately 1 psi)

REMOVE THE AIR FILTER
(if so equipped)

Let the engine idle, place a burning match or cigarette at the inlet. The pump should draw in the smoke. If not, have it serviced by your dealer.

stores the vapor when the engine is stopped. When the engine runs, manifold vacuum draws the vapor from the canister. Instead of being released into the atmosphere, the fuel vapor takes part in the normal combustion process.

Exhaust Gas Recirculation

The exhaust gas recirculation (EGR) system is used to reduce the emission of nitrogen oxides (NOx). Relatively inert exhaust gases are introduced into the combustion process to slightly reduce peak temperatures. This reduction in temperature reduces the formation of NOx.

Figure 31 provides a simple test of this system.

ENGINE NOISES

Often the first evidence of an internal engine trouble is a strange noise. That knocking, clicking, or tapping which you never heard before may be warning you of impending trouble.

While engine noises can indicate problems, they are sometimes difficult to interpret correctly; inexperienced mechanics can be seriously misled by them.

Professional mechanics often use a special stethoscope which looks similar to a doctor's stethoscope for isolating engine noises. You can do nearly as well with a "sounding stick" which can be an ordinary piece of doweling or a section of small hose. By placing one end in contact with the area to which you want to listen and the other end near your ear, you can hear

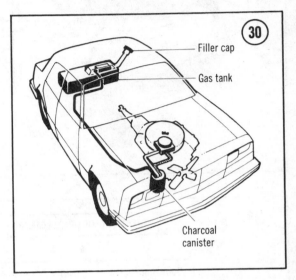

Filler cap

Gas tank

Charcoal canister

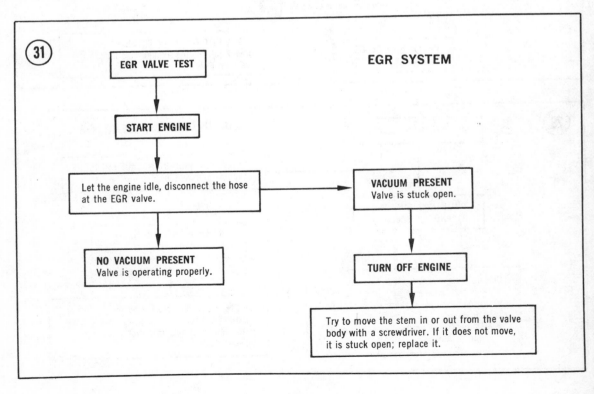

EGR SYSTEM

EGR VALVE TEST

START ENGINE

Let the engine idle, disconnect the hose at the EGR valve.

NO VACUUM PRESENT
Valve is operating properly.

VACUUM PRESENT
Valve is stuck open.

TURN OFF ENGINE

Try to move the stem in or out from the valve body with a screwdriver. If it does not move, it is stuck open; replace it.

sounds emanating from that area. The first time you do this, you may be horrified at the strange noises coming from even a normal engine. If you can, have an experienced friend or mechanic help you sort the noises out.

Clicking or Tapping Noises

Clicking or tapping noises usually come from the valve train, and indicate excessive valve clearance.

If your vehicle has adjustable valves, the procedure for adjusting the valve clearance is explained in Chapter Three. If your vehicle has hydraulic lifters, the clearance may not be adjustable. The noise may be coming from a collapsed lifter. These may be cleaned or replaced as described in the engine chapter.

A sticking valve may also sound like a valve with excessive clearance. In addition, excessive wear in valve train components can cause similar engine noises.

Knocking Noises

A heavy, dull knocking is usually caused by a worn main bearing. The noise is loudest when the engine is working hard, i.e., accelerating hard at low speed. You may be able to isolate the trouble to a single bearing by disconnecting

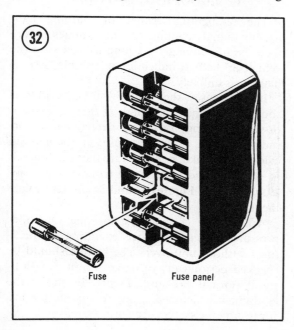

Fuse   Fuse panel

the spark plugs one at a time. When you reach the spark plug nearest the bearing, the knock will be reduced or disappear.

Worn connecting rod bearings may also produce a knock, but the sound is usually more "metallic." As with a main bearing, the noise is worse when accelerating. It may even increase further just as you go from accelerating to coasting. Disconnecting spark plugs will help isolate this knock as well.

A double knock or clicking usually indicates a worn piston pin. Disconnecting spark plugs will isolate this to a particular piston, however, the noise will *increase* when you reach the affected piston.

A loose flywheel and excessive crankshaft end play also produce knocking noises. While similar to main bearing noises, these are usually intermittent, not constant, and they do not change when spark plugs are disconnected.

Some mechanics confuse piston pin noise with piston slap. The double knock will distinguish the piston pin noise. Piston slap is identified by the fact that it is always louder when the engine is cold.

ELECTRICAL ACCESSORIES

Lights and Switches (Interior and Exterior)

1. *Bulb does not light* — Remove the bulb and check for a broken element. Also check the inside of the socket; make sure the contacts are clean and free of corrosion. If the bulb and socket are OK, check to see if a fuse has blown or a circuit breaker has tripped. The fuse panel (**Figure 32**) is usually located under the instrument panel. Replace the blown fuse or reset the circuit breaker. If the fuse blows or the breaker trips again, there is a short in that circuit. Check that circuit all the way to the battery. Look for worn wire insulation or burned wires.

If all the above are all right, check the switch controlling the bulb for continuity with an ohmmeter at the switch terminals. Check the switch contact terminals for loose or dirty electrical connections.

2. *Headlights work but will not switch from either high or low beam* — Check the beam selector switch for continuity with an ohmmeter

at the switch terminals. Check the switch contact terminals for loose or dirty electrical connections.

3. *Brake light switch inoperative* — On mechanically operated switches, usually mounted near the brake pedal arm, adjust the switch to achieve correct mechanical operation. Check the switch for continuity with an ohmmeter at the switch terminals. Check the switch contact terminals for loose or dirty electrical connections.

4. *Back-up lights do not operate* — Check light bulb as described earlier. Locate the switch, normally located near the shift lever. Adjust switch to achieve correct mechanical operation. Check the switch for continuity with an ohmmeter at the switch terminals. Bypass the switch with a jumper wire; if the lights work, replace the switch.

Directional Signals

1. *Directional signals do not operate* — If the indicator light on the instrument panel burns steadily instead of flashing, this usually indicates that one of the exterior lights is burned out. Check all lamps that normally flash. If all are all right, the flasher unit may be defective. Replace it with a good one.

2. *Directional signal indicator light on instrument panel does not light up* — Check the light bulbs as described earlier. Check all electrical connections and check the flasher unit.

3. *Directional signals will not self-cancel* — Check the self-cancelling mechanism located inside the steering column.

4. *Directional signals flash slowly* — Check the condition of the battery and the alternator (or generator) drive belt tension (**Figure 4**). Check the flasher unit and all related electrical connections.

Windshield Wipers

1. *Wipers do not operate* — Check for a blown fuse or circuit breaker that has tripped; replace or reset. Check all related terminals for loose or dirty electrical connections. Check continuity of the control switch with an ohmmeter at the switch terminals. Check the linkage and arms

for loose, broken, or binding parts. Straighten out or replace where necessary.

2. *Wiper motor hums but will not operate* — The motor may be shorted out internally; check and/or replace the motor. Also check for broken or binding linkage and arms.

3. *Wiper arms will not return to the stowed position when turned off* — The motor has a special internal switch for this purpose. Have it inspected by your dealer. Do not attempt this yourself.

Interior Heater

1. *Heater fan does not operate* — Check for a blown fuse or circuit breaker that has tripped. Check the switch for continuity with an ohmmeter at the switch terminals. Check the switch contact terminals for loose or dirty electrical connections.

2. *Heat output is insufficient* — Check the heater hose/engine coolant control valve usually located in the engine compartment; make sure it is in the open position. Ensure that the heater door(s) and cable(s) are operating correctly and are in the open position. Inspect the heat ducts; make sure that they are not crimped or blocked.

COOLING SYSTEM

The temperature gauge or warning light usually signals cooling system troubles before there is any damage. As long as you stop the vehicle at the first indication of trouble, serious damage is unlikely.

In most cases, the trouble will be obvious as soon as you open the hood. If there is coolant or steam leaking, look for a defective radiator, radiator hose, or heater hose. If there is no evidence of leakage, make sure that the fan belt is in good condition. If the trouble is not obvious, refer to **Figures 33 and 34** to help isolate the trouble.

Automotive cooling systems operate under pressure to permit higher operating temperatures without boil-over. The system should be checked periodically to make sure it can withstand normal pressure. **Figure 35** shows the equipment which nearly any service station has for testing the system pressure.

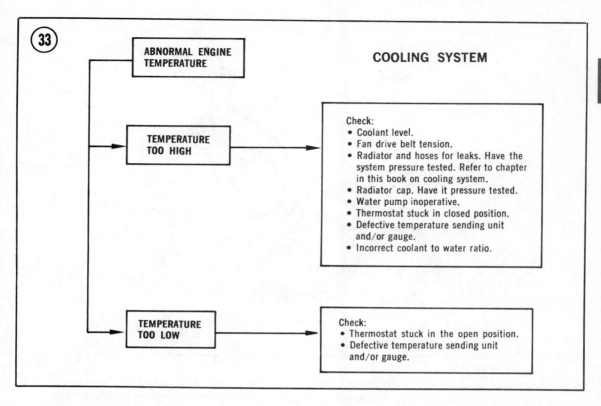

2

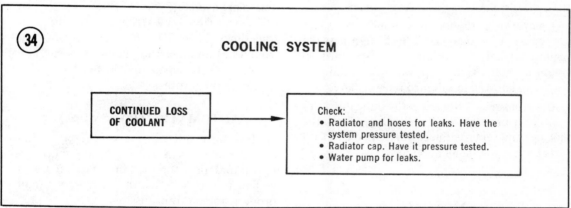

CLUTCH

All clutch troubles except adjustments require transmission removal to identify and cure the problem.

1. *Slippage* — This is most noticeable when accelerating in a high gear at relatively low speed. To check slippage, park the vehicle on a level surface with the handbrake set. Shift to 2nd gear and release the clutch as if driving off. If the clutch is good, the engine will slow and stall. If the clutch slips, continued engine speed will give it away.

Slippage results from insufficient clutch pedal free play, oil or grease on the clutch disc, worn pressure plate, or weak springs.

2. *Drag or failure to release* — This trouble usually causes difficult shifting and gear clash, especially when downshifting. The cause may be excessive clutch pedal free play, warped or bent pressure plate or clutch disc, broken or

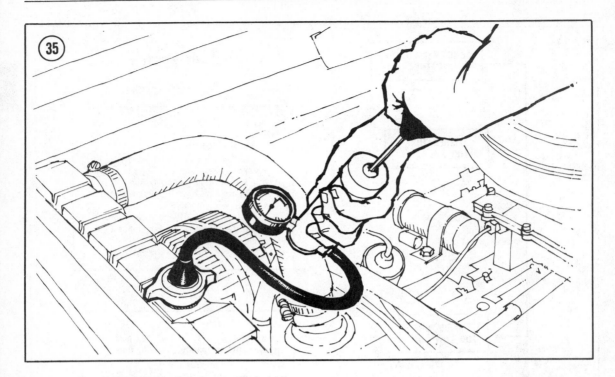

loose linings, or lack of lubrication in pilot bearing. Also check condition of transmission main shaft splines.

3. *Chatter or grabbing* — A number of things can cause this trouble. Check tightness of engine mounts and engine-to-transmission mounting bolts. Check for worn or misaligned pressure plate and misaligned release plate.

4. *Other noises* — Noise usually indicates a dry or defective release or pilot bearing. Check the bearings and replace if necessary. Also check all parts for misalignment and uneven wear.

MANUAL
TRANSMISSION/TRANSAXLE

Transmission and transaxle troubles are evident when one or more of the following symptoms appear:

   a. Difficulty changing gears

   b. Gears clash when downshifting

   c. Slipping out of gear

   d. Excessive noise in NEUTRAL

   e. Excessive noise in gear

   f. Oil leaks

Transmission and transaxle repairs are not recommended unless the many special tools required are available.

Transmission and transaxle troubles are sometimes difficult to distinguish from clutch troubles. Eliminate the clutch as a source of trouble before installing a new or rebuilt transmission or transaxle.

AUTOMATIC TRANSMISSION

Most automatic transmission repairs require considerable specialized knowledge and tools. It is impractical for the home mechanic to invest in the tools, since they cost more than a properly rebuilt transmission.

Check fluid level and condition frequently to help prevent future problems. If the fluid is orange or black in color or smells like varnish, it is an indication of some type of damage or failure within the transmission. Have the transmission serviced by your dealer or competent automatic transmission service facility.

BRAKES

Good brakes are vital to the safe operation of the vehicle. Performing the maintenance speci-

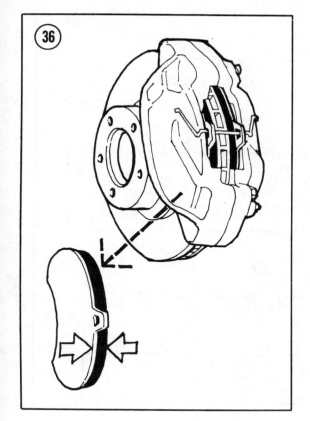

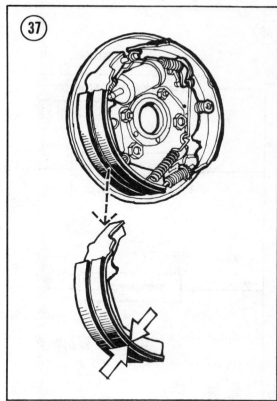

fied in Chapter Three will minimize problems with the brakes. Most importantly, check and maintain the level of fluid in the master cylinder, and check the thickness of the linings on the disc brake pads **(Figure 36)** or drum brake shoes **(Figure 37)**.

If trouble develops, **Figures 38 through 40** will help you locate the problem. Refer to the brake chapter for actual repair procedures.

STEERING AND SUSPENSION

Trouble in the suspension or steering is evident when the following occur:

a. Steering is hard
b. Car pulls to one side
c. Car wanders or front wheels wobble
d. Steering has excessive play
e. Tire wear is abnormal

Unusual steering, pulling, or wandering is usually caused by bent or otherwise misaligned suspension parts. This is difficult to check

without proper alignment equipment. Refer to the suspension chapter in this book for repairs that you can perform and those that must be left to a dealer or suspension specialist.

If your trouble seems to be excessive play, check wheel bearing adjustment first. This is the most frequent cause. Then check ball-joints (refer to Suspension chapter). Finally, check tie rod end ball-joints by shaking each tie rod. Also check steering gear, or rack-and-pinion assembly to see that it is securely bolted down.

TIRE WEAR ANALYSIS

Abnormal tire wear should be analyzed to determine its causes. The most common causes are the following:

a. Incorrect tire pressure
b. Improper driving
c. Overloading
d. Bad road surfaces
e. Incorrect wheel alignment

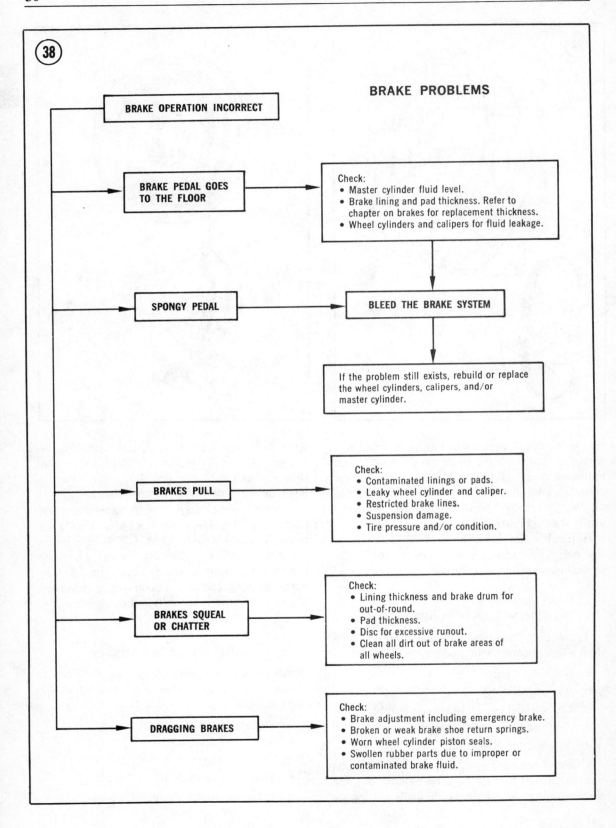

(38)

BRAKE PROBLEMS

BRAKE OPERATION INCORRECT

BRAKE PEDAL GOES TO THE FLOOR → Check:
• Master cylinder fluid level.
• Brake lining and pad thickness. Refer to chapter on brakes for replacement thickness.
• Wheel cylinders and calipers for fluid leakage.

SPONGY PEDAL → **BLEED THE BRAKE SYSTEM**

If the problem still exists, rebuild or replace the wheel cylinders, calipers, and/or master cylinder.

BRAKES PULL → Check:
• Contaminated linings or pads.
• Leaky wheel cylinder and caliper.
• Restricted brake lines.
• Suspension damage.
• Tire pressure and/or condition.

BRAKES SQUEAL OR CHATTER → Check:
• Lining thickness and brake drum for out-of-round.
• Pad thickness.
• Disc for excessive runout.
• Clean all dirt out of brake areas of all wheels.

DRAGGING BRAKES → Check:
• Brake adjustment including emergency brake.
• Broken or weak brake shoe return springs.
• Worn wheel cylinder piston seals.
• Swollen rubber parts due to improper or contaminated brake fluid.

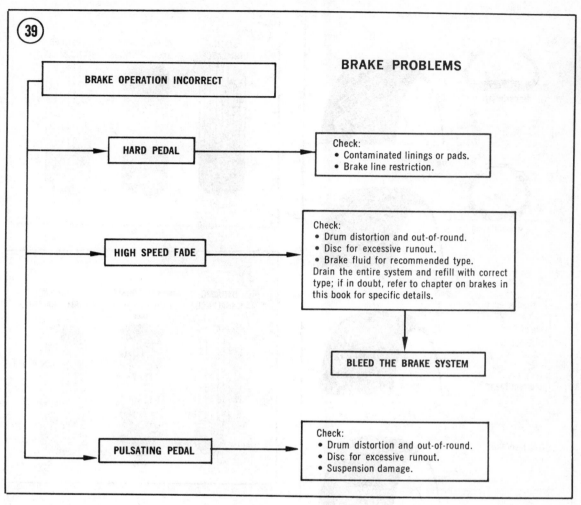

(39) **BRAKE PROBLEMS**

BRAKE OPERATION INCORRECT

HARD PEDAL

Check:
• Contaminated linings or pads.
• Brake line restriction.

HIGH SPEED FADE

Check:
• Drum distortion and out-of-round.
• Disc for excessive runout.
• Brake fluid for recommended type.
Drain the entire system and refill with correct type; if in doubt, refer to chapter on brakes in this book for specific details.

BLEED THE BRAKE SYSTEM

PULSATING PEDAL

Check:
• Drum distortion and out-of-round.
• Disc for excessive runout.
• Suspension damage.

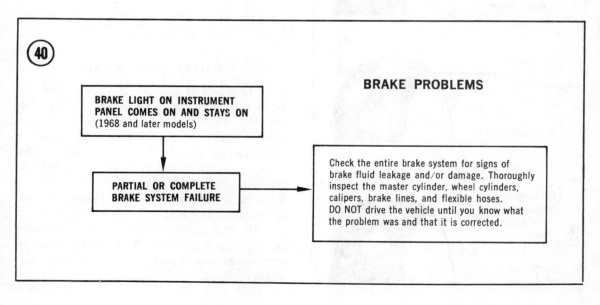

(40) **BRAKE PROBLEMS**

BRAKE LIGHT ON INSTRUMENT PANEL COMES ON AND STAYS ON
(1968 and later models)

PARTIAL OR COMPLETE BRAKE SYSTEM FAILURE

Check the entire brake system for signs of brake fluid leakage and/or damage. Thoroughly inspect the master cylinder, wheel cylinders, calipers, brake lines, and flexible hoses.
DO NOT drive the vehicle until you know what the problem was and that it is corrected.

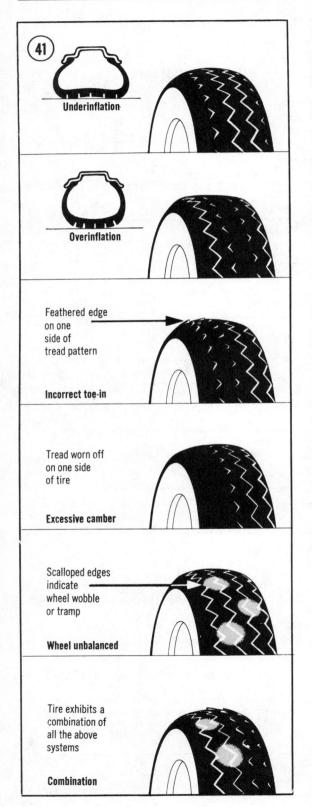

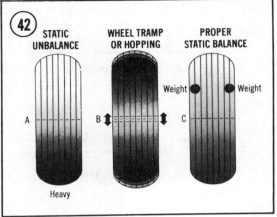

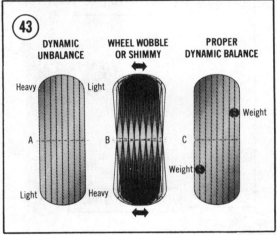

Figure 41 identifies wear patterns and indicates the most probable causes.

WHEEL BALANCING

All four wheels and tires must be in balance along two axes. To be in static balance (**Figure 42**), weight must be evenly distributed around the axis of rotation. (A) shows a statically unbalanced wheel; (B) shows the result — wheel tramp or hopping; (C) shows proper static balance.

To be in dynamic balance (**Figure 43**), the centerline of the weight must coincide with the centerline of the wheel. (A) shows a dynamically unbalanced wheel; (B) shows the result — wheel wobble or shimmy; (C) shows proper dynamic balance.

LUBRICATION, MAINTENANCE
AND TUNE-UP

This chapter deals with the normal maintenance necessary to keep your Corvette running properly. **Table 1** lists the maintenance intervals for cars given normal use. Some procedures are done at fuel stops; others are done at specified mileage or time intervals.

Cars driven under severe conditions require more frequent maintenance. This is specified in **Table 1**. Such conditions include:

a. Frequent short trips.
b. Stop-and-go driving.
c. Extremely cold weather.
d. Trailer towing.
e. Dusty conditions.

Some maintenance procedures are described under *Tune-up* at the end of the chapter. Other steps are described in the following chapters. Chapter references are included with these steps. **Tables 1-4** are at the end of the chapter.

HOISTING, JACKING AND
LIFT POINTS

Corvette design requires that special precautions be taken when raising the car with a jack or a hoist and when positioning jackstands. Incorrect jack or jackstand placement can cause suspension or drive train damage. The service jack provided with the car is intended only for emergency use in changing a flat tire. Refer to the Owner's Manual when using this jack. Do not use it to lift the car up while performing other services.

A floor jack or other type of hydraulic jack is recommended for raising the front or rear of the car when required for service. Always place jackstands at the appropriate points to hold the car stable. Relying upon a single jack to hold the car without the use of jackstands can lead to serious physical injury.

When lifting the front of the car, place your jack (and jackstand) under the outer end of the lower control arms. To lift the rear of the car, place your jack (and jackstands) under the metal frame "birdcage" just forward of the rear wheels. *Do not* place a jack under the differential carrier, rear suspension arms or fiberglass body panels.

FUEL STOP CHECKS

Many of the following services were once routinely made by the service station attendants when you stopped for gas. With the advent of the self-service station and the extra cost of "full service," you may want to perform the checks yourself. Although simple to perform, they are important, as such checks give an indication of the need for other maintenance.

1. With the engine cold and off, pull out the engine oil dipstick (**Figure 1**). Wipe the dipstick with a clean rag and reinsert it in the dipstick tube. Be sure to push the dipstick all the way down. Pull the dipstick out again and check the oil level on the end of the dipstick. Reinsert the dipstick and push it all the way into the dipstick tube. Some dipsticks

have "ADD" and "FULL" lines. Others read
"ADD 1 QT." and "OPERATING RANGE." In
either case, keep the oil level above the "ADD"
line. Top up to the "FULL" or "OPERATING
RANGE" mark on the dipstick, if necessary, using
only an SF, SF/CC or SF/CD oil. See **Table 2** for
proper oil viscosity. Add oil through the hole in the
valve cover (**Figure 2**).

2. Check coolant level in the recovery tank (**Figure
3**) using the dipstick built into the tank cap. It
should be at the "FULL COLD" mark on the
dipstick when the engine is cold and at the "FULL
HOT" mark when the engine is hot.

> *WARNING*
> *Do not remove the radiator cap when*
> *the engine is warm or hot. If this is*
> *unavoidable, cover the cap with a thick*
> *rag or wear heavy leather gloves. Turn*
> *the cap slowly counterclockwise against*
> *the first stop (about 1/4 turn). Let all*
> *pressure (hot coolant and steam)*
> *escape. Then depress the cap and turn*
> *counterclockwise to remove. If the cap*
> *is removed too soon, scalding coolant*
> *may escape and cause a serious burn.*

Top up as needed with a 50/50 mixture of
ethylene glycol antifreeze and water, adding it to
the recovery tank, not the radiator. If the recovery
tank is empty, check the radiator level as well.

3. Check battery electrolyte level (not required on
sealed batteries). On unsealed batteries with
filler/vent caps, it should be even with the bottom
of the split vent wells. See **Figure 4**. If the level is
low, add distilled water until the level contacts the
bottom of the vent well. Do not overfill, as this will
result in loss of electrolyte and shorter battery life.

4. Check fluid level in the windshield washer tank.
See **Figure 5**. It should be kept full, except during
winter months when filling it only 3/4 full will
allow for expansion if the fluid freezes. Use
windshield washer solvent, following the
manufacturer's instructions for proper dilution.

> *CAUTION*
> *Do not use radiator antifreeze in the*
> *washer tank. The runoff may damage*
> *the car's paint.*

5. Check fluid level in the brake master cylinder
reservoirs (**Figure 6**). Make sure the brake fluid in
each reservoir is above the embossed fill line on
the outside of the reservoir. If you cannot
determine the fluid level visually, clean the area
around each reservoir cap. Depress the center of
the cap while pulling up on its edge to remove the

cap (**Figure 7**). Top up, if necessary, with DOT 3
brake fluid as specified in **Table 3**.

> *WARNING*
> *Do not use fluid from a previously*
> *opened container that is only part full.*
> *Brake fluid absorbs moisture and*
> *moisture in the brake lines can reduce*
> *braking efficiency.*

6. Check fluid level in the power steering pump
reservoir (**Figure 8**). With the engine at normal

3

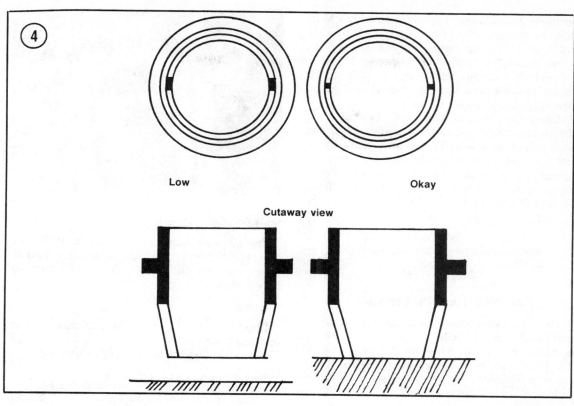

Low

Okay

Cutaway view

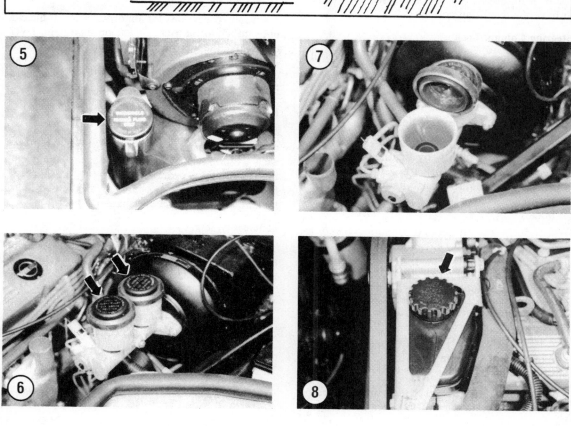

operating temperature (upper radiator hose hot), turn the steering wheel from lock-to-lock several times, then shut the engine off and remove the power steering pump dipstick (**Figure 9**). The fluid should be between the "HOT" and "COLD" marks on the dipstick. Top up if necessary with power steering fluid. Install the dipstick.

7. Check tire pressures. This should be done when the tires are cold in the morning or after the car has been parked for at least 3 hours after being driven less than one mile. When the tires heat up from driving, the air inside them expands and gives false high-pressure readings. See the tire placard affixed to the left front door edge for recommended tire pressure.

> *NOTE*
> *Maintain the temporary-use spare tire at 60 psi.*

OWNER SAFETY CHECKS

The following simple checks should be performed on a daily basis during normal operation of the car. Some are driveway checks. The others can be performed while driving. If any result in unsatisfactory operation, see your dealer to have the condition corrected.

Steering Column Lock

The ignition key should turn to LOCK only when the transmission selector is in PARK (automatic transmission) or REVERSE (manual transmission).

Parking Brake and Transmission PARK Mechanism

Check holding ability by setting the parking brake with the car on a fairly steep hill. If equipped with an automatic transmission, place the transmission selector lever in "PARK" and release all brakes.

> *WARNING*
> *You should not expect the PARK mechanism to hold the car by itself even on a level surface. Always set the parking brake **after** placing the transmission selector in PARK. When parking on an incline, you should also turn the wheels to the curb before shutting off the engine.*

Automatic Transmission Shift Indicator

Make sure the transmission shift indicator accurately indicates the shift position selected.

Starter Safety Switch

The starter should operate only in PARK or NEUTRAL positions (automatic transmission) or with the clutch fully depressed (manual transmission).

Steering

Check the steering mechanism to make sure it operates freely and does not have excessive play or make harsh sounds when turning or parking.

Wheel Alignment and Balance

Visually check tires for abnormal wear. If the car pulls either to the right or left on a straight, level road, have the wheel alignment checked. Excessive vibration of the steering wheel or front of the car while driving at normal highway speeds usually indicates the need for wheel balancing.

Brakes

Observe brake warning light during braking action. Also check for changes in braking action, such as pulling to one side, unusual sounds or increased brake pedal travel. If the brake pedal feels spongy, there is probably air in the hydraulic system. Bleed the brakes (Chapter Eleven).

Exhaust System

Be alert to any smell of fumes in the car or to any changes in the sound of the exhaust system that might indicate leakage.

Defroster

Turn on the heater, then move the control to the defrost (DEF) position and check the amount of air directed to the windshield.

Rear View Mirrors and Sun Visors

Make sure that the friction mounts are adjusted so that mirror and visors stay in selected positions.

Horn

Check the horn to make sure that it works properly.

Lap and Shoulder Belts

Check all components for proper operation. Make sure that the anchor bolts are tight. Check the belts for fraying.

Head Restraints

Make sure that head restraints, if so equipped, adjust up and down properly and that no components are missing, loose or damaged.

Lights and Buzzers

Make sure that all interior lights and buzzers are working. These include the seat belt reminder light and buzzer, ignition key buzzer, interior lights, instrument panel illumination and warning lights.

Check all exterior lights for proper operation. These include the headlights, license plate lights, side marker lights, parking lights, turn or directional signals, backup lights and hazard warning lights.

Glass

Check for any condition that could obscure vision or be a safety hazard. Correct as required.

Door Latches

Verify positive closing, latching and locking action.

Hood Latches

Verify that the hood closes firmly by lifting up on the hood after closing it. Check for missing, broken or damaged parts.

Fluid Leaks

Check under the vehicle after it has been parked for awhile for evidence of fuel, water or oil leaks. Water dripping from the air conditioner drain tube after use is normal. Immediately determine and correct the cause of any leaking gasoline fumes or liquids to avoid possible fire or explosion.

Tires and Wheels

Visually check tire condition. Look for nails, cuts, excessive wear or other damage. Remove all stones or other objects wedged in the tread. Check tire side walls for cuts or other damage. Check tire valve for air leaks; replace valve if necessary. Replace any valve caps that are missing. Check tire pressure with a reliable pressure gauge and adjust air pressure as needed.

SCHEDULED MAINTENANCE

Table 1 provides a complete vehicle maintenance and lubrication schedule, recommended by Chevrolet. The schedule is intended only as a guide. If your car is subjected to conditions such as heavy dust, continuous short trips or pulling trailers, more frequent servicing will be required.

The following is a brief explanation of each of the services listed in **Table 1**. Use only those that apply to your vehicle.

Engine Oil and Filter

Engine oil should be selected to meet the demands of the temperatures and driving conditions anticipated. Chevrolet recommends the use of an oil designated API SF, SF/CC or SF/CD. Multi-viscosity oils are recommended. To select the exact viscosity range, refer to **Table 2**. The rating and viscosity range are clearly marked on the top of the oil can.

Change the engine oil and filter at the intervals specified in **Table 1**.

To drain the oil and change the filter, you will need:

    a. Drain pan (6 quarts or more capacity).
    b. Oil can spout or can opener and funnel.
    c. Filter wrench.
    d. Appropriate type and quantity of new oil.
    e. Adjustable wrench.
    f. New oil filter.

There are several ways to discard the old oil safely. The easiest way is to pour it from the drain pan into a gallon bleach or milk container. The oil can then be taken to a service station for recycling. Check local regulations before disposing of oil in your household trash. Never allow oil to drain onto the ground.

The drain pan can be cleaned with solvent and paint thinner, if available. If not, hot water and dishwashing liquid will work.

1. Warm the engine to operating temperature, then shut it off.

2. Place the drain pan under the crankcase drain plug (**Figure 10**). Remove the plug with the wrench and let the oil drain for at least 10 minutes. Check condition of the drain plug gasket and replace if damaged. Reinstall the plug and gasket and tighten the plug to 20 ft.-lb. (27 N•m).

3. Move the drain pan beneath the oil filter (**Figure 11**). Unscrew the oil filter counterclockwise. Use a filter wrench if the filter is too tight or too hot to remove by hand.

4. Wipe the gasket surface on the engine block clean with a paper towel.

5. Coat the neoprene gasket on the new filter with clean engine oil.

6. Screw the filter onto the engine *by hand* until the gasket just touches the engine block. At this point, there will be a very slight resistance when turning the filter.

7. Tighten the filter another 3/4 turn *by hand*. If the filter wrench is used, the filter will probably be overtightened. Improper filter tightening can result in an oil leak.

8. Remove the oil filler cap from the valve cover (**Figure 12**).

9. Pour the new oil into the engine. Wipe up any spills on the valve cover with a clean cloth.

10. Start the engine and let it idle. The oil pressure light in the instrument panel driver information center will remain on for a few seconds, then go out. The digital display will gradually increase to a normal pressure reading.

> *CAUTION*
> *Do not race the engine to make the oil pressure light go out or the digital display increase. It takes time for the oil to reach all parts of the engine and racing it could damage dry parts.*

11. While the engine is running, check the area under and around the drain plug and oil filter for leaks.

12. Turn the engine off. Let the oil settle for several minutes, then recheck the level on the dipstick. Add oil, if necessary, to bring the level up to the "FULL" or "OPERATING RANGE" mark, but *do not overfill*. Make sure the dipstick is fully reinserted in the dipstick tube.

Chassis and Suspension Lubrication

Inspect and lubricate the following components or systems at the intervals specified in **Table 1**:
a. Upper and lower control arm ball-joints.
b. Steering linkage ball-joints.
c. Transmission shift linkage contacting faces.
d. Hood latch and hinges.
e. Door hinges, jamb switch and lock cylinder.
f. Gas tank filler door hinges.
g. Rear hatch hinges, latch and lock.
h. Parking brake pulley, cable and linkage.
i. Throttle linkage.

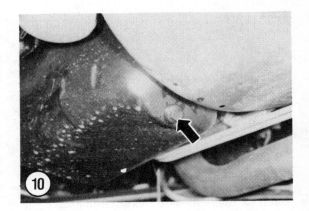

Brake System

Check brake lines and hoses for proper routing and connection. Look for binding, leaking, chafing, cracks or other defects. Correct any defects found.

Check rotor surface condition. Check the lining thickness through the inspection hole in the top of the caliper. If the lining is worn to the approximate thickness of the pad, remove the brake pads and measure the lining. Replace all pads if any lining is worn to within 1/32 in. of any point on the pad.

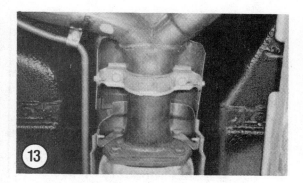

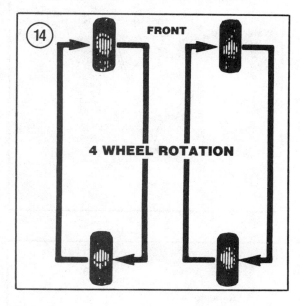

FRONT

4 WHEEL ROTATION

Outer disc brake pads contain a wear sensor to make noise when the linings require replacement. The spring clip indicator is an integral part of the pad. As the lining wears, the clip touches the rotor and makes a warning sound.

Exhaust System

Inspect the complete exhaust system including the catalytic converter for open holes, seams, loose connections or other unsafe conditions. Check for broken, damaged, missing or out-of-position components. Pay particular attention to exhaust and converter heat shield condition (**Figure 13**, typical). Whenever the muffler requires replacement, replace the exhaust pipe(s) to the rear of the muffler to maintain exhaust system integrity.

Rear Axle and Manual Transmission

Rear axle and manual transmission/overdrive unit lubricants do not require changing during the life of the vehicle, but fluid levels should be checked at specified intervals. With the engine at operating temperature, the rear axle, transmission and overdrive lubricant levels should be at the bottom of their respective filler plug holes.

The lubricant in limited slip differentials should be drained and refilled at the first 7,500 mile interval. Be sure to use 4 oz. of limited-slip additive (GM part No. 1052358 or equivalent) when refilling the differential.

Suspension and Steering

Check front and rear suspension and steering systems for worn, damaged, loose or missing parts. Inspect power steering line and hoses for binding, cracks, chafing, leaks and other defects. Correct as required.

Throttle Linkage

Check for damaged or missing parts. Correct any interference or binding.

Throttle Body Mounting Bolts (1984)

Check throttle body mounting bolt torque. If not within 8-14 ft.-lb. (11-19 N•m), retorque to this specification.

Tire Rotation

Inspect the tires for cracks, bumps, bulges or other defects. Look for signs of excessive wear. If the car is equipped with 16 in. aluminum wheels (but does not have the performance handling package), rotate the tires according to **Figure 14**. Readjust tire pressure to the specifications listed on the tire placard affixed to the left front door edge.

On Corvettes equipped with standard 15 in. aluminum wheels or with 16 in. wheels *and* the performance handling package, the rear wheels are wider than the front wheels and should not be rotated by the usual method. To rotate tires on such vehicles:

1. Remove the wheels from the vehicle.
2. Dismount the tires from the wheels.
3. Rotate the tires (but not the wheels) according to **Figure 14** and remount the tires to the wheels.

NOTE
If the car is equipped with P255/50VR16 tires, an arrow on the sidewall indicates the required direction of rotation for best performance. Make sure such tires are mounted correctly when rotating tires by this procedure.

4. Rebalance the tires and install the wheels to the car in their original location.

Drive Belt

A single (serpentine) belt is used to drive all accessories. All belt driven accessory units are rigidly mounted, with belt tension maintained by a spring-loaded tensioner. See **Figure 15** (1984) or **Figure 16** (1985-on). Drive belt tension can only be checked between the alternator and air pump. Belt tension should be between 120-140 lbs. (534-623 N). If it is not, check the tensioner. If the indicator mark on the tensioner is outside the operating range, the tensioner is worn and must be replaced. See **Figure 17** (typical). If tension is incorrect but the tensioner is within its operating range, replace the belt.

Cracks may be discovered in the belt ribs during periodic inspections. Such cracks will not affect belt performance and should not be considered abnormal. The belt requires replacement only if it slips or if segments of one or more ribs in the belt are missing.

To remove or install the drive belt:

1. Lift the tensioner from the belt using a 1/2 in. breaker bar.

2. Slip the belt from under the tensioner and remove it from the accessory pulleys.

3. Installation is the reverse of removal. Check drive belt tension with the tension gauge.

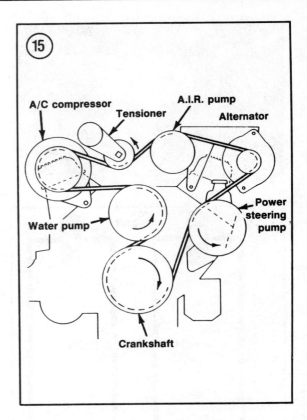

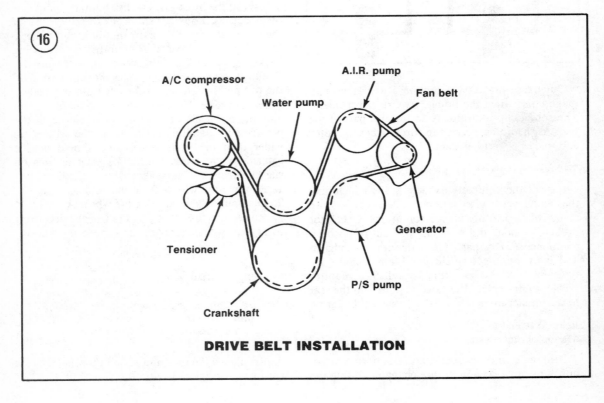

DRIVE BELT INSTALLATION

Throttle Body Hoses

Check injection unit hoses for proper routing and connection. Check hose condition and replace any that are cracked, split or deteriorated.

Overdrive Unit

Change fluid and filter at the intervals stated in **Table 1**. See Chapter Eight.

Automatic Transmission Fluid

Check fluid level. See Chapter Eight.

Cooling System

WARNING
Personal injury is possible. Perform the
cooling system service when the engine
is cold.

Visually inspect the level and condition of the coolant in the recovery tank (**Figure 3**). Top up, if necessary, with a 50/50 mixture of ethylene glycol antifreeze and water. If the coolant looks dirty or rusty, flush the radiator and replace the coolant as described in Chapter Six. Inspect all radiator and heater hoses. Replace any hoses that are cracked, deteriorated or extremely soft or spongy. Make sure all hoses are correctly installed and all clamps are securely tightened.

Fuel Filter

Before opening any fuel connection on a TBI-equipped engine, fuel pressure must be relieved to reduce the risk of fire and personal injury. See *System Pressure Relief,* Chapter Five.

The disposable inline filter canister is located on the right frame rail approximately in the middle of the vehicle (**Figure 18**). To replace the filter:
1. Relieve the system pressure. See Chapter Five.
2. Securely block the wheels that remain on the ground. Raise the vehicle and place it on jackstands.
3. Cover each fuel hose connection with a clean cloth to collect the small amount of fuel discharged when the connection is opened.
4. Loosen each clamp screw. Slide the clamp back on the fuel hose about 3 inches.
5. Remove the bracket clamp screw from the frame.
6. Disconnect the hoses from the filter canister.
7. Remove the filter canister. Remove the bracket and install it on the new filter.
8. Installation is the reverse of removal. Make sure the arrow on the filter canister faces in the direction of fuel flow. If fuel fitting uses an O-ring, make sure it is in good condition; if not, replace the O-ring. Tighten all connections to 22 ft.-lb. (30 N•m).

Fuel Tank, Cap and Lines

Inspect the fuel tank, cap and lines for leaks or damage. Remove the fuel cap and check the gasket for an even filler neck imprint.

Spark Plugs, Engine Timing and Ignition Wiring

See *Tune-up* in this chapter.

Cooling System

Drain, flush and refill every 2 years or 30,000 miles. See *Cooling System Flushing* in Chapter Six.

PCV System Check

Inspect the system as described under *Crankcase Ventilation System* in Chapter Five.

Air Cleaner System and Filter

Inspect the 1984 system as described under *Thermostatic (Thermac) Air Cleaner* in Chapter Five.

To replace the filter on 1984 models, remove the 2 nuts holding the air cleaner cover in place (**Figure 19**). Remove the cover and lift out the old filter

(**Figure 20**). Wipe the inside of the air cleaner housing with a damp paper towel to remove dust, dirt and debris. Install a new filter. Fit the cover back in place and tighten the attaching nuts finger-tight.

To replace the filter on 1985 and later models, unscrew the milled plastic knob on the screw at each side of the front of the air cleaner housing. See **Figure 21**. Remove the cover and filter from the front of the housing assembly. Lift out and discard the old filter (**Figure 22**). Wipe the inside of the filter housing with a damp paper towel to remove dust, dirt and debris. Install the new filter in the cover. Position cover and filter on air cleaner housing, engage the cover screws in the housing and tighten the plastic knobs evenly and alternately until finger-tight.

Crankcase Ventilation Filter (1984)

Remove the air cleaner cover and filter. Reach inside the snorkel containing the crankcase ventilation filter and remove the retaining clip from the filter case (**Figure 23**). Reach underneath the snorkel and disconnect the filter from the housing and vent hose. Installation is the reverse of removal.

Exhaust Gas Recirculation (EGR) System

Inspect the system as described in Chapter Five.

Automatic Transmission Fluid

Drain and refill the fluid at intervals specified in **Table 1**.
1. Raise the front of the car with a jack and place it on jackstands.
2. Place a drain pan under the transmission.
3. Loosen all pan attaching bolts (**Figure 24**) a few turns. Tap one corner of the pan with a rubber hammer to break it loose and let the fluid drain.
4. When the fluid has drained to the level of the pan flange, remove the pan bolts at the rear and along both sides of the pan. This will let the pan drop at one end and drain slowly.
5. When all fluid has drained, remove the pan and let the screen/filter drain.
6. Discard the pan gasket. Clean the pan thoroughly with solvent and lint-free cloths or paper towels.
7. Remove the screen/filter-to-valve body bolts. Remove the screen/filter assembly and gasket. Discard the gasket.

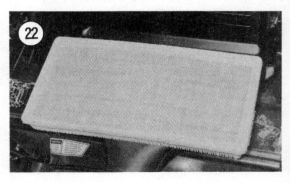

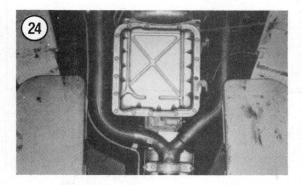

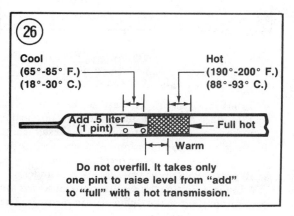

Cool
(65°-85° F.)
(18°-30° C.)

Hot
(190°-200° F.)
(88°-93° C.)

Add .5 liter
(1 pint) → ⌷ — Full hot

← Warm →

**Do not overfill. It takes only
one pint to raise level from "add"
to "full" with a hot transmission.**

8. Clean screen thoroughly in solvent and dry with compressed air. Replace paper or felt-type filters.

9. Install a new gasket or O-ring (as required) to the screen/filter. Install the screen/filter to the valve body and tighten the attaching bolts securely.

10. Install the oil pan with a new gasket. Tighten the attaching bolts in an alternating pattern to 10-13 ft.-lb. (14-18 N•m).

11. Fill the transmission through the filler tube with approximately 4 quarts of DEXRON II automatic transmission fluid. Start the engine and let it idle for 2 minutes.

12. Set the parking brake, block the wheels and place the transmission in PARK. Move the selector lever through each gear range, pausing long enough for the transmission to engage. Return to the PARK position.

13. Remove the dipstick (**Figure 25**) and wipe it clean. Reinsert the dipstick in the filler tube until it seats completely.

14. Remove the dipstick and check the fluid level. It should be in the crosshatch area between the "ADD" and "FULL" marks (**Figure 26**). Reinstall the dipstick.

CAUTION
Do not overfill the transmission. This will cause foaming and a loss of fluid through the vent, which will result in a premature transmission failure.

TUNE-UP

The tune-up consists of a series of inspections, adjustments and parts replacements to compensate for wear and deterioration of engine components. Regular tune-ups are especially important to modern engines. Emission control systems, improved electrical systems and other advances make these engines especially sensitive to improperly operating or incorrectly adjusted parts.

Since proper engine operation depends upon a number of inter-related system functions, a tune-up consisting of only 1 or 2 corrections will seldom bring lasting results. Instead, a thorough, systematic procedure of analysis and correction will pay dividends in improved power, performance and operating economy.

The procedure presented in this chapter requires a series of visual and mechanical checks and adjustments. The instruments required are described in detail in Chapter One. Tune-up specifications are provided on the Vehicle Emission Control Information (VECI) decal located in the engine compartment. To prevent loss of this information in the event of decal

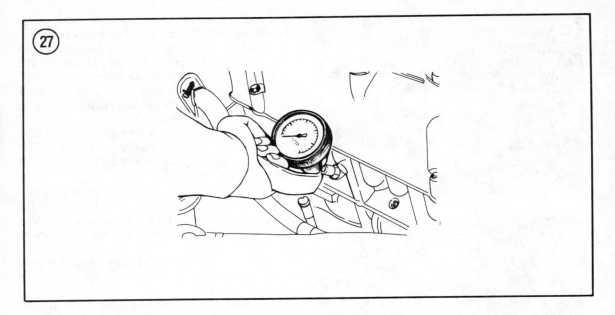

damage, it is a good idea to copy the specifications on a 3×5 in. file card and keep it in the glove compartment.

> *NOTE*
> *Chevrolet does not provide general tune-up specifications for 1984 models. You must refer to the VECI decal for this information.*

A tune-up consists of the following:
a. Compression check.
b. Ignition system work.
c. Throttle body inspection.

Compression Test

Whenever the spark plugs are removed from the engine, it is a good idea to run a compression test. The compression test measures the compression pressure built up in each cylinder. Its results can be used to assess general cylinder and valve condition. In addition, it can warn of developing problems inside the engine.
1. Warm the engine to normal operating temperature (upper radiator hose hot).
2. Remove all spark plugs. See *Spark Plug Removal* in this chapter.
3. Disconnect the ignition switch feed wire at the distributor. This is the pink wire from the ignition coil.
4. Connect a remote starter switch to the starter solenoid according to manufacturer's instructions. Leave the ignition key in the OFF position.
5. Connect a compression tester to the No. 1 cylinder following the manufacturer's instructions. See **Figure 27**.

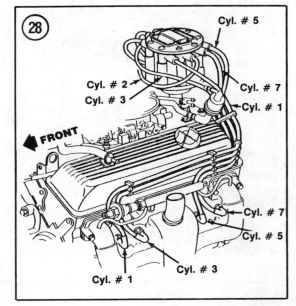

> *NOTE*
> *The No. 1 cylinder is the front cylinder in the left bank. See **Figure 28**.*

6. Crank the engine at least 5 turns with the remote start switch or until there is no further increase in compression shown on the tester gauge.
7. Remove the compression tester and record the reading. Relieve the tester pressure valve.
8. Repeat Step 6 and Step 7 for each cylinder.

When interpreting the results, actual readings are not as important as the differences in readings. The

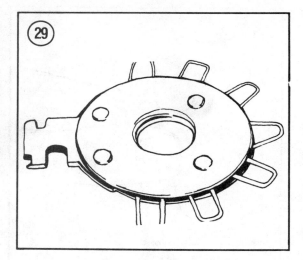

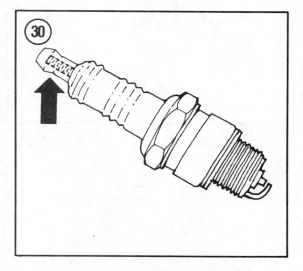

Spark Plug Removal

CAUTION
Whenever the spark plugs are removed, dirt from around them can fall into the spark plug holes. This can cause expensive engine damage.

1. Blow out any foreign matter from around the spark plugs with compressed air. Use a compressor if you have one. Another method is to use a can of compressed inert gas, available from photo stores.
2. Disconnect the spark plug wires by twisting the wire boot back and forth on the plug insulator while pulling upward. Use of a spark plug wire removal tool is recommended, as pulling on the wire instead of the boot may cause internal damage to the wire.
3. Remove the plugs with a 5/8 in. spark plug socket. Keep the plugs in order so you know which cylinder they came from.
4. Examine each spark plug. Compare its condition with the illustrations in Chapter Two. Spark plug condition indicates engine condition and can warn of developing trouble.
5. Discard the plugs. Although they could be cleaned, regapped and reused if in good condition, they seldom last very long. New plugs are inexpensive and far more reliable.

Spark Plug Gapping and Installation

New plugs should be carefully gapped to ensure a reliable, consistent spark. Use a special spark plug tool with a wire gauge. See **Figure 29** for one common type.

1. Refer to the Vehicle Emission Control Information (VECI) label located under the hood for the proper plug type and gap.
2. Remove the plugs from the box. Tapered seat plugs do not use gaskets. Some plug brands may have small end pieces that must be screwed on (**Figure 30**) before the plugs can be used.
3. Insert the appropriate size wire gauge between the spark plug electrodes. If the gap is correct, there will be a slight drag as the wire is pulled through. If there is no drag or if the wire will not pull through, bend the side electrode with the gapping tool (**Figure 31**) to change the gap and then remeasure with the wire gauge.

CAUTION
Never try to close the electrode gap by tapping the spark plug on a solid surface. This can damage the plug internally. Always use the special tool to open or close the gap.

lowest must be within 75 percent of the highest. A greater difference indicates worn or broken rings, leaking or sticking valves or a combination of these problems.

If the compression test indicates a problem (excessive variation in readings), isolate the cause with a wet compression test. This is done in the same way as the dry compression test, except that about one tablespoon of oil is poured down the spark plug holes before performing Steps 5-7. If the wet compression readings are much greater than the dry compression readings, the trouble is probably due to worn or broken rings. If there is little difference between the wet and dry readings, the problem is probably due to leaky or sticking valves. If 2 adjacent cylinders have low readings during both dry and wet testing, the head gasket may be leaking.

4. Screw each plug in by hand until it seats. Very little effort should be required. If force is necessary, the plug is cross-threaded. Unscrew it and try again.

5. Tighten the spark plugs. If you have a torque wrench, tighten to 15 ft.-lb. (20 N•m). If not, tighten the plugs with your fingers, then tighten an additional 1/16 turn with the plug wrench.

6. Install the wires to their correct cylinder location. Refer to **Figure 28** for the left cylinder bank and **Figure 32** for the right cylinder bank.

Distributor Cap, Wires and Rotor

The distributor cap, wires and rotor should be inspected every 30,000 miles or whenever the spark plugs are replaced.

1. 1985-on—remove the distributor cover (**Figure 33**).

2. Depress the 2 wire harness latches (A, **Figure 34**) and remove the wire harness retainer from the distributor cap.

3. Depress the 4 distributor cap latch screws and turn 90° (B, **Figure 34** shows the 2 front screws; the 2 rear screws are on the back side of the cap). Lift the cap straight up and off to prevent rotor blade damage.

4. Check the carbon button and electrodes inside the distributor cap for dirt, corrosion or arcing. Check the cap for cracks. Replace the cap and rotor as a set, if necessary.

5. Replace the wires if the insulation is melted, brittle or cracked.

6. Loosen the 2 rotor screws. Lift the rotor straight up and off.

7. Wipe the rotor with a clean, damp cloth. Check for burns, arcing, cracks or other defects. Replace the rotor and cap as a set, if necessary.

8. Install the rotor.

9. Install the distributor cap. Depress and rotate the cap latch screws 90° to lock the cap in place.

10. Install the wire harness retainer to the distributor cap. Make sure the 2 latches lock in place.

11. 1985-on—install the distributor cover (**Figure 33**).

Ignition Timing

NOTE
Refer to the VECI label in the engine compartment. Follow all instructions and specifications on the label.

1. Connect a timing light to the engine according to manufacturer's instructions. Refer to **Figure 28** for the No. 1 cylinder plug wire.

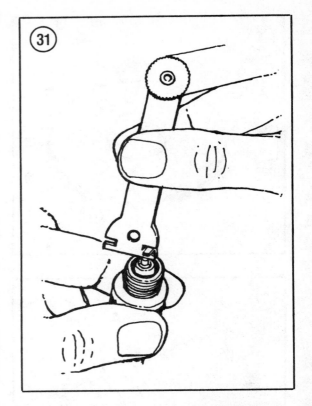

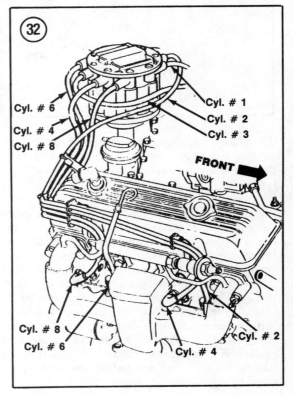

2. Disconnect the 4-terminal EST connector at the distributor to allow the engine to operate in the bypass timing mode.

3. Locate the timing mark on the crankshaft balancer or pulley and mark it with white paint. See **Figure 35**. The paint makes the marks easier to see under the timing mark.

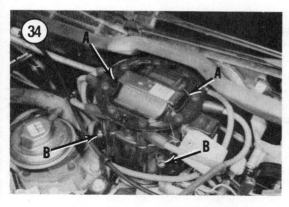

4. Start the engine and let it idle. Point the timing light at the marks. They will appear to stand still or waver slightly under the light.

WARNING
Keep your hands and hair clear of all drive belts and pulleys. Although they seem to be standing still, they are actually spinning at more than 10 times per second and can cause serious injury.

5. If the timing is incorrect, loosen the distributor hold-down bolt (**Figure 36**) enough to rotate the distributor body.

WARNING
Never touch the distributor's thick wires when the engine is running. This can cause a painful shock, even if the insulation is in perfect condition.

6. Grasp the distributor cap and rotate the body clockwise or counterclockwise as required to align the timing marks. Tighten the hold-down bolt snugly and recheck the timing.

7. Shut the engine off. Remove the test equipment. Reconnect the 4-terminal EST connector. Perform any other steps specified on the VECI label.

Idle Speed Adjustment

No attempt should be made to adjust the idle speed on the throttle body fuel injection assembly. An idle air control (IAC) assembly mounted on the throttle body maintains the correct idle speed according to electrical impulses from the electronic control module (ECM). Attempting to adjust the system will only make matters worse. If idle speed seems to require adjustment, see your Chevrolet dealer.

Fast Idle Speed Adjustment

The fast idle speed is controlled by the ECM and IAC assembly and cannot be adjusted.

Table 1 MAINTENANCE SCHEDULE

Every 7,500 miles or 12 months	• Engine oil [1] • Chassis lubrication • Check brake system • Check exhaust system • Check rear axle and manual transmission fluid levels • Check/adjust drive belts • Check suspension and steering • Check throttle linkage
At 7,500 miles	• Check throttle body mounting torque (1984)
At first 7,500 miles, then every 15,000 miles	• Replace oil filter • Check and rotate tires
At first 7,500 miles, then every 30,000 miles	• Check throttle body hoses
Every 15,000 miles	• Check automatic transmission fluid [1] • Check cooling system [2] • Replace fuel filter
Every 30,000 miles	• Replace spark plugs • Change overdrive unit fluid and filter • Check ignition timing • Check ignition wiring • Check PCV system
Every 30,000 miles or 24 months	• Drain, flush and refill cooling system
Every 30,000 miles or 36 months	• Check air cleaner system operation • Replace air cleaner filter • Replace crankcase ventilation filter • Check EGR system operation
Every 100,000 miles	• Change automatic transmission fluid and filter [1]

1. SEVERE SERVICE OPERATION: If the vehicle is operated under any of the following conditions, change engine oil @ 3,000 miles or 3 month intervals and oil filter @ alternate oil changes. Clean and regap spark plugs every 6,000 miles. Change automatic transmission fluid and filter every 100,000 miles.
  a. Extended idle or low-speed operation (short trips, stop-and-go driving).
  b. Trailer towing.
  c. Operation @ temperatures below 10° F for 60 days or more with most trips under 10 miles.
  d. Very dusty or muddy conditions.
2. Check coolant protection and condition once a year.

Table 2 OIL VISCOSITIES

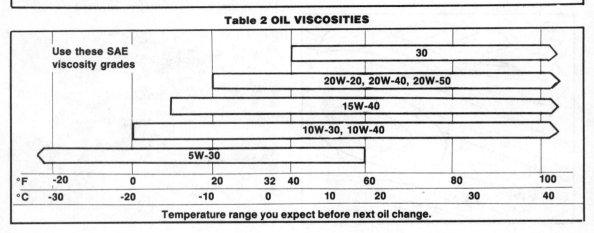

Temperature range you expect before next oil change.

Table 3 RECOMMENDED LUBRICANTS

Engine crankcase	API service SF, SF/CC or SF/CD oil
Engine coolant	Ethylene glycol antifreeze meeting GM specification 1825M (part No. 1052753) or equivalent
Brake fluid	Delco Supreme II or other DOT 3 fluid
Power steering pump	GM power steering fluid or equivalent
Manual transmission	SAE 80W or SAE 80W-90 GL-5 gear lubricant
Overdrive unit	DEXRON II or equivalent
Automatic transmission fluid	DEXRON II or equivalent
Rear axle	GM part No. 1052271 and 4 ounces of GM part No. 1052358 or equivalent
Chassis and parking brake cables	Chassis grease meeting GM specification 6031M or equivalent
Shift linkage, hood latch, all hinges	Engine oil
Key lock cylinders	WD-40 or equivalent
Windshield washer	GM Optikleen solvent (part No. 1051515) or equivalent

Table 4 APPROXIMATE REFILL CAPACITIES

	qt.	pt.
Engine crankcase*		
With filter change	6.0	
Without filter change	5.0	
Automatic transmission		
After rebuild		10.0
Fluid change		7.0
Manual transmission		2.0
Overdrive unit		4.0
Differential		4.0
Cooling system	14.5	

* Includes one qt. for oil cooler.

CHAPTER FOUR

ENGINE

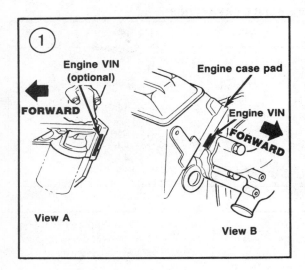

View A

Engine VIN (optional)

FORWARD

Engine case pad

Engine VIN

FORWARD

View B

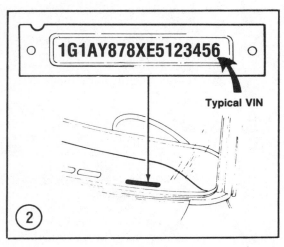

1G1AY878XE5123456

Typical VIN

The Corvette is equipped with a 350 cid (5.7L) V8 engine manufactured by Chevrolet. The firing order is 1-8-4-3-6-5-7-2. The No. 1 cylinder is the front cylinder on the left bank.

The chain-driven camshaft is made of cast iron and is supported by 5 bearings. A camshaft gear drives the distributor and oil pump. The cast iron (1984-1985) or aluminum (1986-on) cylinder heads have individual intake and exhaust ports. Integral valve guides are used, with rocker arms held on individual pressed studs. A ball pivot valve train is used, with camshaft motion transferred through the hydraulic lifters to the rocker arms by pushrods. Roller lifters are used on 1987 engines.

The oil pump is driven by the camshaft and is mounted at the bottom of the engine block.

The crankshaft is supported by 5 main bearings, with the No. 5 bearing providing the crankshaft thrust surfaces.

The cylinder block is cast iron with full length water jackets around each cylinder.

Engine specifications (**Table 1**) and tightening torques (**Table 2**) are at the end of the chapter.

VEHICLE IDENTIFICATION NUMBER

The Vehicle Identification Number (VIN) is the official identification for title and vehicle registration. The VIN may be located on a boss beside the oil filter or on the engine case pad near the water pump (**Figure 1**). The engine code is the 8th digit/letter of the VIN.

The VIN is stamped on a gray-colored plate fastened to the upper left corner of the instrument panel close to the windshield on the driver's side (**Figure 2**). It can be read from outside the car.

GASKET SEALANT

Room temperature vulcanizing (RTV) sealant is used instead of pre-formed gaskets between numerous engine mating surfaces. This black silicone gel is supplied in tubes and is available from your Chevrolet dealer (part No. 1052366). Moisture in the air causes RTV to cure. Always place the cap on the tube as soon as possible when using RTV. RTV has a shelf life of one year and will not cure properly when the shelf life has expired. Check the expiration date on RTV tubes before using and keep partially used tubes tightly sealed.

Applying RTV Sealant

Clean all RTV residue from mating surfaces. The secret of a non-leaking seal with RTV lies in clean surfaces that are free of all oil and dirt. Remove all RTV material from blind attaching holes, as it can cause a hydraulic effect and affect bolt torque.

Apply RTV sealant in a continuous bead about 1/8 in. (3 mm) thick. Run the sealant on the inner

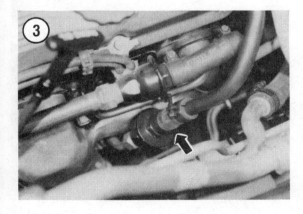

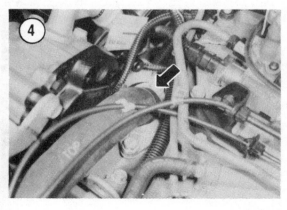

side of mounting holes. Torque mating parts within 10 minutes after application.

ENGINE REMOVAL (1984)

WARNING
Have the air conditioning system discharged by an air conditioning specialist before beginning this procedure.

WARNING
The engine is heavy, awkward to handle and has sharp edges. It may shift or drop suddenly during removal. To prevent serious injury, always observe the following precautions.
1. Never place any part of your body where a moving or falling engine may trap, cut or crush you.
2. If you must push the engine during removal, use a board or similar tool to keep your hands out of danger.
3. Be sure the hoist is designed to lift engines and has enough load capacity for your engine.
4. Be sure the hoist is securely attached to safe lifting points on the engine.
5. The engine should not be difficult to lift with a proper hoist. If it is, stop lifting, lower the engine back onto its mounts and make sure the engine has been completely separated from the vehicle.

1. Disconnect the negative battery cable.
2. Place a suitable container under the radiator drain valve. Drain the cooling system. See Chapter Six.
3. Remove the air cleaner. See Chapter Five.
4. Disconnect the left and right AIR hoses and the air management hose at their respective check valves (**Figure 3**, typical).
5. Remove both rear braces at the air conditioning compressor.
6. Disconnect the air conditioning compressor wires.
7. Remove the air pump pulley and air control valve adapter from the air pump. Remove the air pump. See Chapter Five.
8. Remove the upper radiator hose at the water outlet. See **Figure 4**. Disconnect the clamp holding the hose to the power steering reservoir brace.
9. Disconnect the alternator wires. Remove the alternator brace. Remove the alternator.
10. Remove the AIR pipe at the intake manifold and power steering reservoir brace.
11. Remove the power steering reservoir brace and power steering pump lower bracket. Move the reservoir, brace, pump and air conditioning wire

loom to the front of the engine compartment out of the way.

12. Use one wrench to hold the fuel inlet nut and another wrench to loosen the fuel line fitting nut. Disconnect the fuel supply and return lines at the throttle body assemblies. See **Figure 5**. Cap the lines to prevent leakage.

13. Remove the air conditioning compressor and idler pulley bracket nuts at the water pump. Remove the lower compressor mounting bolt. Move the bracket forward and remove upper compressor bolt. Place compressor to one side out of the way.

14. Remove the fuel line lower bracket. The bracket is mounted on a cover plate at the lower right front of the engine.

15. Remove the idler pulley bracket.

16. Disconnect lower radiator hose and heater hose at the water pump. Move hoses and fuel lines out of the way.

17. Disconnect the throttle cable from the intake manifold cover bracket and the throttle body assembly. Disconnect throttle rod and cruise control cables, if so equipped. See **Figure 6** and Chapter Five.

18. Disconnect the power brake booster vacuum line and the PCV hose at the intake manifold cover.

19. Disconnect all electrical connections at the TBI units. Disconnect front ground stud, coolant sensor and EGR solenoid leads.

20. Label and disconnect all vacuum lines.

21. Remove the wiring harness at the valve cover clip. Move the air control valve, AIR pipe and wiring harness to the right rear of the engine.

22. Remove the distributor tach filter and ground wires at the intake manifold cover stud. Disconnect the distributor leads at the distributor cap.

23. Disconnect the spark plug wires and remove the distributor cap.

24. Disconnect the heater hose at the intake manifold cover.

25. Remove the distributor. See Chapter Seven.

26. Disconnect the oil pressure sending unit.

27. Remove the rear intake manifold bolt. Remove the wire bracket.

28. Remove the crankshaft pulley.

29. Securely block the wheels that remain on the ground. Raise the vehicle and place it on jackstands.

30. Disconnect the oxygen sensor lead. Disconnect the air management pipe (**Figure 7**). Disconnect exhaust crossover pipe at each manifold (**Figure 7**,

typical) and at the converter (**Figure 8**). Remove the crossover pipe.

31. Disconnect the starter wires.

32. Disconnect the coolant sensor lead at the cylinder head and at the engine block bracket.

33. Disconnect the wire harness from the oil pan and front of the engine block.

34. Disconnect the battery and engine grounds from the rear of the engine block (above the oil filter).

35. Remove the flywheel cover.

36. Automatic transmission—remove torque converter bolts.

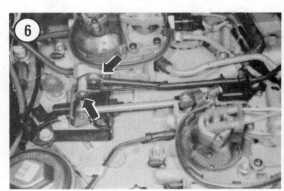

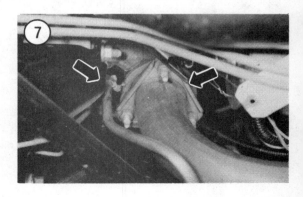

37. Manual transmission—disconnect hydraulic clutch cylinder. See Chapter Eight.

38. Remove the bellhousing bolts on the right side of the engine. Remove the lower first, then the upper to provide access to the center bolt.

39. Remove the bellhousing bolts on the left side of the engine.

40. Place a jack under the engine for support. Remove the right and left motor mount-to-block bolts.

41. Remove the jackstands and lower the vehicle to the ground.

42. Place a jack under the transmission for support.

43. Attach an engine support bracket or hoisting sling. Connect the bracket or sling to the hoist.

> *NOTE*
> *At this point, there should be no hoses, wires or linkage connecting the engine to the vehicle. Recheck this to be sure nothing will hamper engine removal.*

44. Pull forward on the engine until it disengages from the transmission. Remove the engine from the vehicle.

ENGINE REMOVAL (1985-ON)

> *WARNING*
> *Have the air conditioning system discharged by an air conditioning specialist before beginning this procedure.*

> *WARNING*
> *The engine is heavy, awkward to handle and has sharp edges. It may shift or drop suddenly during removal. To prevent serious injury, always observe the following precautions.*
> *1. Never place any part of your body where a moving or falling engine may trap, cut or crush you.*
> *2. If you must push the engine during removal, use a board or similar tool to keep your hands out of danger.*
> *3. Be sure the hoist is designed to lift engines and has enough load capacity for your engine.*
> *4. Be sure the hoist is securely attached to safe lifting points on the engine.*
> *5. The engine should not be difficult to lift with a proper hoist. If it is, stop lifting, lower the engine back onto its mounts and make sure the engine has been completely separated from the vehicle.*

1. Disconnect the negative battery cable.

2. Place a suitable container under the radiator drain valve. Drain the cooling system. See Chapter Six.

3. Unclamp and remove the flexible air intake duct from the throttle body and air cleaner duct. See **Figure 9**.

4. Remove both rear braces at the air conditioning compressor.

5. Disconnect the air conditioning compressor wires.

6. Relieve the fuel system pressure. See Chapter Five.

7. Use one wrench to hold the fuel inlet nut and another wrench to loosen the fuel line fitting nut. Disconnect the fuel supply and return lines at the fuel rail. Plug the lines to prevent leakage. See **Figure 10**.

8. Remove the air conditioning compressor and idler pulley bracket fasteners.

9. Disconnect the heater hoses at the bulkhead.

10. Remove the nut holding the fuel line bracket to the fuel pump cover plate on the engine. Remove the bracket from the stud and move the fuel line assembly out of the way. See **Figure 10**.

11. Disconnect the upper radiator hose at the water outlet (**Figure 11**).

12. Remove the air conditioning compressor mounting bolt. Place compressor to one side out of the way. Remove the compressor mounting bracket.

13. Disconnect the fuel injection harness at the engine.

14. Disconnect the throttle cable from the throttle body assembly. Disconnect throttle rod and cruise control cables, if so equipped. See **Figure 12**.

15. Remove the distributor shield or cover (**Figure 13**). Remove the distributor cap and disconnect the 4-wire distributor connector.

16. Remove the detent cable bracket at the intake manifold.

17. Remove the distributor. See Chapter Seven.

18. Disconnect and remove the oil pressure sending unit.

19. Label and disconnect all vacuum lines connected to the engine.

20. Disconnect the power steering hoses at the steering gearbox. Plug the lines and cap the fittings.

21. Remove the crankshaft pulley as described in this chapter.

22. Disconnect the wiring harness at the bulkhead connectors.

23. Disconnect the AIR hose at the converter check valve.

24. Disconnect the lower radiator hose and heater hose at the water pump.

25. Remove the upper radiator hose from the radiator shroud bracket.

26. Raise the vehicle and place it on jackstands.

27. Disconnect the AIR pipes at the exhaust manifold and catalytic converter. Disconnect the

exhaust crossover pipe hanger. Disconnect the heat shields at the crossover pipe and converter. Disconnect the oxygen sensor lead and remove the crosssover pipe.

28. Remove the flywheel cover.

29. Automatic transmission—remove torque converter bolts.

30. Manual transmission—disconnect hydraulic clutch cylinder. See Chapter Eight.

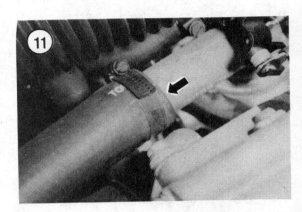

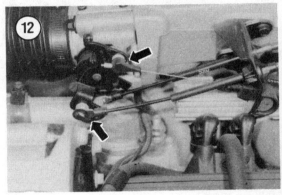

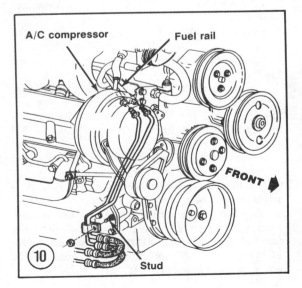

31. Loosen the motor mount through-bolts. Remove the motor mount-to-engine block bolts.
32. Disconnect the engine knock sensor lead. Disconnect the battery and engine grounds from the rear of the engine block (above the oil filter).
33. Remove the right rear intake manifold bolt and install a lifting eye.
34. Remove the bellhousing bolts on the right side of the engine. Remove the lower first, then the upper to provide access to the center bolt.
35. Remove the bellhousing bolts on the left side of the engine.
36. Remove the jackstands and lower the vehicle to the ground.
37. Place a jack under the transmission for support.
38. Attach an engine hoisting sling to the lifting eye.

NOTE
At this point, there should be no hoses, wires or linkage connecting the engine to the vehicle. Recheck this to be sure nothing will hamper engine removal.

39. Pull forward on the engine until it disengages from the transmission. Remove the engine from the vehicle.

ENGINE INSTALLATION

Engine installation is the reverse of removal, plus the following:
1. Lower the engine into the vehicle. Leave the hoist attached and holding the engine weight until all mount and mount fasteners have been installed and torqued to specifications.
2. If equipped with an automatic transmission, thoroughly clean all converter-to-drive plate bolts and coat them with Loctite 271 or equivalent before installation.
3. Tighten all fasteners to specifications. See **Table 2**.
4. Fill the engine with an oil recommended in Chapter Three.
5. Fill the cooling system. See Chapter Six.

DISASSEMBLY CHECKLISTS

To use the checklists, remove and inspect each part in the order mentioned. To reassemble, go through the checklists backwards, installing the parts in order. Each major part is covered under its own heading in this chapter, unless otherwise noted.

Decarbonizing or Valve Service

1. Remove the valve cover(s).
2. Remove the intake and exhaust manifolds.
3. Remove the rocker arms and camshaft.

4. Remove the cylinder head(s).
5. Remove and inspect the valves. Inspect valve guides and seats, repairing or replacing as required.
6. Assemble by reversing Steps 1-5.

Valve and Ring Service

1. Perform *Decarbonizing or Valve Service* in this chapter.
2. Remove the oil pan.
3. Remove the pistons with the connecting rods.
4. Remove the piston rings. It is not necessary to separate the pistons from the connecting rods unless a piston, connecting rod or piston pin needs repair or replacement.
5. Assemble by reversing Steps 1-4.

General Overhaul

1. Remove the engine. Remove the clutch (Chapter Eight) from manual transmission vehicles.
2. Remove the flywheel or drive plate.
3. Remove the front mount brackets and oil pressure sending unit from the engine.
4. If available, mount the engine on an engine stand. These can be rented from equipment rental dealers. The stand is not absolutely necessary, but it will make the job much easier.
5. Check the engine for signs of coolant or oil leaks.
6. Clean the outside of the engine.
7. Remove all hoses and tubes connected to the engine.
8. Remove the intake and exhaust manifolds.
9. Remove the thermostat. See Chapter Six.
10. Remove the rocker arms.
11. Remove the crankshaft pulley/vibration damper and timing case cover.
12. Remove the camshaft.
13. Remove the water pump. See Chapter Six.
14. Remove the cylinder heads.
15. Remove the oil pan and oil pump.
16. Remove the pistons and connecting rods.
17. Remove the crankshaft.
18. Inspect the cylinder block.
19. Assemble by reversing Steps 1-17.

VALVE COVERS

The valve covers are manufactured of epoxy-coated die-cast magnesium and are mounted to the cylinder heads with RTV sealant. Raised rocker cover rails are used on 1987 engines to improve oil sealing. To remove the valve covers without damage, it may be necessary to bump the front of the cover with a rubber mallet and block of wood. If this does not loosen the cover sufficiently for removal, *carefully* pry the cover free, taking care not to distort the sealing flanges.

1984 Removal (Right Side)

1. Disconnect the negative battery cable.
2. Remove the air cleaner. See Chapter Five.
3. Disconnect the AIR hose from the exhaust check valve.
4. Disconnect the fuel inlet and return lines at the TBI assembly. Use one wrench to hold the inlet nut and another wrench to loosen the fuel line fitting.
5. Remove the 2 rear braces and the lower mounting bolt at the air conditioning compressor.
6. Remove the drive belt. See Chapter Three.
7. Remove the idler pulley bracket nuts at the water pump.

> *WARNING*
> *The air conditioning system contains pressurized refrigerant which can cause frostbite if it touches skin and blindness if it touches the eyes. If discharged near an open flame, the refrigerant forms poisonous gas. Never disconnect air conditioning system lines unless the system has been discharged and evacuated by a professional.*

8. Slide the air conditioning compressor bracket forward. Remove the compressor upper mounting bolt. Remove the compressor.
9. Remove the valve cover bolts.
10. Bend the bracket back at the rear of the head and remove the valve cover.

1984 Removal (Left Side)

1. Disconnect the negative battery cable.
2. Remove the air cleaner. See Chapter Five.
3. Disconnect the PCV hoses at the PCV valve (**Figure 14**).
4. Disconnect the power brake booster line at the intake manifold.
5. Remove the drive belt. See Chapter Three.
6. Disconnect the radiator hose bracket at the power steering pump brace.
7. Remove the alternator. See Chapter Seven.
8. Remove the valve cover bolts.
9. Disconnect the spark plug wires.
10. Bend the bracket back at the rear of the head and remove the valve cover.

1985-on Removal (Right Side)

1. Disconnect the negative battery cable.
2. Remove the injector harness cover.
3. Disconnect the AIR hose from the AIR pipe.
4. Disconnect the heater hoses at the throttle body (A, **Figure 15**).

5. Disconnect all electrical leads at the idle air control (IAC), throttle position sensor (TPS) and injectors. See B, **Figure 15** for location of IAC and TPS wires.
6. Disconnect the spark plug wires at the valve cover wire loom.
7. Remove the valve cover bolts. Remove the valve cover.

1985-on Removal (Left Side)

1. Disconnect the negative battery cable.
2. Remove the injector harness cover. See A, **Figure 16**.

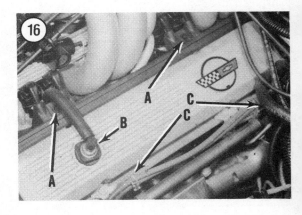

3. Disconnect the PCV valve at the valve cover. See B, **Figure 16**.

4. Disconnect the spark plug wires at the valve cover wire loom. See C, **Figure 16**.

5. Loosen the air pump bolts and remove the drive belt. Remove the air pump and lower mounting bracket.

6. Remove the valve cover bolts. Remove the valve cover.

Installation (Both Sides)

Installation is the reverse of removal, plus the following:

1. Clean the sealing surface on the valve cover and cylinder head with degreaser and a putty knife to remove all RTV sealant residue. The sealing surfaces must be perfectly clean and dry.

2. Run a 1/8 in. (3 mm) bead of RTV sealant around the valve cover sealing surface, flowing it on the inner side of the attaching holes.

3. Tighten cover bolts to 50 in.-lb. (6 N•m) while RTV is still wet.

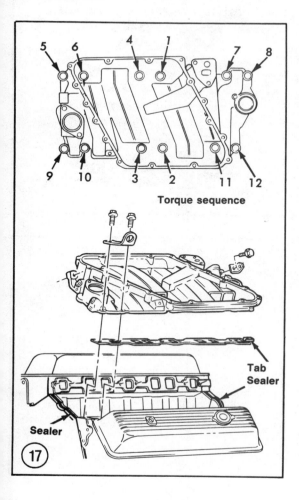

Torque sequence

Tab Sealer

Sealer

(17)

INTAKE MANIFOLD

Removal/Installation (1984)

Refer to **Figure 17** for this procedure.

1. Disconnect the negative battery cable.

2. Remove the air cleaner assembly. See Chapter Five.

3. Relieve the fuel injection system pressure (Chapter Five). Disconnect the fuel inlet and return lines from the TBI assembly. Use one wrench to hold the inlet nut and another wrench to loosen the fuel line fitting.

4. Disconnect all electrical fittings.

5. Label and disconnect all vacuum lines.

6. Disconnect the throttle cable. See **Figure 6** and Chapter Five. Disconnect the throttle rod and cruise control cable, if so equipped. Disconnect cable(s) from bracket(s).

7. Remove the intake manifold cover nuts and bolts. Remove the cover.

8. Drain the cooling system. See Chapter Six.

9. Disconnect the upper radiator hose at the water outlet (**Figure 4**). Remove the radiator hose bracket at the power steering pump brace.

10. Remove the distributor. See Chapter Seven.

11. Disconnect the heater hose at the rear of the intake manifold.

12. Remove the air pump. See Chapter Five.

13. Disconnect the ECM coolant temperature sensor.

14. Remove the intake manifold bolts. Remove the intake manifold.

15. Clean the gasket and seal surfaces on the manifold, engine block and cylinder heads with degreaser and a putty knife to remove all RTV and gasket residue.

16. Install new gaskets on the cylinder heads with the blocked openings at the rear of the engine. Bend the gasket tab flush with the rear face of the head, then run a 3/16 in. (5 mm) bead of RTV sealant on the front and rear ridges of the cylinder case. See **Figure 17**.

17. Reverse Steps 1-14 to install the intake manifold. Use Loctite 1052624 or equivalent on the manifold bolts and tighten to specifications in the sequence shown in **Figure 17**. Tighten all other fasteners to specifications.

Removal/Installation (1985-on)

1. Disconnect the negative battery cable.

2. Drain the cooling system. See Chapter Six.

3. Unclamp and remove the flexible air intake duct from the throttle body and air cleaner duct. See **Figure 9**.

4. Disconnect all electrical leads and coolant hoses at the throttle body. See **Figure 15**.

5. Disconnect all vacuum lines and breather hoses at the throttle body.

6. Remove the distributor shield or cover (**Figure 13**).

7. Disconnect the brake booster vacuum pipe and all vacuum hoses from the plenum.

8. Relieve the fuel system pressure. See Chapter Five.

9. Use one wrench to hold the fuel inlet nut and another wrench to loosen the fuel line fitting nut. Disconnect the fuel supply and return lines at the fuel rail. Plug the lines to prevent leakage. See **Figure 10**. Disconnect the fuel line bracket from the intake manifold.

10. Disconnect the cold start injector line at the fuel rail.

11. Disconnect all vacuum lines at the EGR and pressure regulator control valves.

12. Remove both injector harness covers (**Figure 16** shows left side cover). Disconnect the wiring harness from each injector.

13. Disconnect the PCV pipe at the valve cover and remove the breather tube.

14. Remove the fuel rail. See Chapter Five.

15. Remove the distributor. See Chapter Seven.

16. Disconnect the EGR solenoid leads.

17. Disconnect the ECM coolant temperature and cold start injector sensors.

18. Disconnect the ground lead and upper radiator hose at the water outlet.

19. Remove the intake manifold bolts. Remove the intake manifold.

20. Clean the gasket and seal surfaces on the manifold, engine block and cylinder heads with degreaser and a putty knife to remove all RTV and gasket residue.

21. Install new gaskets on the cylinder heads with the blocked openings at the rear of the engine. Bend the gasket tab flush with the rear face of the head, then run a 3/16 in. (5 mm) bead of RTV sealant on the front and rear ridges of the cylinder case. See **Figure 17**.

22. Reverse Steps 1-19 to install the intake manifold. Use Loctite 1052624 or equivalent on the manifold bolts. Follow the upper tightening sequence shown in **Figure 18** and tighten those 6 bolts snugly, then tighten all bolts to specifications (**Table 2**) following the lower sequence shown in **Figure 18**.

EXHAUST MANIFOLD

Removal/Installation (Right Manifold)

Refer to **Figure 19** for this procedure.

1. Disconnect the negative battery cable.

2. Remove the air cleaner. See Chapter Five.

3. Drain the cooling system. See Chapter Six.

4. Remove the air conditioning compressor rear brace.

5. Disconnect the AIR hoses at the check valves (**Figure 3**).

6. Disconnect the heater hose at the rear of the intake manifold.

7. Disconnect the spark plug wires and place out of the way.

8. Remove the spark plugs. See Chapter Three.

9. Remove the temperature sending unit in the right cylinder head.

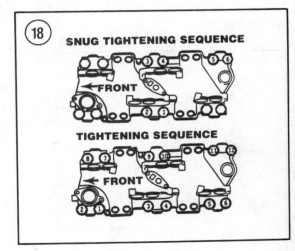

SNUG TIGHTENING SEQUENCE

←FRONT

TIGHTENING SEQUENCE

←FRONT

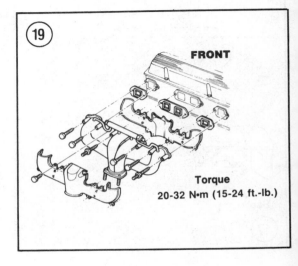

FRONT

Torque
20-32 N•m (15-24 ft.-lb.)

10. Securely block the wheels that remain on the ground. Raise the front of the vehicle and place it on jackstands.

11. Disconnect the crossover pipe and air management pipe at the exhaust manifold (**Figure 7**).

12. Remove the 2 rear bolts from the exhaust manifold.

13. Disconnect the dipstick tube at the manifold.

14. Remove the jackstands and lower the vehicle.

15. Remove the remaining manifold bolts. Remove the manifold.

16. **Clean the mating surfaces on the cylinder head.**

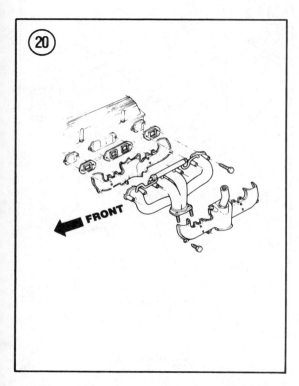

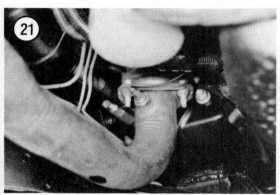

17. Installation is the reverse of removal. Tighten all fasteners to specifications.

Removal/Installation
(Left Manifold)

Refer to **Figure 20** for this procedure.

1. Disconnect the negative battery cable.

2. Remove the air cleaner. See Chapter Five.

3. Disconnect the PCV hose at the intake manifold cover and valve cover.

4. Disconnect the AIR hose at the check valve.

5. Disconnect rear alternator brace from manifold.

6. Raise the front of the vehicle and place it on jackstands.

7. Disconnect the crossover pipe at the exhaust manifold (**Figure 21**).

8. Remove the jackstands and lower the vehicle to the ground.

9. Remove the manifold bolts. Remove the manifold.

10. Clean mating surface on cylinder head.

11. Installation is the reverse of removal. Tighten all fasteners to specifications.

Manifold Inspection

1. Check the intake and exhaust manifolds for cracks or distortion. Replace if distorted or if cracks are found.

2. Check the gasket surfaces for nicks or burrs. Small burrs may be removed with an oilstone.

3. Place a straightedge across the manifold gasket surfaces. Measure horizontally and diagonally. If there is any gap between the straightedge and the gasket surface, measure it with a feeler gauge.

4. The gasket surface must be flat within 0.006 in. (0.15 mm) per foot of manifold length. If not, replace the manifold.

ROCKER ARMS

Removal

Each rocker arm moves on its own pivot ball. The rocker arm and pivot ball are retained by a capscrew.

It is not necessary to remove the rocker arm for pushrod replacement; simply loosen the rocker arm nut and move the arm away from the pushrod.

To remove the entire assembly, proceed as follows:

1. Remove the valve cover as described in this chapter.

2. Remove the rocker arm nuts, rocker arm balls, rocker arms and pushrods.

3. Place each rocker arm assembly in a separate container or use a rack to keep them separated for reinstallation in the same position as removed.

4. 1987—unbolt and remove the roller lifter retainers and restrictors.

5. All engines—remove the valve lifters with a pencil-type magnet. Place lifters in a rack in order of removal for reinstallation in their original location.

Inspection

Clean all parts with solvent and use compressed air to blow out the oil passages in the pushrod. Check each rocker arm, pivot ball and pushrod for scuffing, pitting or excessive wear. If a pushrod is worn from lack of oil, it will be necessary to replace that pushrod's hydraulic valve tappet and rocker arm as well.

Installation

If new rocker arms and rocker arm balls are being installed, coat bearing surfaces with Molykote or equivalent.

1. Install the valve lifters. On 1987 engines, install roller lifter restrictors and retainers. Install the pushrods and make sure they seat in the lifter sockets.

2. Install rocker arms, rocker arm balls and rocker arm nuts. Tighten nuts until all lash is eliminated.

3. Crank engine to align torsional damper mark with "0" mark on the timing tab. As the damper mark nears the "0" mark on the timing tab, place a finger on the No. 1 valves. They should not be moving (No. 1 firing position). If the valves move, the engine is in the No. 6 firing position. Crank it over one more time to bring the No. 1 cylinder into firing position.

4. With the engine in the No. 1 firing position, refer to **Figure 22** and adjust the No. 1, 2, 5 and 7 intake and the No. 1, 3, 4 and 8 exhaust valves as follows:

   a. Back off the rocker arm stud nut until play can be felt in the pushrod.

   b. Tighten the nut to the point that all pushrod-to-rocker arm clearance is removed. This can be determined by rotating the pushrod while tightening the nut (**Figure 23**). When the pushrod does not rotate easily, clearance has been eliminated.

   c. Now tighten the nut one additional turn to center the hydraulic lifter plunger. No other adjustment is required.

5. Crank the engine one revolution to the No. 6 firing position. Refer to **Figure 22** and adjust the

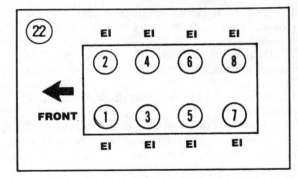

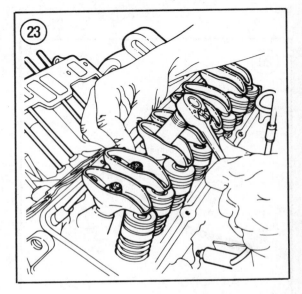

No. 3, 4, 6 and 8 intake and No. 2, 5, 6 and 7 exhaust valves as described in Step 4.

6. Install the valve covers as described in this chapter.

CAMSHAFT

Removal

1. Remove the engine from the car as described in this chapter.

2. Remove the valve covers as described in this chapter.

3. Remove the rocker arms and valve lifters as described in this chapter.

4. Remove the torsional damper, front cover and timing chain as described in this chapter.

> *CAUTION*
> *All camshaft journals are the same diameter and care must be taken to prevent bearing damage while performing Step 5.*

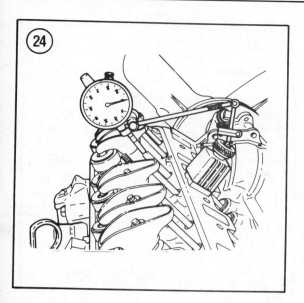

5. Withdraw camshaft from the block with a slow, careful rotating motion.

Inspection

1. Check the journals and lobes for signs of wear or scoring. Lobe pitting in the toe area is not sufficient reason for replacement, unless the lobe lift loss exceeds specifications.

> *NOTE*
> *If you do not have precision measuring equipment, have Step 2 done by a machine shop.*

2. Measure the camshaft journal diameters with a micrometer. Replace the camshaft if the journals are more than 0.001 in. (0.025 mm) out-of-round.

Installation

> *NOTE*
> *When installing a new camshaft, coat the lobes with Molykote or equivalent.*

1. Lubricate the camshaft journals with SAE 30W engine oil.
2. Install the camshaft with a rotating motion.
3. Reverse Steps 1-4 of *Removal* in this chapter to complete installation.

Bearing Replacement

Camshaft bearings can be replaced without complete engine disassembly. Camshaft bearing remover/installer tool part No. J-6098 is required for this procedure.

1. Remove the camshaft and crankshaft as described in this chapter.

2. Drive the camshaft rear plug from the block.

3. Install the nut and thrust washer to tool part No. J-6098. Index the tool pilot in the front cam bearing. Install the puller screw through the pilot.

4. Install tool part No. J-6098 with its shoulder facing the front intermediate bearing and the threads engaging the bearing.

5. Hold the puller screw with one wrench. Turn the nut with a second wrench until the bearing has been pulled from its bore.

6. Repeat Steps 3-5 to remove remaining bearings (except front and rear).

7. Remove the tool and index it to the rear bearing to remove the rear intermediate bearing from the block.

8. Remove the front and rear bearings by driving them toward the center of the block.

9. Installation is the reverse of removal. Use the same tool to pull the new bearings into their bores. Index the front bearing oil holes so they are equidistant from the 6 o'clock position. Index the rear bearing oil hole at the 12 o'clock position. Index all other bearing oil holes at the 5 o'clock position (toward left side of engine and even with bottom of cylinder bore).

10. Coat outer diameter of new camshaft rear plug with sealant part No. 1052080 or equivalent and install flush to 1/32 in. (0.8 mm) deep.

Lobe Lift Measurement

Camshaft lobe lift is measured with the camshaft in the block and the cylinder head in place. Refer to **Figure 24** for this procedure.
1. Remove the valve covers and rocker arm assemblies as described in this chapter.
2. Install a dial indicator with ball socket adapter part No. J-8520 to fit over the pushrod.
3. Turn the crankshaft in the direction of rotation until the valve lifter seats on the heel of the cam lobe. This positions the pushrod at its lowest point.
4. Zero the dial indicator, then slowly rotate the crankshaft until the pushrod is in its fully raised position. Record the total lift.
5. Repeat Steps 2-4 for each pushrod. If all lobes are within specifications (**Table 1**), reinstall the rocker arm assemblies and adjust the valves as described in this chapter.
6. If one or more lobes are worn beyond specifications, replace the camshaft as described in this chapter.

4

TORSIONAL DAMPER

Removal/Installation

> *CAUTION*
> *The inertial weight section of the damper is assembled to the hub by a bonded rubber sleeve. Follow the procedure below using the specified tools or you may destroy the damper tuning.*

This procedure requires the use of GM puller part No. J-23523. Refer to **Figure 25**.

1. Disconnect the negative battery cable.
2. Remove the drive belt. See Chapter Three.
3. Remove the crankshaft pulley. Remove the damper bolt.
4. Install puller part No. J-23523 on damper. Tighten puller screw and remove damper.
5. Lubricate the front cover seal contact area on the damper with SAE 30W engine oil.
6. Position the damper over the crankshaft key.
7. Install threaded end of puller part No. J-23523 in the crankshaft so that at least 1/2 in. (13 mm) of the tool thread is engaged. Install plate, thrust bearing and nut.
8. Pull the damper into position as shown in **Figure 26**.
9. Remove the tool and reverse Steps 1-3 to complete installation.

Crankcase Front Cover

Refer to **Figure 27** for this procedure.

1. Remove the torsional damper as described in this chapter.
2. Remove the pulley and air control valve adapter from the air pump. Remove the air pump. See Chapter Five.
3. Relieve the fuel injection system pressure (Chapter Five). Disconnect the fuel supply and return lines at the TBI assembly (1984) or fuel rail (1985-on). Use one wrench to hold the inlet nut and another wrench to loosen the fuel line fitting.

> *WARNING*
> *The air conditioning system contains pressurized refrigerant which can cause frostbite if it touches skin and blindness if it touches the eyes. If discharged near an open flame, the refrigerant forms poisonous gas. Never disconnect air conditioning system lines unless the system has been discharged and evacuated by a professional.*

4. Remove the air conditioning compressor rear braces and lower mounting bolt. Remove compressor bracket nuts at water pump. Slide bracket forward and remove compressor mounting bolt. Disconnect electrical wires from the compressor and place the unit to one side out of the way.

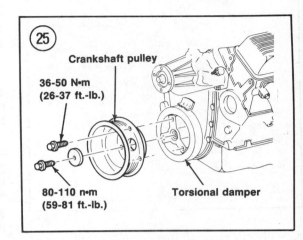

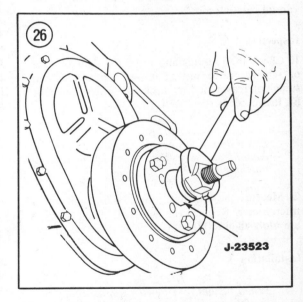

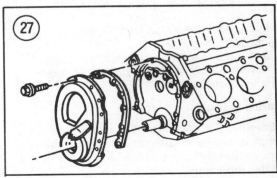

5. Disconnect the air pump hose at the right exhaust manifold.

6. Remove air conditioning compressor mounting bracket.

7. Remove upper air pump bracket with power steering reservoir. Remove lower air pump bracket.

8. Drain the cooling system. See Chapter Six.

9. Disconnect the radiator and heater hoses at the water pump.

10. Remove the water pump. See Chapter Six.

11. Remove the front cover bolts and front cover.

12. Clean the block and front cover sealing surfaces of all oil, grease and gasket or RTV sealant residue. Use degreaser and a putty knife.

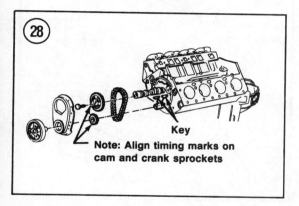

Key

Note: Align timing marks on cam and crank sprockets

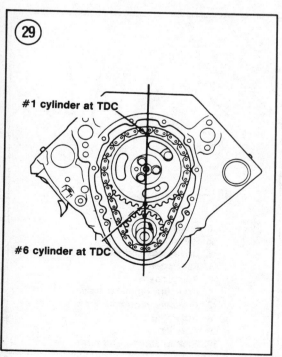

#1 cylinder at TDC

#6 cylinder at TDC

13. Apply a 1/8 in. (3 mm) bead of RTV sealant at the joint formed by the cylinder block and oil pan.

14. Install a new gasket to the cover with gasket sealant.

15. Install the cover-to-oil pan seal. Coat the bottom of the seal with SAE 30W engine oil. Position cover over crankshaft end.

16. Loosely install cover-to-block upper screws.

CAUTION
Do not force cover on dowels in Step 17. This will distort the cover flange or holes.

17. Align dowels in block with corresponding cover holes. Depress and hold cover in this position while tightening screws in an alternating pattern.

18. Reverse Steps 1-10 to complete installation. Tighten all fasteners to specifications (**Table 2**).

TIMING CHAIN AND SPROCKET

Removal

Refer to **Figure 28** for this procedure.

1. Remove front cover as described in this chapter.

2. Rotate crankshaft to align timing marks as shown in **Figure 29**.

NOTE
The camshaft sprocket is a light fit on the camshaft. A light blow with a plastic mallet on the lower sprocket edge should dislodge it.

3. Remove the camshaft sprocket bolt. Remove the sprocket and chain.

Installation

Refer to **Figure 28** and **Figure 29** for this procedure.

1. Install the timing chain on the camshaft sprocket.

2. Hold the sprocket vertically with the chain hanging down. Align the camshaft and crankshaft sprocket marks as shown in **Figure 29**.

3. Align the camshaft dowel with the sprocket hole. Position the sprocket on the camshaft.

4. Install camshaft sprocket bolts and draw sprocket onto camshaft by tightening the bolts to specifications (**Table 2**).

5. Lubricate the timing chain with SAE 30 engine oil.

6. Install the front cover as described in this chapter.

OIL PAN AND PUMP

A one-piece pan gasket is used on 1986 and later V8 engines in place of the 2-piece gasket and front/rear seals on earlier engines. The V8 gasket is installed with a very slight amount of RTV sealant (part No. 1052751) at the front and rear corners of the pan. Excessive sealant will prevent the gasket from making a proper seal and can result in an oil leak.

Oil Pan Removal

Refer to **Figure 30** (typical) for this procedure.
1. Disconnect the negative battery cable.
2. Block the rear wheels, then raise the front of the vehicle with a jack and place it on jackstands.
3. Drain the engine oil. See Chapter Three.
4. Remove the starter brace nut. Remove starter bolts and move starter to one side.
5. Remove the flywheel cover.
6. Remove the oil pan bolts. Remove the oil pan.
7. Remove and discard the oil pan gasket. Remove and discard the front and rear seals, if used.

Oil Pan Inspection

1. Clean the pan thoroughly in solvent.
2. Check the pan for dents or warped gasket surfaces. Straighten or replace the pan as required.
3. Check the pan for cracks. Repair or replace the pan as required.

Oil Pan Installation

Refer to **Figure 30** (typical) for this procedure.
1. Clean any RTV sealant or gasket residue from the oil pan rail on the engine block.
2A. 1-piece gasket:
   a. Apply a very slight amount of RTV sealant (part No. 1052751) at the front and rear corners of the pan.
     b. Place the gasket on the oil pan flange and install a pan attaching bolt at each corner to hold the gasket in position.
2B. 2-piece gasket:
   a. Place the gaskets on the oil pan flanges and install a pan attaching bolt at each end to hold the gasket in position.
     b. Install the front and rear seals on the engine block.
3. Carefully place the oil pan in position. Tighten the corner bolts finger-tight.

4. Make sure the gasket is properly aligned and not pinched, then install the remaining pan bolts finger-tight.
5. Tighten all bolts to specifications (**Table 4**). Work from the center outward in each direction.
6. Reverse Steps 1-5 of *Oil Pan Removal* in this chapter to complete installation.

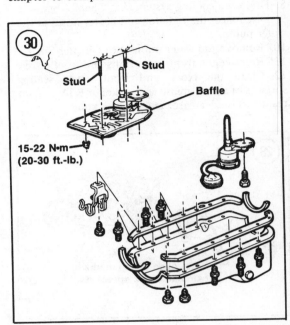

15-22 N•m
(20-30 ft.-lb.)

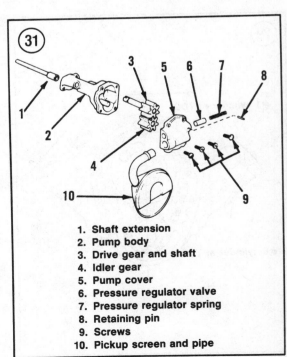

1. Shaft extension
2. Pump body
3. Drive gear and shaft
4. Idler gear
5. Pump cover
6. Pressure regulator valve
7. Pressure regulator spring
8. Retaining pin
9. Screws
10. Pickup screen and pipe

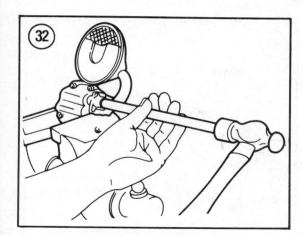

Oil Pump Removal/Installation

Some 1986-on V8 engines use a baffle over the oil pump (**Figure 30**).

1. Remove the oil pan as described in this chapter. If equipped with a baffle over the oil pump, remove the fasteners holding it in place and remove the baffle.

2. Remove the pump-to-rear main bearing cap bolt. Remove the oil pump and drive shaft.

3. Installation is the reverse of removal. Make sure slot on top of drive shaft aligns with drive tang on lower end of distributor drive shaft.

Oil Pump Disassembly/Assembly

Refer to **Figure 31** for this procedure.

1. Remove the cover bolts and cover.

2. Scribe marks on the gear teeth for reinstallation indexing.

3. Remove the idler gear, drive gear and shaft from the pump body.

4. Remove the pressure regulator valve pin, spring and valve.

5. Remove the pickup tube/screen *only* if it needs replacement. Secure the pump body in a vise with protective jaws and separate the tube from the cover.

> *NOTE*
> *Do not twist, shear or collapse the tube when installing it in Step 6.*

6. If the pickup tube/screen was removed, install a new one. Secure the pump body in a vise with protective jaws. Apply sealer to the new tube and tap in place with a plastic mallet and tool part No. J-8369 (**Figure 32**).

7. Assembly is the reverse of disassembly. Use a new cover gasket and tighten cover bolts to specifications (**Table 2**). Rotate pump drive shaft by hand to check for binding.

Oil Pump Inspection

The pump body and gears are serviced as an assembly. If one or the other is worn or damaged, replace the entire pump. No wear specifications are provided by Chevrolet.

1. Clean all parts thoroughly in solvent. Brush the inside of the body and the pressure regulator chamber to remove all dirt and metal particles. Dry with compressed air, if available.

2. Check the pump body and cover for cracks or excessive wear.

3. Check the pump gears for damage or excessive wear.

4. Check the drive gear shaft-to-body fit for excessive looseness.

5. Check the inside of the pump cover for wear that could allow oil to leak around the ends of the gears.

6. Check the pressure regulator valve for a proper fit.

CYLINDER HEADS

Aluminum cylinder heads are used on 1986 engines. Power tools should not be used to remove or install aluminum heads. Be sure to torque heads properly in the specified order to avoid possible warpage.

1984 Removal (Right Side)

1. Disconnect the negative battery cable.

2. Remove the intake manifold as described in this chapter.

3. Remove the valve cover a described in this chapter.

4. Disconnect air control valve hose at check valve.

5. Remove the 2 rear braces and the lower mounting bolt at the air conditioning compressor.

6. Remove the drive belt. See Chapter Three.

7. Remove the idler pulley bracket nuts at the water pump.

8. Disconnect air management pipe at exhaust manifold. Remove 2 rear manifold bolts. Disconnect crossover pipe at exhaust manifold. See **Figure 7**.

9. Remove dipstick at manifold.

10. Remove jackstands and lower vehicle to the ground.

11. Remove the exhaust manifold.

12. Disconnect spark plug cable holder at rear of head.

13. Loosen rocker arm nuts. Remove pushrods.

14. Remove head bolts. Remove cylinder head. Remove and discard the head gasket.

> *NOTE*
> *Place the head on its side to prevent damage to the head gasket surface.*

1985-on Removal (Right Side)

1. Disconnect the negative battery cable.
2. Remove the intake manifold as described in this chapter.
3. Disconnect the AIR hose from the exhaust check valve.

WARNING
The air conditioning system contains pressurized refrigerant which can cause frostbite if it touches skin and blindness if it touches the eyes. If discharged near an open flame, the refrigerant forms poisonous gas. Never disconnect air conditioning system lines unless the

4. Remove both rear braces at the air conditioning compressor. Remove the lower compressor mounting bolt. Remove the compressor bracket nuts at the water pump. Slide the bracket forward and disconnect the compressor wires. Remove upper compressor bolt. Place compressor to one side out of the way.
5. Remove the valve cover as described in this chapter.
6. Disconnect the AIR hose at the converter check valve.
7. Remove the spark plugs. See Chapter Three.
8. Remove the temperature sending unit.
9. Disconnect the AIR pipe at the exhaust manifold.
10. Raise front of vehicle and place it on jackstands.
11. Remove the 2 rear exhaust manifold bolts. Disconnect crossover pipe at manifold. Remove dipstick at manifold.
12. Remove jackstands and lower vehicle to the ground.
13. Remove the exhaust manifold.
14. Disconnect spark plug cable holder at rear of head.
15. Loosen rocker arm nuts. Remove pushrods.
16. Remove head bolts. Remove the cylinder head. Remove and discard the head gasket.

NOTE
Place the head on its side to prevent damage to the head gasket surface.

1984-on Removal (Left Side)

1. Disconnect the negative battery cable.
2. Remove intake manifold as described in this chapter.
3. Remove the alternator. See Chapter Seven.
4. Remove the valve cover as described in this chapter.
5. Remove exhaust manifold as described in this chapter.

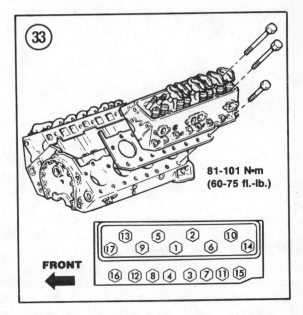

81-101 N•m
(60-75 fl.-lb.)

FRONT

6. Remove upper air pump bracket with power steering pump reservoir.
7. Disconnect the spark plug cable holder at the rear of the head.
8. Disconnect ground wire at rear of head.
9. Disconnect temperature sending unit wire.
10. Remove the pushrods.
11. Remove the head bolts. Remove the cylinder head. Remove and discard the head gasket.

CAUTION
Place the head on its side to prevent damage to the head gasket surface.

Decarbonizing

1. Without removing the valves, remove all deposits from the combustion chambers, intake ports and exhaust ports. Use a fine wire brush dipped in solvent or make a scraper from hardwood. Be careful not to scratch or gouge the combustion chambers.
2. After all carbon is removed from the combustion chambers and ports, clean the entire head in solvent.
3. Clean away all carbon on the piston tops. Do not remove the carbon ridge at the top of the cylinder bore.
4. Remove the valves as described in this chapter.
5. Clean the pushrod guides, valve guide bores and all bolt holes. Use a cleaning solvent to remove dirt and grease.
6. Clean the valve with a fine wire brush or buffing wheel.

Inspection

1. Check the cylinder head for signs of oil or water leaks before cleaning.

2. Clean the cylinder head thoroughly in solvent. While cleaning, look for cracks or other visible signs of damage. Look for corrosion or foreign material in the oil and water passages. Clean the passages with a stiff spiral brush, then blow them out with compressed air.

3. Check the cylinder head studs for damage and replace if necessary.

4. Check the rocker arm studs for wear or damaged threads. Replace if necessary.

Installation

1. Be sure the cylinder head and engine block gasket surfaces and bolt holes are clean. Dirt in the block bolt holes or on the head bolt threads will affect bolt torque.

2. Check all visible oil and water passages for cleanliness.

NOTE
*Use gasket sealer on steel gaskets. **Do not** use sealer on composition steel/asbestos gaskets.*

3. Install a new head gasket on the cylinder head dowel pins in the block with the words "This Side Up" facing up. If the gasket is not marked in this manner, be sure its bead faces up.

4. Carefully lower the cylinder head in place on the dowel pins and gasket.

5. Coat the head bolt threads with sealing compound (part No. 1052080 or equivalent) and install the bolts finger-tight.

6. Tighten head bolts a little at a time following the sequence shown in **Figure 33** until the specified torque (**Table 2**) is reached.

7. Reverse Steps 1-13 (1984 right head), Steps 1-15 (1985 right head) or Steps 1-10 (left head) of *Removal* in this chapter.

VALVES AND VALVE SEATS

Some of the following procedures must be done by a dealer or a machine shop, since they require special knowledge and expensive machine tools. Others, while possible for the home mechanic, are difficult or time-consuming. A general practice among those who do their own service is to remove the cylinder head, perform all disassembly except valve removal and take the head to a machine shop for inspection and service. Since the cost is low relative to the required effort and equipment, this is usually the best approach, even for experienced mechanics. The following procedures are given to acquaint the home mechanic with what the dealer or machine shop will do.

Valve Removal

1. Remove the cylinder head as described in this chapter.

2. Remove the rocker arm assemblies as described in this chapter.

3. Compress the valve spring with a compressor like the one shown in **Figure 34**. Remove the valve stem keys and release the spring tension.

4. Remove the valve spring cap or rotator, oil shedder, valve spring and damper assembly.

5. Pry the stem seal off with a screwdriver blade and discard it. Remove valve spring shims, if used.

CAUTION
Remove any burrs from the valve stem key grooves before removing the valves or the valve guides will be damaged.

6. Remove the valve and repeat Steps 3-5 on each remaining valve.

7. Arrange the parts in order so they can be returned to their original positions when reassembled.

Inspection

1. Clean the valves with a fine wire brush or buffing wheel. Discard any cracked, warped or burned valves.

2. Measure valve stems at the top, center and bottom for wear. A machine shop can do this when the valves are ground. Also measure the length of each valve and the diameter of each valve head.

NOTE
Check the thickness of the valve edge or margin after the valves have been

4

ground. Any valve with a margin of less than 1/32 in. (0.787 mm) should be discarded.

3. Remove all carbon and varnish from the valve guides with a stiff spiral wire brush.

NOTE
The next step assumes that all valve stems have been measured and are within specifications. Replace valves that have worn stems before performing this step.

4. Measure the valve guide clearance as follows:
   a. Attach a dial indicator to one side of the valve cover gasket rail on the head. Position the indicator so that side-to-side valve stem movement will cause a direct movement of the indicator plunger. The indicator plunger should touch the valve stem just above the valve guide. See **Figure 35**.
   b. Drop the valve head about 1/16 in. off the valve seat. Move the valve stem with light pressure from side to side and take indicator reading. If reading exceeds the specified tolerance (**Table 1**), have the valve guide reamed and oversize valves installed by a dealer or automotive machine shop.

5. Have the valve spring height checked by a dealer or automotive machine shop. Springs should be replaced if not within 10 lb. (44 N) of the specified load (without dampers). See **Table 1**.

6. Inspect the valve seat inserts. If worn or burned, they must be reconditioned. This is a job for a dealer or machine shop, although the procedure is described in this chapter.

Valve Guide Reaming

Worn valve guides must be reamed to accept a valve with an oversize stem. These are available in 3 sizes for both intake and exhaust valves. Reaming must be done by hand (**Figure 36**) and is a job best left to an experienced machine shop. The valve seat must be refaced after the guide has been reamed.

Valve Seat Reconditioning

1. Cut the valve seats to the specified angle (**Table 1**) with a dressing stone. Remove only enough metal to obtain a good finish.
2. Use tapered stones to obtain the specified seat width when necessary.
3. Coat the corresponding valve face with Prussian blue dye.
4. Insert the valve into the valve guide.

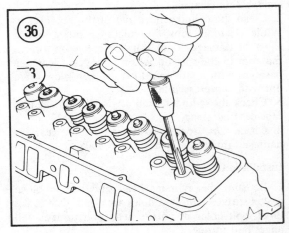

5. Apply light pressure to the valve and rotate it approximately 1/4 turn.
6. Lift the valve out. If it seats properly, the dye will transfer evenly to the valve face.
7. If the dye transfers to the top of the valve face, lower the seat. If it transfers to the bottom of the valve face, raise the seat.

Valve Installation

1. Coat the valves with oil and install them in the cylinder head.
2. Install the valve spring shim (if used), valve spring, damper assembly, oil shedder and valve cap or rotator on the valve.

NOTE
Install all parts in the same positions from which they were removed.

3. Compress the spring with a spring compressor **(Figure 34)** and install the oil seal in the lower groove of the valve stem. Make sure it lies flat and is not twisted.

4. Install the valve keys and release the compressor tool. Make sure both keys seat properly in the upper groove of the valve stem.

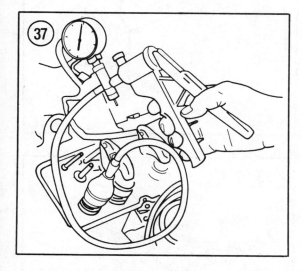

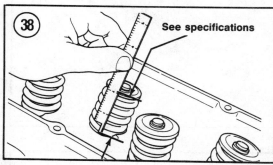

See specifications

Measure between rod cap and crank throw

5. Check each valve stem oil seal for leakage by placing a leak detector (part No. J-23994) over the end of the valve stem against the cap or rotator. Connect a hand vacuum pump to the detector and apply 6-8 in. Hg vacuum. See **Figure 37**. If air leaks past the seal, it is incorrectly installed.

6. Measure the installed spring height between the top of the spring seat (or shim, if used) and the top of the oil shedder, as shown in **Figure 38**. If greater than the specified height, install an extra spring seat shim about 1/16 in. thick and remeasure the height.

VALVE LIFTERS

The lifters used in all engines require special handling and test equipment. If any are suspect, remove them and have their leakdown rate tested by a dealer or qualified specialist.

Removal/Installation

1. Remove the intake manifold as described in this chapter.

2. Remove the rocker arm assemblies and pushrods as described in this chapter.

3. 1987—unbolt and remove the roller lifter retainers and restrictors.

4. Remove the valve lifters with a pencil-type magnet. Arrange lifters in a rack in the sequence of removal for reinstallation in their original position.

5. Installation is the reverse of removal.

PISTON/CONNECTING ROD ASSEMBLY

Piston Removal

1. Remove the cylinder head and oil pan as described in this chapter.

2. Pack the cylinder bore with clean shop rags. Remove the carbon ridge at the top of the cylinder bore with a ridge reamer. These can be rented for use. Vacuum out the shavings, then remove the shop rags.

3. Rotate the crankshaft so the connecting rod is centered in the bore.

4. Measure the clearance between each connecting rod and the crankshaft journal flange with a feeler gauge **(Figure 39)**. If the clearance exceeds specifications in **Table 1**, replace the connecting rod during reassembly.

NOTE
Mark the cylinder number on the top of each piston with quick-drying paint.

*Check for cylinder numbers or identification marks on the connecting rod and cap. If they are not visible, make your own (**Figure 40**).*

5. Remove the nuts holding the connecting rod cap. Lift off the cap, together with the lower bearing insert.

NOTE
If the connecting rod caps are difficult to remove, tap the studs with a wooden hammer handle.

6. Use a wooden hammer handle to push the piston and connecting rod from the bore.
7. Remove the piston rings with a ring remover (**Figure 41**).

Piston Pin
Removal/Installation

The piston pins are press-fitted to the connecting rods and hand-fitted to the pistons. Removal requires the use of a press and support stand. This is a job for a dealer or machine shop equipped to fit the pistons to the pin, ream the pin bushings to the correct diameter and install the pistons and pins on the connecting rods.

Piston Clearance Check

Unless you have precision measuring equipment and know how to use it properly, have this procedure done by a machine shop.
1. Measure the piston diameter with a micrometer (**Figure 42**). Measure just below the rings at right angles to the piston pin bore.
2. Measure the cylinder bore diameter with a bore gauge (**Figure 43**). Measure at the top, center and

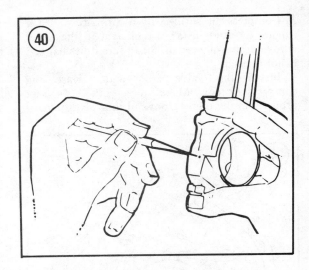

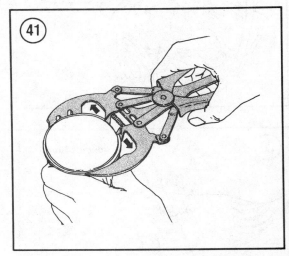

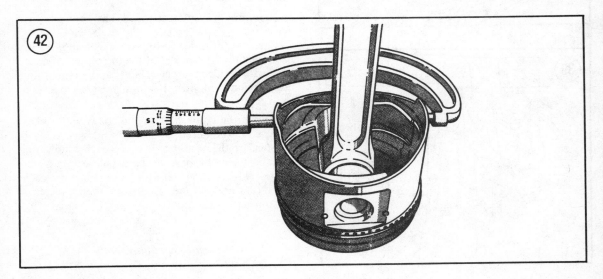

bottom of the bore, in front-to-rear and side-to-side directions.

3. Subtract the piston diameter from the largest cylinder bore reading. If the difference exceeds specifications (**Table 1**), the cylinder must be rebored and oversized pistons installed.

Piston Ring Fit/Installation

1. Check the ring gap of each piston ring. To do this, position the ring at the bottom of the ring travel area and square it by tapping gently with an inverted piston. See **Figure 44**.

NOTE
If the cylinders have not been rebored, check the gap at the bottom of the ring travel, where the cylinder is least worn.

2. Measure the ring gap with a feeler gauge as shown in **Figure 45**. Compare with specifications. If the measurement is not within specifications, the rings must be replaced as a set.

3. Check ring grooves for binding by rolling the ring around its respective groove as shown in **Figure 46**. If binding occurs at any point, dress the ring groove with a fine-cut file.

4. Check the side clearance of the rings as shown in **Figure 47**. Place the feeler gauge alongside the ring all the way into the groove. If the measurement is not within specifications, either the rings or the ring grooves are worn. Inspect and replace as necessary.

4

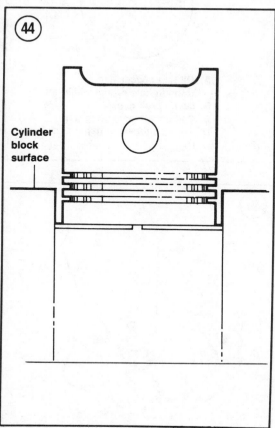

Cylinder
block
surface

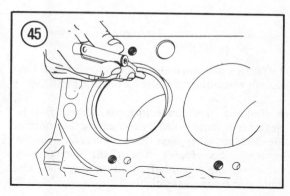

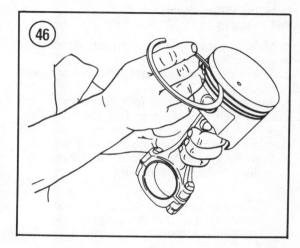

5. Using a ring expander tool (**Figure 41**), carefully install the oil control ring, then the compression rings.

> *NOTE*
> *Oil rings consists of 3 segments. The wavy segment goes between the flat segments to act as a spacer. Upper and lower flat segments are interchangeable. The top sides of both compression rings are marked and must face upward.*

6. Position the ring gaps as shown in **Figure 48**.

Connecting Rod Inspection

Have the connecting rods checked for straightness by a dealer or a machine shop.

Connecting Rod Bearing Clearance Measurement

1. Place the connecting rods and upper bearing halves on the proper connecting rod journals.
2. Cut a piece of Plastigage the width of the bearing. Place the Plastigage on the journal, then install the lower bearing half and cap.

> *NOTE*
> *Do not place Plastigage over the journal oil hole.*

3. Tighten the connecting rod cap to specifications. Do not rotate the crankshaft while the Plastigage is in place.
4. Remove the connecting rod caps. Bearing clearance is determined by comparing the width of the flattened Plastigage to the markings on the envelope. See **Figure 49**. If the clearance is excessive, the crankshaft must be reground and undersize bearings installed.

Installing Piston/Connecting Rod Assembly

1. Make sure the pistons are correctly installed on the connecting rods.
2. Make sure the ring gaps are positioned as shown in **Figure 48**.
3. Slip short pieces of hose over the connecting rod studs to keep them from nicking the crankshaft. Tape will work if you do not have the right diameter hose, but it is more difficult to remove.
4. Immerse the entire piston in clean engine oil. Coat the cylinder wall with oil.

> *CAUTION*
> *Use extreme care in Step 5 to prevent the connecting rod from nicking the crankshaft journal.*

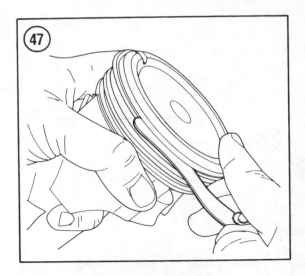

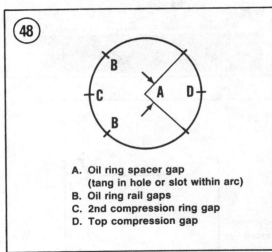

A. Oil ring spacer gap
(tang in hole or slot within arc)
B. Oil ring rail gaps
C. 2nd compression ring gap
D. Top compression gap

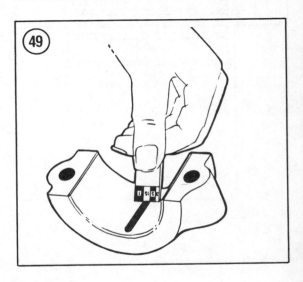

5. Install the piston/connecting rod assembly in its cylinder as shown in **Figure 50**. Make sure the number painted on the top of the piston before removal corresponds to the cylinder number, counting from the front of the engine.

6. Clean the connecting rod bearings carefully, including the back sides. Coat the journals and bearings with clean engine oil. Place the bearings in the connecting rod and cap.

7. Remove the protective hose or tape and install the connecting rod cap. Make sure the rod and cap

marks align. Tighten the cap nuts to specifications (**Table 2**).

8. Check the connecting rod big-end play as described under *Piston Removal*.

REAR MAIN OIL SEAL

Replacement

A 2-piece seal is used on 1984-1986 engines; a 1-piece seal is used on 1987 engines.

Two-piece Seal Replacement

1. Fabricate a seal installation tool as shown in **Figure 51** to protect the seal bead when positioning the new seal.

2. Remove the oil pan and oil pump as described in this chapter.

3. Remove the rear main bearing cap. Pry the oil seal from the bottom of the cap with a small screwdriver as shown in **Figure 52**.

4. Remove the upper half of the seal with a brass pin punch. Tap one end of seal with punch until other end protrudes far enough to be removed with pliers. See **Figure 53**.

5. Clean all sealant from bearing cap and crankshaft with a non-abrasive cleaner.

6. Coat new seal lips and bead with light engine oil. Do not let oil touch seal mating ends.

7. Position tip of seal installer tool (fabricated in Step 1) between crankshaft and seal seat. Position seal between crankshaft and tip of tool so seal bead touches tool tip. Make sure oil seal lip faces toward front of engine. See **Figure 54**.

8. Use seal installer tool as a shoehorn to roll seal around crankshaft, protecting seal bead from sharp corners of seal seating surface. Keep tool in position until seal is properly seated, with both ends flush with the block.

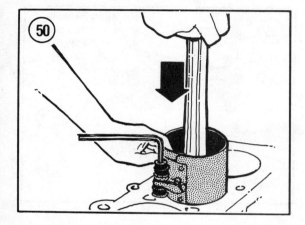

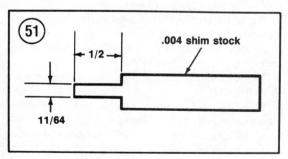

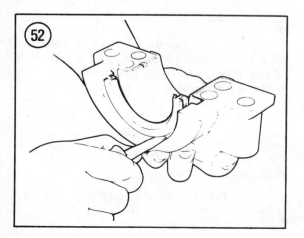

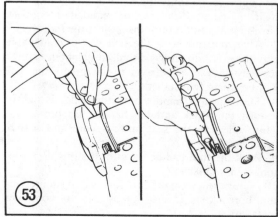

9. Remove tool carefully to prevent pulling seal out with it.

10. Use seal installer tool as a shoehorn again and install seal half in bearing cap. Feed seal into cap with light thumb and finger pressure.

11. Apply sealant to the areas shown in **Figure 55**. Keep sealant off the seal split line.

12. Install bearing cap and tighten to 10-12 ft.-lb. (14-16 N•m). Tap end of crankshaft to the rear, then to the front to align thrust surfaces.

13. Retighten bearing cap to specifications (**Table 2**).

One-piece Seal Replacement

The rear main oil seal on 1987 engines is located in a cast aluminum retainer installed on the rear of the block. Whenever the retainer is removed, a new seal and gasket must be installed. The seal can be installed without removing the engine from the vehicle.

1. Securely block the rear wheels. Raise the vehicle with a jack and place it on jackstands.

2. Support the engine with a jack and remove the transmission. See Chapter Nine.

3. Remove the flywheel as described in this chapter.

4. Pry the old seal from the retainer with a small screwdriver or awl. Use the pry notches provided in the retainer and work carefully to avoid scratching the outer diameter of the crankshaft.

5. Carefully clean and inspect the inner diameter of the seal bore and the outer diameter of the crankshaft for nicks or burrs which could affect seal performance. If any are found, the engine must be removed, disassembled and the defects corrected before a new seal is installed.

6. Lubricate the inner diameter of a new seal with clean engine oil. Install seal on mandril of tool part No. J-35621 until it bottoms against the tool collar.

7. Align the tool with the rear of the crankshaft and thread tool screws in place. Tighten screws securely with a screwdriver to make sure the seal will be squarely installed.

8. Turn the tool handle until the collar is tightly against the block and the handle has bottomed. This will push the seal into its bore and seat it properly.

9. Back the tool handle off until it stops. Remove tool from crankshaft.

10. Check seal to make sure it is seated squarely in the bore, then reverse Steps 1-3 to complete installation.

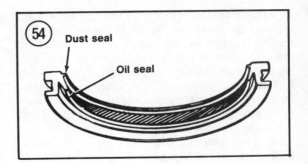

Dust seal
Oil seal

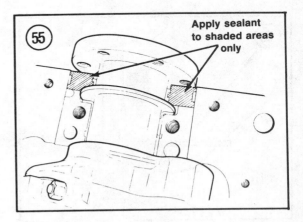

Apply sealant to shaded areas only

If the retainer requires removal:

1. Raise the vehicle with a jack and place it on jackstands.

2. Support the engine with a jack and remove the transmission. See Chapter Nine.

3. Remove the flywheel and oil pan as described in this chapter.

4. Unscrew and remove retainer/seal assembly. Remove and discard the gasket.

5. Clean all gasket residue from retainer and block mating surfaces.

6. Fit a new gasket over the stud on the block and install retainer. Tighten screws to 120-150 in.-lb. (13-16 N•m).

7. Apply a small quantity of sealer part No. 1052751 or equivalent to front and rear corners of oil pan, then reinstall with same gasket.

8. Install a new seal as described in this chapter.

CRANKSHAFT

Removal

Refer to **Figure 56** (typical) for this procedure.

1. Remove the engine from the vehicle as described in this chapter.

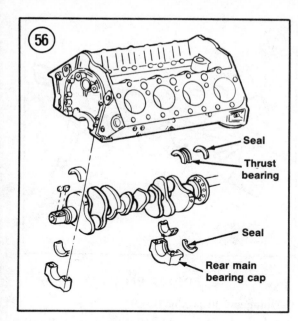

Inspection

1. Clean the crankshaft thoroughly with solvent. Blow out the oil passages with compressed air.

NOTE
If you do not have precision measuring equipment, have a machine shop perform Step 2.

2. Check the crankpins and main bearing journals for wear, scoring and cracks. Check all journals against specifications for out-of-roundness and taper. See **Table 1**. If necessary, have the crankshaft reground.

Main Bearing
Clearance Measurement

Main bearing clearance is measured with Plastigage in the same manner as the connecting rod bearing clearance, described in this chapter. Excessive clearance requires that the bearings be replaced, the crankshaft reground or both.

Installation

1. Install the main bearing inserts with their lubrication groove in the cylinder block.
2. Lubricate the bolt threads with SAE 30W engine oil.
3. Install the cap bearing inserts.
4. Install the crankshaft in the block.
5. Install the bearing caps with their arrows pointing toward the front of the engine and tighten the bolts finger-tight.
6. Tighten all main bearing cap bolts (except the rear main cap) to specifications (**Table 2**).
7. Tighten the rear main cap to 10-12 ft.-lb. (14-16 N•m), then tap the end of the crankshaft to the rear and back again with a lead hammer to align the bearing thrust surfaces.
8. Retorque all main bearing caps to specifications (**Table 2**).

2. Remove the starter motor. See Chapter Seven.
3. If equipped with manual transmission, remove the clutch. See Chapter Eight.
4. Remove the flywheel/drive plate as described in this chapter.
5. Remove the spark plugs. See Chapter Three.
6. Remove the crankshaft pulley and torsional damper as described in this chapter.
7. Remove the oil pan and pump assembly as described in this chapter.
8. Remove the front cover and crankshaft timing gear as described in this chapter.
9. Remove the connecting rod bearing caps and bearings. Move the rod/piston assemblies away from the crankshaft.
10. Unbolt and remove the main bearing caps with bearing inserts.

NOTE
If the caps are difficult to remove, lift the bolts partway out, then pry the caps from side to side.

11. Check the caps for identification numbers or marks. If none are visible, clean the caps with a wire brush. If marks still cannot be seen, make your own with quick-drying paint.
12. Lift the crankshaft from the engine block and place it on a clean workbench.
13. Remove the bearing inserts from the block. Place the bearing caps and inserts in order on a clean workbench.

End Play Measurement

1. Pry the crankshaft to the front of the engine with a large screwdriver.
2. Measure the crankshaft end play at the front of the No. 5 bearing with a feeler gauge. Compare to specifications in **Table 1**.
3. If the end play is excessive, replace the No. 5 bearing. If less than specified, check the bearing faces for imperfections.

FLYWHEEL OR DRIVE PLATE

Removal/Installation

1. Remove the engine as described in this chapter.
2. If equipped with manual transmission, remove the clutch. See Chapter Eight.
3. Unbolt the flywheel or drive plate from the crankshaft. Remove the flywheel or drive plate.
4. Installation is the reverse of removal. Tighten bolts to specifications in a diagonal pattern. Wipe all oil, grease and other contamination from the flywheel surface before installing the clutch on manual transmission engines.

Inspection

1. Visually check the flywheel or drive plate surfaces for cracks, deep scoring, excessive wear, heat discoloration and checking.
2. Check surface flatness with a straightedge and feeler gauge.
3. Inspect the ring gear teeth for cracks, broken teeth or excessive wear. If severely worn, check the starter motor drive teeth for similar wear or damage. Replace as indicated.

NOTE
The ring gear can only be replaced on manual transmission vehicles. It is welded to and balanced as part of the torque converter drive plate assembly on automatic transmission vehicles and must be replaced with the drive plate.

PILOT BUSHING

The pilot bushing is located inside the rear end of the crankshaft on manual transmission vehicles. It supports the transmission input shaft.
1. Remove the engine as described in this chapter.
2. Remove the clutch. See Chapter Eight.
3. Soak a replacement bushing in engine oil while performing Steps 4-6.
4. Remove the bushing lubricating wick (if used). Fill the crankshaft bushing bore with chassis grease.
5. Insert a dummy shaft or clutch aligning tool into the bushing and tap with a soft hammer. The hydraulic pressure caused by the grease should force the bushing out easily. If it does not, remove the bushing with a bushing puller and slide hammer.
6. Clean the bore thoroughly of all grease.
7. Install the oil-soaked bushing on the end of the dummy shaft or clutch aligning tool.
8. Install the bushing using the dummy shaft or aligning tool as a driver.
9. Install the bushing lubricating wick (if used).

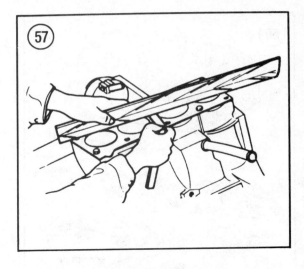

CYLINDER BLOCK

Cleaning and Inspection

1. Clean the block thoroughly with solvent. Remove any RTV sealant residue from the machined surfaces. Check all core plugs for leaks and replace any that are suspect. See *Core Plugs* in this chapter. Remove any plugs that seal oil passages. Check oil and coolant passages for sludge, dirt and corrosion while cleaning. If the passages are very dirty, have the block boiled out by a machine shop. Blow out all passages with compressed air. Check the threads in the head bolt holes to be sure they are clean. If dirty, use a tap to true up the threads and remove any deposits.

2. Examine the block for cracks. To confirm suspicions about possible leak areas, use a mixture of 1 part kerosene and 2 parts engine oil. Coat the suspected area with this solution, then wipe dry and immediately apply a solution of zinc oxide dissolved in wood alcohol. If any discoloration appears in the treated area, the block is cracked and should be replaced.

3. Check the cylinder block deck or top surface for flatness. Place an accurate straightedge on the block. If there is any gap between the block and straightedge, measure it with a feeler gauge (**Figure 57**). Measure from end to end and from corner to corner.

4. Measure the cylinder bores with a bore gauge (**Figure 43**) as described in Step 2, *Piston Clearance Check* in this chapter. If the cylinders exceed maximum tolerances, they must be rebored. Reboring is also necessary if the cylinder walls are badly scuffed or scored. Before boring, install all main bearing caps and tighten the cap bolts to specifications.

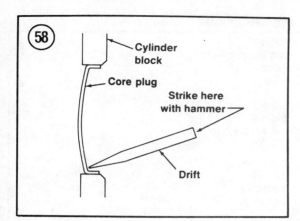

Cylinder block

Core plug

Strike here with hammer

Drift

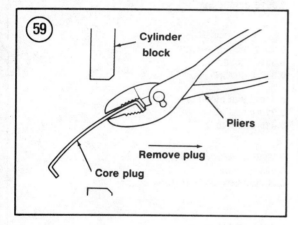

Cylinder block

Pliers

Remove plug

Core plug

CORE PLUGS

The condition of all core plugs in the block should be checked whenever the engine is out of the vehicle for service. If any signs of leakage or corrosion are found around one core plug, replace them all.

Removal/Installation

CAUTION
Do not drive core plugs into the engine casting. It will be impossible to retrieve them and they can restrict coolant circulation, resulting in serious engine damage.

1. Tap the bottom edge of the core plug with a hammer and drift. Use several sharp blows to push the bottom of the plug inward, tilting the top out (**Figure 58**).
2. Grip the top of the plug firmly with pliers. Pull the plug from its bore (**Figure 59**) and discard.
3. Clean the plug bore thoroughly to remove all traces of the old sealer.
4. Apply a light coat of Loctite Stud N' Bearing mount or equivalent to the plug bore.
5. Install the new core plug with an appropriate size driver or socket. The sharp edge of the plug should be at least 0.02 in. (0.5 mm) inside the lead-in chamfer.
6. Repeat Steps 1-5 to replace each remaining core plug.

Table 1 ENGINE SPECIFICATIONS

Type	90° V8
Displacement	350 cid (5.7 liter)
Bore	4.000 in
Stroke	3.480 in
Cylinder arrangement	
Left bank	1-3-5-7
Right bank	2-4-6-8
Firing order	1-8-4-3-6-5-7-2
Cylinder bore	
Maximum out-of-round	0.0020 in.
Maximum taper	
Thrust side	0.0005 in.
Relief side	0.0010 in.
Piston	
Clearance	0.0025-0.0035 in.
Piston rings	
Clearance	
Top	0.0012-0.0032 in.
Bottom	0.0012-0.0032 in.
Oil	0.002-0.007 in.
Gap	
Top	0.010-0.020 in.
Bottom	0.010-0.025 in.
Oil	0.015-0.055 in.
Piston pin	
Diameter	0.9270-0.9273 in.
Clearance	0.001 in. max.
Fit in rod	0.0008-0.0016 in. interference
Crankshaft	
Main journal diameter	
Front	2.4484-2.4493 in.
Intermediate	2.4481-2.4490 in.
Rear	2.4479-2.4488 in.
Main journal taper	0.0010 in. max.
Main journal out-of-round	0.0010 in. max.
Main bearing clearance	
Front	0.0008-0.0020 in.
Intermediate	0.0011-0.0023 in.
Rear	0.0017-0.0032 in.
End play	0.002-0.006 in.
Crankpin diameter	2.0986-2.0998 in.
Crankpin taper	0.001 in. max.
Crankpin out-of-round	0.001 in. max.
Rod bearing clearance	0.0013-0.0035 in.
Rod side clearance	0.014 in.
Camshaft	
Journal diameter	1.8682-1.8692 in.
End play	0.004-0.012 in.
Lobe lift	
Intake	
1984-1986	0.2733
1987	0.4040

(continued)

Table 1 ENGINE SPECIFICATIONS (continued)

Lobe lift (cont.)	
Exhaust	
1984-1986	0.2820
1987	0.4150
Valve system	
Lifter	Hydraulic
Rocker arm ratio	1.50:1
Valve lash	One turn down from zero lash
Face angle	
Intake and exhaust	45°
Seat angle	
Intake and exhaust	46°
Seat runout	0.002 in.
Seat width	
Intake	1/32-1/16 in.
Exhaust	1/16-1/32 in.
Stem clearance	0.0010-0.0027 in.
Valve spring free length	2.03 in.
Valve spring load	
Intake	
Closed	76-84 lb. @ 1.70 in.
Open	194-206 lb. @ 1.25 in.
Exhaust	
Closed	76-84 lb. @ 1.61 in.
Open	194-206 lb. @ 1.16 in.
Damper	
Free length	1.86 in.
Approximate number of coils	4

Table 2 TIGHTENING TORQUES

Fastener	in.-lb.	ft.-lb.
Camshaft sprocket		20
Clutch pressure plate		30
Connecting rod cap		45
Crankcase front cover	80	
Crankshaft pulley		26-37
Cylinder head bolts		
1984-1985		65
1986-on		
Long and medium		65
Short		60
Distributor hold-down clamp		25
Engine mount		
To engine		30-44
To mount bracket		21-25
Exhaust manifold		20
Flywheel		60
Flywheel housing		30
Flywheel housing cover	80	
Intake manifold		
1984		30
1985-on		35
Intake manifold cover		11-18
Main bearing cap		80
Oil filter	(continued)	25

Table 2 TIGHTENING TORQUES (continued)

Fastener	in.-lb.	ft.-lb.
Oil filter bypass valve	80	
Oil pan attaching bolts/nuts		
1/4-20	80	
5/16-18	165	
Oil pan drain plug		20
Rocker arm		
Stud		50
Cover	50	
Spark plug		22
Temperature sending unit		20
Thermostat housing		30
Torsional damper		60
Water outlet		20
Water pump		30

CHAPTER FIVE

FUEL, EXHAUST AND EMISSION CONTROL SYSTEMS

This chapter consists of service procedures for the air cleaner, fuel injection system, fuel pump, fuel tank and lines, the exhaust system and fuel-related emission controls.

THERMOSTATICALLY CONTROLLED (THERMAC) AIR CLEANER SYSTEM (1984)

The 1984 Thermac system furnishes the throttle body assembly with temperature-regulated air to reduce hydrocarbon emissions and improve driveability. The air cleaner assembly has separate air intakes for each throttle body. Fresh air ducting located in the hood connects to the air cleaner intakes through hood seals. The left air intake is also connected to a heat stove surrounding the exhaust manifold to provide heated intake air. Each air intake contains a vacuum-operated air control valve to regulate air flow. The left side is temperature-controlled. The right side opens only under wide-open throttle, high load conditions to supply additional air as required.

Fresh air and heated air intake is modulated by the air control valve in each air cleaner intake. These valves are operated by a vacuum motor mounted under the valve and connected to it by an operating rod. **Figure 1** shows the major components in the 1984 Corvette air cleaner.

When the engine is first started, the air cleaner draws hot air from near the exhaust manifold through the heat stove tube. See **Figure 2**. As the

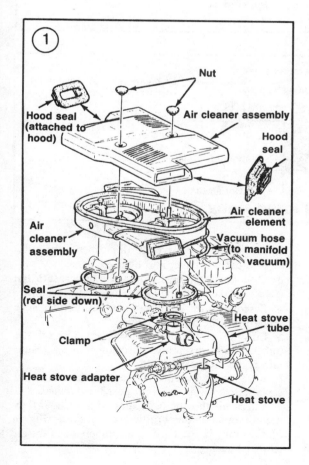

①

Nut

Hood seal (attached to hood)

Air cleaner assembly

Hood seal

Air cleaner element

Air cleaner assembly

Vacuum hose (to manifold vacuum)

Seal (red side down)

Clamp

Heat stove tube

Heat stove adapter

Heat stove

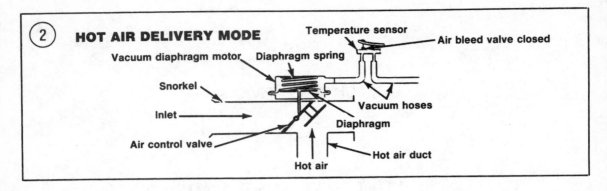

② **HOT AIR DELIVERY MODE**

Temperature sensor — Air bleed valve closed
Vacuum diaphragm motor — Diaphragm spring
Snorkel
Inlet
Air control valve
Vacuum hoses
Diaphragm
Hot air duct
Hot air

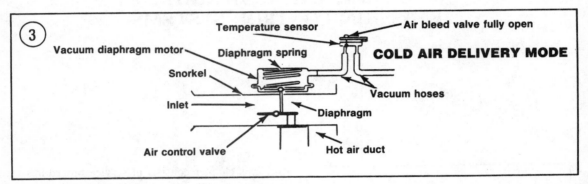

③ Temperature sensor — Air bleed valve fully open
Vacuum diaphragm motor — Diaphragm spring — **COLD AIR DELIVERY MODE**
Snorkel
Inlet
Vacuum hoses
Diaphragm
Air control valve
Hot air duct

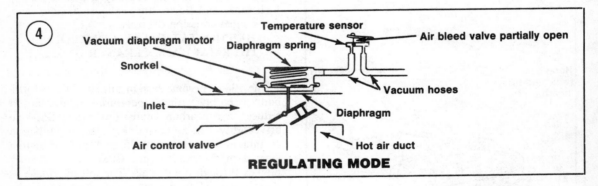

④ Temperature sensor — Air bleed valve partially open
Vacuum diaphragm motor — Diaphragm spring
Snorkel
Inlet
Air control valve
Vacuum hoses
Diaphragm
Hot air duct
REGULATING MODE

engine warms up, the air valve changes position to block off air from the exhaust manifold (**Figure 3**). This allows the air cleaner to draw intake air from the outside air ducting in the hood.

At intermediate temperatures, air reaching the throttle body assembly is a blend of outside and pre-heated air. Blending is regulated by a bi-metal thermal switch in the air cleaner. This thermal switch controls the position of the air control valve (**Figure 4**).

Air cleaner filter replacement is described in Chapter Three.

Housing Removal/Installation

Refer to **Figure 1** for this procedure.

1. Unscrew and remove the air cleaner cover nuts.
2. Remove the cover and filter element.
3. Disconnect the heat stove tube underneath the left air intake from the heat stove.
4. Disconnect the crankcase ventilation filter hose underneath the right air intake.
5. Lift the air cleaner housing up and off the throttle body assembly. Disconnect the vacuum line at the intake manifold.
6. Remove air cleaner housing and place it on a clean flat surface to prevent possible damage.
7. Check the throttle body mounting seals. If they are not found on the throttle body air horns (**Figure 5**), they may be attached to the underside of the air cleaner housing.

8. Installation is the reverse of removal. If the old mounting seal is missing or damaged, install a new one with the red side facing down to prevent a vacuum leak.

Air Cleaner Operational Check

1. Set the parking brake and block the front wheels.
2. Remove the air cleaner cover and filter element.
3. Check the heated air tube and heat stove adapter (**Figure 1**) for cracks or other damage. Repair or replace as needed.

4. Look into the left air intake. The air valve should be in the down (heat off) position (**Figure 3**).
5. Depress the air valve with one finger and check for binding or sticking.
6. Start the engine. The air valve should immediately move to the up (heat on) position (**Figure 2**).
7. Open and close the throttle quickly while watching the position of the air valve. It should move partially toward the down (heat off) position, then return to the up (heat on) position. As the engine warms up, the valve should gradually move to the down (heat off) position.
8. If the air valve does not operate as described, check for a vacuum leak in the system or mechanical binding of the air valve linkage. If none are found, check vacuum motor operation. See *Vacuum Motor Test* in this Chapter.

Thermal Switch Operational Check

1. Remove the air cleaner cover. Tape a candy thermometer as close as possible to the thermal switch on the air inlet side of the switch. See **Figure 6**. Install the air cleaner cover without the attaching nuts.
2. Start the engine and warm to normal operating temperature (upper radiator hose hot). Shut the engine off.
3. Disconnect the vacuum line at the air cleaner thermal switch. Connect a hand vacuum pump and apply 14 in. Hg vacuum. The thermal switch vent valve should open and the vacuum drop to zero.
4. Remove the air cleaner cover and cool the thermal switch with an ice pack. Once the switch temperature drops below approximately 40° F (5° C), apply 14 in. Hg vacuum. If the switch is working properly, the vacuum should be maintained.
5. If the switch does not operate as described in Step 3 and Step 4, replace it.

Vacuum Motor Test

1. Disconnect the vacuum line at the vacuum motor located underneath the air intake. See **Figure 7**. Connect a hand vacuum pump to the nipple.
2. Apply approximately 6-8 in. Hg vacuum to the vacuum motor.
3. With the vacuum trapped, the air valve should be in the up (heat on) position. If it is not, replace the vacuum motor.

Vacuum Motor Replacement

1. Remove the air cleaner assembly from the engine as described in this chapter.

2. Turn the air cleaner housing over and place it on a clean flat surface.

3. Disconnect the vacuum line at the vacuum motor to be replaced (**Figure 7**).

4. Drill through the spot welds on the retaining strap holding the vacuum motor to the air intake. Remove the retaining strap.

5. Lift the motor from the air intake and rotate it to disengage the linkage from the air valve door.

6. Installation is the reverse of removal. Install the sheet metal screw included with the new motor to hold it to the air intake. Make sure the screw does not interfere with air valve operation.

7. Connect a hand vacuum pump to the motor nipple and apply 6-8 in. Hg vacuum to the motor to check air valve for proper operation.

8. Connect the vacuum line to the motor and reinstall the air cleaner housing.

Temperature Sensor Replacement

1. Remove the air cleaner as described in this chapter.

2. Turn the housing over and disconnect the 2 vacuum lines at the sensor (**Figure 8**).

3. Pry the sensor retaining clip tabs open. Note position of the old sensor (**Figure 9**) and remove it from the air cleaner housing.

4. Install a new sensor in the same relative position. Press down on the sensor edges and install the retaining clip on the hose connectors.

5. Reconnect the 2 vacuum lines to the sensor nipples from which they were removed.

6. Reinstall the air cleaner assembly.

AIR CLEANER SYSTEM
(1985-ON)

A remote air cleaner assembly mounted on the upper radiator support is used with 1985 and later Corvettes. A flexible air intake duct containing a mass air flow sensor connects the air cleaner assembly to the throttle body. The use of the mass air flow sensor and a manifold air temperature sensor eliminates the need for a Thermac air cleaner system. Air cleaner service is reduced to periodic filter changes. See Chapter Three.

THROTTLE BODY
FUEL INJECTION (1984)

The 1984 Corvette is equipped with a Rochester Model 400 throttle body injection (TBI) unit. This incorporates a pair of throttle body injection units mounted in front and rear positions on the intake

manifold cover (**Figure 10**) and connected by a common throttle rod and fuel line. This arrangement permits each TBI unit to supply the proper air-fuel mixture through long runners in the intake manifold to the cylinder bank on the opposite side of the engine, thus the name "Crossfire Fuel Injection."

Each TBI unit consists of 2 major sub-assemblies: a throttle body containing a throttle lever and throttle valve and a fuel meter body containing an integral fuel pressure regulator (rear unit) or accumulator (front unit). Each throttle body is fitted with an idle air control (IAC) assembly which maintains idle speed according to direction from the electronic control module (ECM). A throttle position sensor (TPS) on the rear unit relays throttle valve position to the ECM. A special swirl plate positioned directly below each throttle valve improves mixture distribution.

An electrically operated injector in each TBI unit meters fuel into the intake air stream under the direction of the ECM. The ECM receives electrical signals from various sensors, refers to its stored program memory and calculates the precise amount and timing of fuel required by the engine. The length of each injection period is modified by the ECM to accommodate special engine conditions such as cranking, cold starts, elevation, acceleration and deceleration.

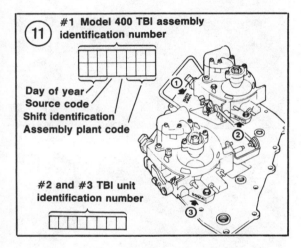

(10)

Rear TBI unit   Front TBI unit

Throttle position sensor   Fuel tube

Intake manifold cover   Throttle rod and bearing assembly

(11) #1 Model 400 TBI assembly identification number

Day of year
Source code
Shift identification
Assembly plant code

#2 and #3 TBI unit identification number

System Operation

Filtered fuel is supplied to the TBI units by an electric fuel pump mounted in the fuel tank. When the ignition switch is turned ON, a fuel pump relay activates the in-tank pump for 1.5-2 seconds to prime the injectors. If the ECM does not receive a reference signal from the distributor within this time span, it shuts down the fuel pump.

Fuel flow is controlled by varying the duration of injection according to signals from the ECM. Excess fuel passes through a pressure regulator and is then returned to the fuel tank. The throttle position sensor informs the ECM of throttle valve position. The idle air control assembly maintains a pre-programmed idle speed according to direction from the ECM.

Since the TBI system is electronically controlled, no attempt should be made to adjust the idle speed. Owner service should be limited to replacement and overhaul only. If the TBI system is not working properly, take the car to a dealer for diagnosis and adjustment.

System Pressure Relief

Before opening any fuel connection on a TBI-equipped engine, fuel pressure must be relieved to reduce risk of fire and personal injury.

1. Place the transmission in NEUTRAL or PARK.

2. Set the parking brake and block the drive wheels.

3. Remove the fuel pump fuse from the fuse block.

4. Crank the engine. The engine will start and run until the fuel remaining in the lines is used up. When the engine stops, crank the engine again for 3 seconds. This will dissipate any remaining fuel pressure and permit safe disconnection of the fuel lines.

5. When fuel system service has been completed and all lines reconnected, install the fuel pump fuse in the fuse block.

6. Turn the ignition switch to ON, but do not start the engine. Inspect system connections for leaks and repair if necessary before starting the engine.

Throttle Body Identification

Rochester TBI units are identified by a code stamped on the mounting flange near the rear hold-down bolt (**Figure 11**). Write the codes down and take them along when buying an overhaul kit. The complete TBI assembly is identified by a code stamped on the manifold. Write this code down and use it if the entire TBI assembly requires replacement.

Preparation For Overhaul

Before removing and disassembling any TBI unit, be sure you have the proper overhaul kit, a sufficient quantity of fresh carburetor cleaner and the proper tools.

CAUTION
TBI units may use Torx drive fasteners instead of the usual Phillips head screws. Do not try to remove a Torx drive screw with any tool other than a Torx driver or the head will be damaged and require drilling out to remove the screw.

Work slowly and carefully, follow the disassembly/assembly procedures, refer to the exploded drawing of the TBI unit when necessary and do not apply excessive force at any time.

It is not necessary to disassemble TBI unit linkage or remove throttle synchronizing screws when overhauling a TBI unit.

Check all gasket mating surfaces for nicks or burrs and replace any parts that have a damaged gasket surface.

TBI Unit
Removal/Installation

This procedure can be used to remove either individual TBI unit from the manifold. Relieve the fuel injection system pressure as described in this chapter.

1. Remove the air cleaner as described in this chapter.
2. Disconnect all electrical connectors at the throttle body.
3. Disconnect the throttle linkage at the throttle body to be removed. Disconnect the transmission detent rod and cruise control cable, if so equipped. See **Figure 12**.

> *NOTE*
> *The throttle rod is permanently attached to the rear TBI unit and no attempt should be made to detach it. If the rod and bearing assembly requires replacement, replace the entire rear TBI unit. A retaining collar on the front unit throttle lever is welded in place to maintain the factory synchronization setting. If front throttle body replacement is necessary, grind off the weld and remove the collar.*

4. Remove and discard the retaining clip on the front TBI throttle lever stud. A replacement clip is supplied in the overhaul kit.
5. Label and disconnect all vacuum lines from the throttle body.
6. Disconnect the fuel supply line (rear unit) or fuel return line (front unit) as required. Use one wrench to hold the fuel inlet nut on the throttle body and another wrench to loosen the fuel line fitting from the inlet nut. Disconnect the interconnecting fuel tube at the unit to be removed. **Figure 13** shows the rear unit lines; the front unit is similar.
7. Remove the bolts holding the throttle body to the manifold cover. Remove the throttle body.
8. Installation is the reverse of removal. Tighten attaching bolts to 10-14 ft.-lb. (14-19 N•m). Have a dealer check and adjust throttle valve synchronization.

TBI Assembly
Removal/Installation

This procedure is used to remove both TBI units and the manifold cover as an assembly. Relieve the fuel injection system pressure as described in this chapter before starting this procedure.

1. Remove the air cleaner as described in this chapter.

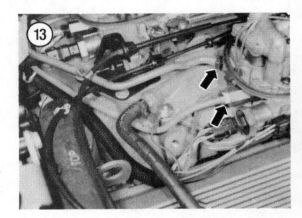

2. Label and disconnect all vacuum lines at the TBI assembly.

3. Disconnect all electrical connectors.

4. Disconnect the throttle cable (**Figure 12**).

5. Disconnect the transmission detent cable and cruise control cable, if so equipped.

6. Disconnect the fuel supply line (rear unit) and fuel return line (front unit). Use one wrench to hold the fuel inlet nut on the throttle body and another wrench to loosen the fuel line fitting from the inlet nut. See **Figure 14**. Cap the lines to prevent leakage.

7. Remove bolts and nuts from manifold cover. Remove the TBI assembly and manifold cover.

8. Installation is the reverse of removal. Tighten attaching bolts and nuts to 10-14 ft.-lb. (14-19 N•m).

TBI Disassembly

1. Remove the 5 fuel meter cover screws and lockwashers (**Figure 15**).

2. Lift fuel meter cover from throttle body.

WARNING
*Do not remove the 4 screws holding the pressure regulator to the fuel meter cover. See **Figure 16**. The regulator contains a large spring under considerable tension which could cause serious personal injury if released accidentally. The pressure regulator is preset at the factory and is serviced as a complete assembly with the fuel meter cover.*

3. Use a screwdriver as shown in **Figure 17** to lift the injector free of the fuel meter body casting.

4. Remove and discard the fuel meter outlet gasket. If rear unit is being disassembled, remove and discard the pressure regulator dust seal. See **Figure 15**.

NOTE
The fuel injector is serviced as a complete assembly. Do not disassemble

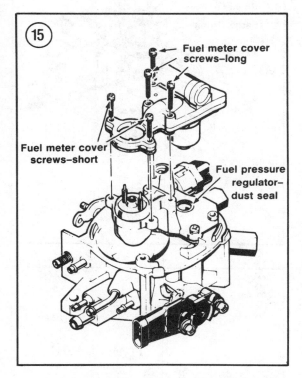

(15)

Fuel meter cover screws–long

Fuel meter cover screws–short

Fuel pressure regulator– dust seal

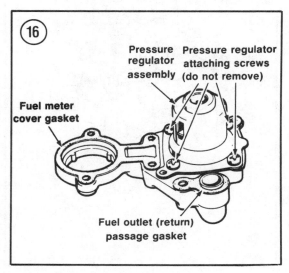

(16)

Pressure regulator assembly

Pressure regulator attaching screws (do not remove)

Fuel meter cover gasket

Fuel outlet (return) passage gasket

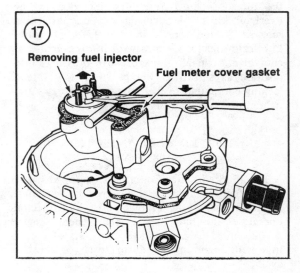

(17)

Removing fuel injector

Fuel meter cover gasket

beyond Step 5 and Step 6. Do not immerse injector in any type of cleaner.

5. Rotate injector fuel filter back and forth to remove from injector base.

6. Remove large O-ring and steel back-up washer from top of fuel meter body injector cavity (**Figure 18**). Remove small O-ring from bottom of injector cavity.

7. Remove fuel inlet and outlet nuts and gaskets from fuel meter body.

8. Remove 3 fuel meter body screws and lockwashers (**Figure 19**). Remove fuel meter body and insulator gasket from throttle body assembly.

> *NOTE*
> *Under normal service conditions, the throttle body need not be immersed in cleaner. If such cleaning is required, the throttle position sensor (TPS) and idle air control (IAC) must be removed. This service should be performed by a dealer.*

Inspection

1. Clean all metal parts and blow dry with compressed air.

2. Inspect casting mating surfaces for damage that might affect gasket sealing.

3. Discard all O-rings.

4. Check injector fuel filter for plugging or damage. Clean or replace as required.

TBI Assembly

Assembly is the reverse of disassembly. Apply the thread locking compound included in the overhaul kit to the fuel meter body attaching screws. Torque screws to 3.5 ft.-lb. (4 N•m). Lubricate injector O-rings with lithium grease or equivalent. Install injector by pressing into position as shown in **Figure 20**. Apply thread locking compound to fuel meter cover screws and tighten to 2.8 ft.-lb. (3 N•m).

PORTED FUEL INJECTION
(1985-ON)

The 1985 and later Corvette is equipped with a ported fuel injection (PFI) system. One injector is located at each of the 8 intake ports. All 8 injectors operate simultaneously once each engine revolution. This produces 2 injections of fuel to mix with incoming air during each combustion cycle.

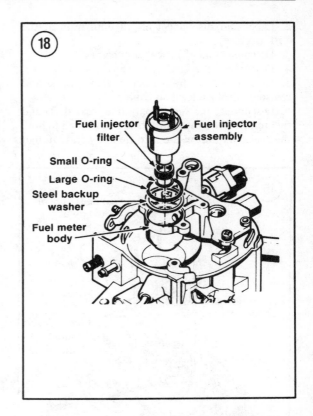

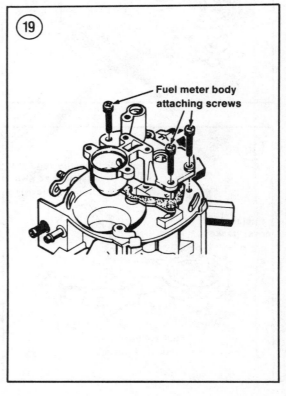

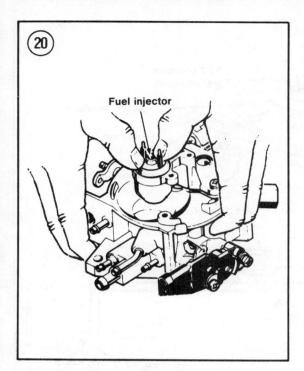

Fuel injector

System Operation

Operation of the PFI system is essentially similar to the TBI system used on 1984 models. The major difference between the systems is in their components. **Figure 21** is a schematic of the PFI system. **Figure 22** shows the PFI system components. The fuel rail is housed under a plenum assembly.

The PFI system is more sophisticated than the TBI system. It can compensate for a weak spark resulting from low battery voltage, shut off fuel completely during a rapid deceleration and use an internal circuit in the oil pressure sending unit as a backup system in case the fuel pump relay malfunctions.

Before opening any fuel connection on the PFI system, the fuel pressure must be relieved as described in this chapter.

Since the PFI system is electronically controlled, no attempt should be made to adjust the idle speed. Owner service should be limited to fuel filter and fuel pump replacement only. If the system is not working properly, take the car to a Chevrolet dealer for diagnosis and adjustment.

5

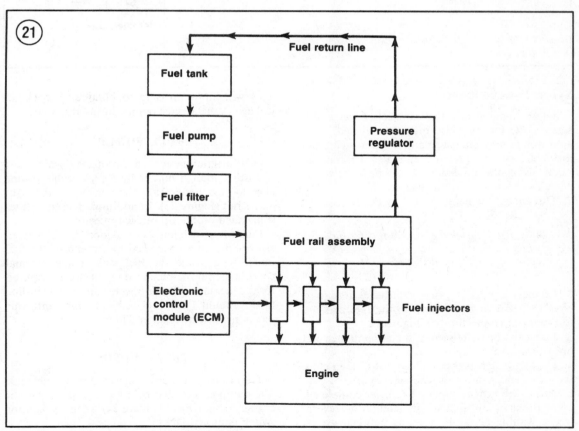

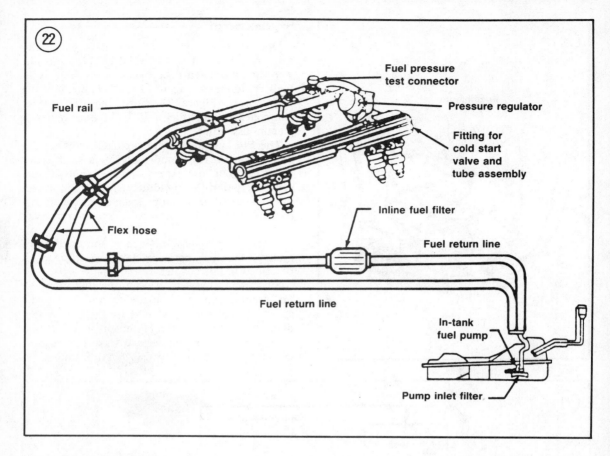

Fuel pressure test connector
Pressure regulator
Fuel rail
Fitting for cold start valve and tube assembly
Inline fuel filter
Flex hose
Fuel return line
Fuel return line
In-tank fuel pump
Pump inlet filter

System Pressure Relief

Before opening any fuel connection on a PFI system, the fuel pressure must be relieved. If an appropriate pressure gauge and bleed hose are not available, system pressure can also be relieved safely using the procedure given under *Throttle Body Fuel Injection* in this chapter.

1. Disconnect the negative battery cable.

> *NOTE*
> *Wrap a shop cloth around the fitting while installing the gauge in Step 2 to collect the fuel, then dispose of it in a safe manner.*

2. Connect a pressure gauge with bleed hose (part No. J-34730-1 or equivalent) to the fuel pressure test point or connector. See **Figure 22**.

3. Insert the bleed hose in a metal container and open the valve.

4. Let the system pressure bleed down, then close the valve and remove the pressure gauge.

5. After fuel system service has been completed, cycle the ignition switch ON and OFF several times, waiting about 10 seconds between cycles.

This will allow pressure to build up. Check for leakage at the service points during this step.

FUEL FILTER

Fuel injection systems are protected against dirt and other foreign matter by a replaceable in-line filter located underneath the vehicle on the right frame rail (**Figure 23**). In addition, a strainer filter is installed on the tip of each injector.

Further protection is provided by a woven, sleeve-type filter connected to the end of the fuel outlet tube inside the fuel tank. Under normal conditions, no maintenance or service is required for the fuel tank filter or injector filters. The in-line filter should be replaced at the intervals recommended in Chapter Three.

FUEL PUMP

The electric fuel pump is located in the fuel tank. The pump is activated by a fuel pump relay in the engine compartment (**Figure 24**) when the ignition switch is turned ON.

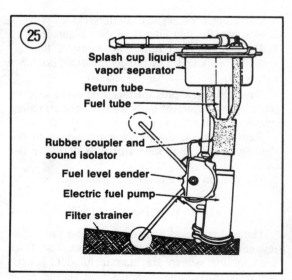

Splash cup liquid
vapor separator

Return tube

Fuel tube

Rubber coupler and
sound isolator

Fuel level sender

Electric fuel pump

Filter strainer

5

The 2 most common fuel pump problems are incorrect pressure and low volume. Low pressure results in a too-lean mixture and too little fuel at high speeds. High pressure will cause engine flooding and result in poor mileage. Low volume also results in too little fuel at high speeds.

If a fuel system problem is suspected, check the fuel filter first. See Chapter Three. If the filter is not clogged or dirty, test the fuel pump pressure.

> *WARNING*
> *Before opening any fuel injection system connections, relieve system pressure as described in this chapter.*

Pressure Test (1984)

1. Remove the air cleaner assembly as described in this chapter. Cap the air cleaner vacuum line on the TBI assembly.
2. Relieve system pressure as described in this chapter.
3. Disconnect the steel fuel tube between the 2 TBI units. Use one wrench to hold the inlet nut and another wrench to loosen the fuel tube fitting.
4. Install a 9-15 psi fuel pressure gauge (part No. J-29658) between the throttle bodies.
5. Start the engine and let the idle stabilize. The pressure gauge should read 9-13 psi. If pressure is less than 9 psi, the fuel filter is restricted or the fuel pump is defective. If pressure is greater than 13 psi,

the fuel return line from the throttle body is restricted or the throttle body pressure regulator is defective.
6. Relieve system pressure and remove the pressure gauge. Start the engine and check for leaks. If none are found, install the air cleaner.

Pressure Test (1985-on)

1. Relieve system pressure as described in this chapter.

> *NOTE*
> *Wrap a shop cloth around the fitting while installing the gauge in Step 2 to collect the fuel, then dispose of it in a safe manner.*

2. Connect a pressure gauge with bleed hose (part No. J-34730-1 or equivalent) to the fuel pressure test point or connector. See **Figure 22**.
3. Start the engine and let the idle stabilize, then shut it off. Leave the ignition switch ON. The pressure gauge should provide a steady 32-40 psi reading. If pressure is less than 32 psi, the fuel filter is restricted or the fuel pump is defective. If pressure is greater than 40 psi, the fuel return line from the fuel rail is restricted or the fuel rail pressure regulator is defective.
4. Relieve system pressure and remove the pressure gauge. Start the engine and check for leaks.

Replacement

The electrical fuel pump is an integral part of the fuel filter, vapor separator and fuel gauge sending unit in the fuel tank (**Figure 25**). The pump can be serviced through the fuel filler door in the body.

1. Disconnect the negative battery cable.
2. Remove the fuel filler door. See **Figure 26**.
3. Remove the fuel tank cap. Remove the fuel tank filler neck seal. Disconnect the drain hose. See **Figure 27**.
4. Disconnect and plug the fuel lines at the sending gauge/vapor separator unit. Remove the attaching screws. Remove the entire unit from the tank.
5. Remove the screws holding the pump to the sending gauge/vapor separator unit. Remove the pump.
6. Installation is the reverse of removal.

FUEL TANK AND LINES

The fuel tank and lines incorporate a fuel vapor (evaporative emission) control system. The hoses used in this system are manufactured of special fuel-resistant material. Regular hose should never be used as a replacement.

WARNING
Before opening any fuel injection system connections, relieve system pressure as described in this chapter.

Fuel Tank
Removal/Installation

Refer to **Figure 28** for this procedure.
1. Disconnect the negative battery cable.
2. Remove the fuel tank filler cap and siphon the tank.

WARNING
Never store gasoline in an open container, since it is an extreme fire hazard. Store gasoline in a sealed metal container away from heat, sparks and flame.

3. Remove the fuel filler door (**Figure 26**).
4. Remove the fuel tank filler neck seal and drain hose (**Figure 27**).
5. Disconnect the sending unit electrical connector and the fuel lines.
6. Securely block the wheels that remain on the ground. Raise the vehicle and place it on jackstands.
7. Remove the spare tire from its carrier.
8. Remove the spare tire carrier.
9. Disconnect the exhaust system at the transmission support (**Figure 29**).
10. Remove the rear muffler brackets at the frame (**Figure 30**). Slide the exhaust system to the rear.
11. Remove the fuel tank strap bolts. Lower the tank to the ground.
12. Installation is the reverse of removal.

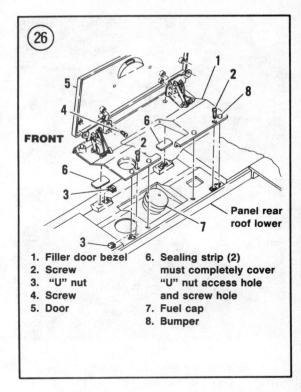

1. Filler door bezel
2. Screw
3. "U" nut
4. Screw
5. Door
6. Sealing strip (2) must completely cover "U" nut access hole and screw hole
7. Fuel cap
8. Bumper

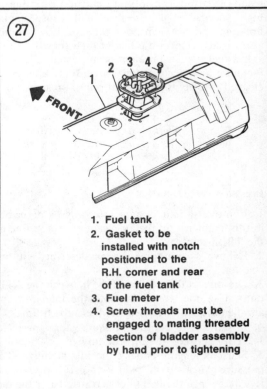

1. Fuel tank
2. Gasket to be installed with notch positioned to the R.H. corner and rear of the fuel tank
3. Fuel meter
4. Screw threads must be engaged to mating threaded section of bladder assembly by hand prior to tightening

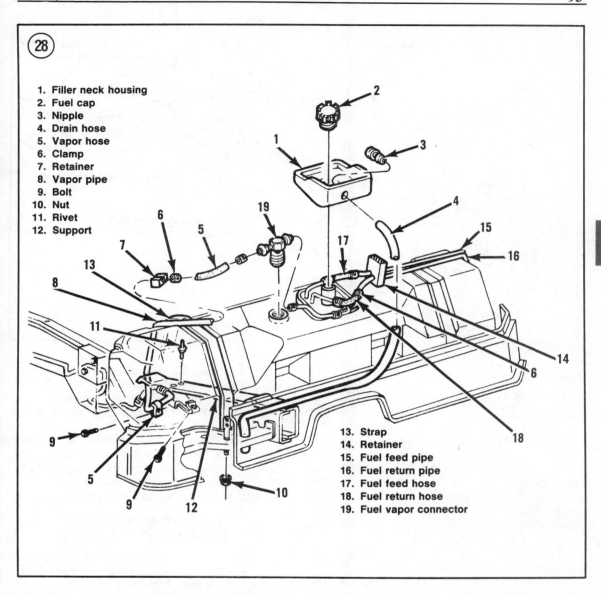

1. Filler neck housing
2. Fuel cap
3. Nipple
4. Drain hose
5. Vapor hose
6. Clamp
7. Retainer
8. Vapor pipe
9. Bolt
10. Nut
11. Rivet
12. Support

13. Strap
14. Retainer
15. Fuel feed pipe
16. Fuel return pipe
17. Fuel feed hose
18. Fuel return hose
19. Fuel vapor connector

5

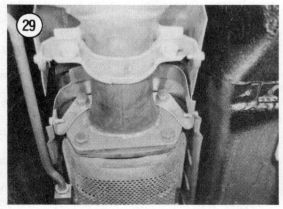

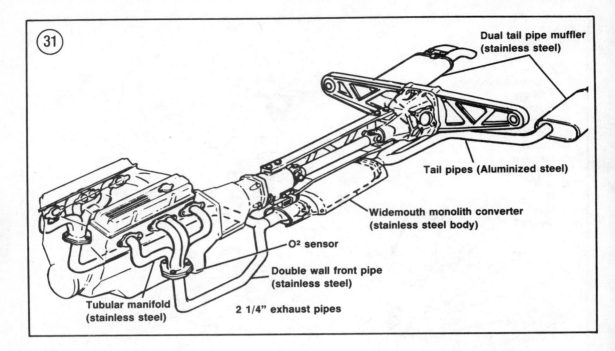

(31)

Dual tail pipe muffler
(stainless steel)

Tail pipes (Aluminized steel)

Widemouth monolith converter
(stainless steel body)

O² sensor

Double wall front pipe
(stainless steel)

Tubular manifold
(stainless steel)

2 1/4" exhaust pipes

Fuel Tank Leaks

The fuel tank contains a pliable polyethylene liner and should be replaced if defective.

EXHAUST SYSTEM

The Corvette exhaust system consists of dual stainless steel exhaust manifolds and a stainless steel dual front pipe assembly connected to a single dual-bed catalytic converter. From the converter, an aluminized dual rear pipe assembly connects to stainless steel mufflers. See **Figure 31**.

The exhaust system should be free of corrosion, leaks, binding, grounding and excessive vibrations. Loose, broken or misaligned clamps, shields, brackets or pipes should be serviced as required to keep the exhaust system in a safe operating condition.

Removal/Installation

WARNING
The exhaust system is very hot under normal operating conditions. To avoid the possibility of a bad burn, it is advisable to work on the system only when it is cool. Be especially careful around the catalytic converter. This device reaches 600° F or more after only a brief period of engine operation.

1. Prior to removal, soak all bolts, nuts and pipe joints with a penetrating oil such as WD-40.
2. Undo the required clamps and hanger brackets.
3. Replace the worn, damaged or corroded component(s).
4. Loosely clamp and align the exhaust components. Start at the front of the system and tighten all clamps and supports to specifications. Be sure there is adequate clearance between the exhaust system and all underbody parts.

COMPUTER COMMAND CONTROL (CCC) SYSTEM

This electronically-controlled system monitors up to 15 different engine/vehicle functions. It may control as many as 9 different operations through an electronic control module (ECM) and various sensors. **Figure 32** shows the operating conditions monitored by the ECM and the systems it controls.

The ECM receives data signals concerning cooling system temperature, crankshaft and distributor rpm, throttle shaft position, manifold pressure and the oxygen content of the exhaust gas. It processes this information and sends back signals to control the air-fuel mixture, distributor advance, canister purge, air management system and other functions.

If a problem develops in the CCC system, a "Check Engine" lamp will light in the warning light section of the instrument panel display. When this happens, return the car to a dealer, who has the

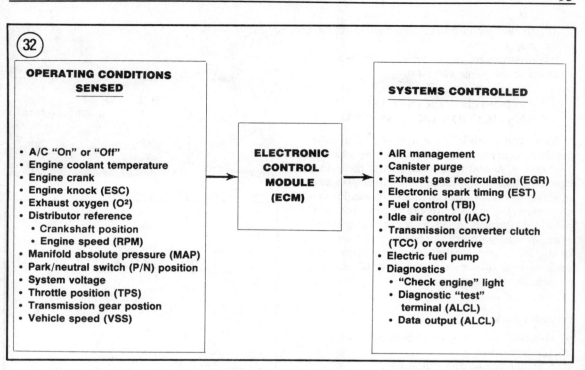

OPERATING CONDITIONS SENSED	ELECTRONIC CONTROL MODULE (ECM)	SYSTEMS CONTROLLED
• A/C "On" or "Off" • Engine coolant temperature • Engine crank • Engine knock (ESC) • Exhaust oxygen (O²) • Distributor reference • Crankshaft position • Engine speed (RPM) • Manifold absolute pressure (MAP) • Park/neutral switch (P/N) position • System voltage • Throttle position (TPS) • Transmission gear postion • Vehicle speed (VSS)		• AIR management • Canister purge • Exhaust gas recirculation (EGR) • Electronic spark timing (EST) • Fuel control (TBI) • Idle air control (IAC) • Transmission converter clutch (TCC) or overdrive • Electric fuel pump • Diagnostics • "Check engine" light • Diagnostic "test" terminal (ALCL) • Data output (ALCL)

5

proper equipment and trained technicians to diagnose this complex system.

EVAPORATIVE EMISSION CONTROL SYSTEM

A fuel a vapor control system is used on all models to prevent gasoline fumes from escaping into the atmosphere. A charcoal canister located in the left front wheel well (**Figure 33**) collects fuel tank vapors when the engine is not running. A canister purge solenoid (**Figure 33A**) controls the purge valve according to directions from the ECM. This prevents canister purge with a cold engine or during idle.

There is no scheduled maintenance. Physical damage, leaks and missing components are the most common causes of evaporative system failure.

System Inspection

1. Check the vapor lines for cracks or loose connections. Replace or tighten as necessary.
2. Check for a deformed fuel tank. Make sure the tank is not cracked and does not leak gasoline.
3. Inspect the charcoal canister (**Figure 33**) for cracks and other damage.
4. Check the vapor hoses and tubes to make sure they slope downhill from the throttle body (1984) or fuel rail (1985-on) assembly to the canister.
5. Check the fuel filler cap for a damaged gasket.

NOTE
Damage or contamination which prevents the filler cap pressure-vacuum valve from working properly can result in deformation of the fuel tank.

6. Repair or replace damaged components as necessary.

Vapor Canister Replacement

1. Label and disconnect the vacuum lines at the
2. Loosen the canister retaining bracket screw (**Figure 33B**). Remove the canister from the bracket.
3. Connect vacuum lines to the new canister purge valve.

4. Install canister in bracket and tighten retaining screw snugly.

5. Make sure the vapor lines are still securely fastened to the purge valve fittings.

POSITIVE CRANKCASE VENTILATION (PCV) SYSTEM

A crankcase ventilation system is used to recycle crankcase vapors into the combustion chambers for burning. A vent hose leading from the right air cleaner intake to the rocker arm cover provides a positive flow of air through the crankcase. Fresh air and crankcase vapors are drawn into the intake manifold through a PCV valve containing a spring-loaded plunger. The position of the plunger in the PCV valve varies depending upon engine vacuum and thus meters the flow of crankcase vapors into the intake manifold.

System Check

1. Remove the PCV valve (**Figure 34**) from the left rocker arm cover.
2. Start the engine and run at idle.
3. Place a thumb over the valve end to check for vacuum. If there is no vacuum, inspect for plugged hoses.
4. Shut the engine off. Shake the valve and listen for the rattle of the check needle in the valve. If no rattle is heard, replace the valve.

AIR INJECTION REACTION (AIR) SYSTEM

The AIR system consists of a belt-driven air pump, ECM control valve, check valves, air switching valve, dual bed catalytic converter and connecting hoses. Typical system configuration is shown in **Figure 35**.

Intake air is drawn through a centrifugal filter fan on the front of the air pump. This air is sent from the pump to the ECM control valve, which directs it either to the exhaust port air injection manifold, to a point in the dual bed converter or dumps it into the air cleaner, according to engine operating condition. The check valve(s) prevents hot exhaust gases from backing up in the system and causing pump damage.

During a cold start or when the Computer Command Control (CCC) system is in open loop, pump air is sent through the air injection manifold to the engine exhaust port area, where it mixes with hot exhaust gases. The extra air promotes a further burning of the mixture, reducing emissions. When the CCC system is in closed loop, the pump

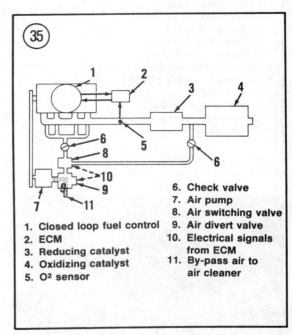

1. Closed loop fuel control
2. ECM
3. Reducing catalyst
4. Oxidizing catalyst
5. O^2 sensor
6. Check valve
7. Air pump
8. Air switching valve
9. Air divert valve
10. Electrical signals from ECM
11. By-pass air to air cleaner

air is sent to the dual bed converter. Under specified conditions such as sudden deceleration, the ECM closes the control valve solenoid and pump air is sent to the air cleaner. An electrical failure of the control valve will also divert pump air to the air cleaner.

Corvettes equipped with a manual transmission also have a decel valve in the system to prevent backfiring during deceleration by allowing air from the air cleaner to flow into the intake manifold and dilute the rich mixture during periods of high manifold vacuum.

Air Pump

The air pump can be distinguished from the alternator by the centrifugal filter fan located on the rotor shaft/drive hub. The pump is serviced by replacement and should not be disassembled.

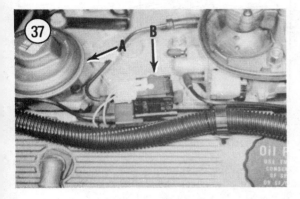

NOTE
There is a small vent hole at the top front of the pump housing. Do not mistake it for a lubrication point. Air pumps require no lubrication.

Air pumps are not noiseless in operation. Pump noise is normal and rises in pitch as engine speed increases. Three types of pump noise may be noticed.

A chirp or squeak is often heard intermittently at low engine speeds. It is usually caused by the pump vanes rubbing in the housing bore, but may also be caused by drive belt slippage if the pump seizes.

A rolling sound heard at all speeds is caused by the bearings. This sound is also normal, but can indicate bearing failure if it reaches an objectionable level.

A continuous knocking noise indicates definite bearing failure. The pump must be replaced.

Air Pump Replacement

1. Compress the drive belt to hold the pump pulley from turning. Loosen pump pulley bolts.
2. Lift the drive belt tensioner with a 1/2 in. breaker bar and slip the drive belt and pulley off the air pump.

3. Disconnect all hoses, vacuum lines and electrical connections from the air control valve (**Figure 36**).
4. Remove the air pump mounting bolts from the alternator bracket and air pump support bracket. Remove the air pump and control valve.
5. If a new pump is to be installed, transfer the air control valve and adapter from the old pump.
6. Installation is the reverse of removal.

Air Management
Functional Test

This test checks for air switching from exhaust port (open loop) to converter (closed loop). The engine coolant must be under 150° F (60° C) when the test is performed. Since the ECM will make the switch from port to converter injection in a matter of a few seconds, the help of an assistant is recommended.

1. Have the assistant start the engine and run it at part-throttle (under 2,000 rpm).
2. Immediately check for air flow at the outlet to the exhaust ports (open loop). If air flow is felt and then stops, the ECM has switched air flow to the converter (closed loop).
3. If the air does not flow as described in Step 2, have a dealer check the system further to determine the malfunction.

EXHAUST GAS RECIRCULATION (EGR) SYSTEM

This system recirculates a calibrated amount of exhaust gas into the incoming air-fuel mixture, lowering the combustion temperature and reducing the formation of oxides of nitrogen (NOx) emissions. Recirculation does not occur during idle or deceleration, when it would cause rough engine operation, or if engine coolant temperature is below a predetermined level. The EGR valve on 1984 models is located on the intake manifold behind the front TBI unit. A solenoid controlled by the ECM regulates vacuum to the EGR valve. See A (EGR valve) and B (solenoid), **Figure 37**. The EGR valve on 1985 and later models is located under the plenum. The solenoid is bracket-mounted beside the distributor at the rear of the intake manifold. See **Figure 38**.

EGR Valve Test

1. With the ignition OFF, push up on the underside of the valve diaphragm with a finger. It should move under finger pressure. If it does not, proceed to Step 7.
2. Connect a tachometer according to manufacturer's instructions.
3. Start the engine and warm to normal operating temperature (upper radiator hose hot).

5

4. Repeat Step 1. Engine rpm should drop noticeably as EGR valve is opened under finger pressure. If there is no rpm change, replace the EGR valve and clean the EGR passages in the intake manifold.

5. Disconnect the EGR solenoid (B, **Figure 35**). Hold a finger under the valve diaphragm and increase engine speed to 1,200 rpm, then return to idle. The valve diaphragm should move up and down.

6. If the valve diaphragm does not move, connect a vacuum gauge first to the engine side and then to the valve side of the EGR solenoid. It should read at least 10 in. Hg on each side. If not, replace the solenoid.

7. Disconnect the vacuum line at the EGR valve and connect a vacuum gauge. It should read at least 10 in. Hg vacuum. If it does not, replace the valve.

EGR Valve
Removal/Installation

1. 1984—Remove the air cleaner as described in this chapter.
2. Disconnect the vacuum line at the EGR valve.
3. Remove the 2 retaining bolts.
4. Remove the EGR valve and gasket.
5. Discard the gasket(s). Clean the manifold mating surface. Install the new EGR valve with a replacement gasket.
6. Install and tighten retaining bolts.
7. Connect the vacuum line to the EGR valve.
8. Install the air cleaner.

EGR Solenoid Replacement

1. Disconnect the negative battery cable.
2. 1984—Remove the air cleaner as described in this chapter.
3. Disconnect the electrical connector at the solenoid.
4. Disconnect the vacuum lines from the solenoid.
5. Remove the attaching nut. Remove the solenoid.
6. Installation is the reverse of removal. Tighten retaining nut to 17 ft.-lb. (24 N•m).

EGR Valve
Cleaning and Inspection

If the valve is operating properly, it can be removed, cleaned and reinstalled.
1. Remove the valve as described in this chapter.
2. Hold the valve in your hand and tap the end of the pintle with a plastic hammer and a gentle snapping motion to remove deposits from the valve seat.

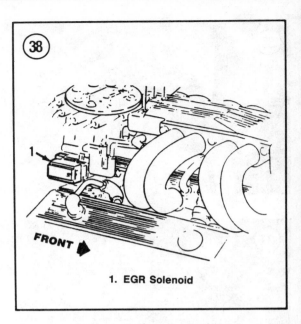

1. EGR Solenoid

3. Clean the valve mounting surface with a wire wheel or wire brush. Clean the pintle with a wire brush.
4. Depress the valve diaphragm. Look through the valve outlet to check the seating area to make sure it is clean. If it is not, repeat Step 2.
5. Check for deposits in the valve outlet and remove with a screwdriver if any are found.
6. Clean the manifold mounting surface and reinstall the valve with a new gasket.

CATALYTIC CONVERTER

The catalytic converter is mounted in the exhaust system between the exhaust manifold pipe and the rear crossover pipe. Carbon monoxide and unburned hydrocarbons in the exhaust gas are oxidized as they pass through the converter. This process changes the harmful pollutants into harmless carbon dioxide and water. The converter also reduces NOx. The converter requires no maintenance other than replacement of the heat shield, if damaged.

OXYGEN SENSOR

An oxygen sensor mounted in the front crossover pipe near the exhaust manifold connection (**Figure 39**) monitors the oxygen content of the exhaust gas and signals the ECM, which evaluates this data in determining injector duration. If the sensor is defective, the vehicle will operate only in open loop. This results in decreased fuel economy and increased emissions.

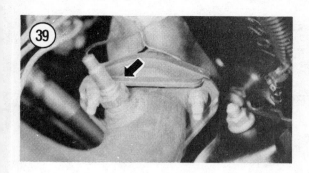

Replacement

1. Start and partially warm the engine. Easy removal of the sensor requires that engine temperature be at least 120° F (48° C). Attempting to remove the sensor when the engine is cold may result in sensor or exhaust pipe thread damage.

2. Shut the engine off. Disconnect the negative battery cable.

3. Securely block the rear wheels. Raise the front of the car and place it on jackstands.

4. Disconnect the electrical connector at the sensor pigtail.

5. Remove the sensor with an appropriate size open-end wrench.

CAUTION
Handle oxygen sensors with care. Keep the louvered end free of dirt, grease and other contamination. Do not clean with solvent, remove the pigtail from the sensor end or drop on a hard surface.

6. If the same sensor is to be reinstalled, wipe its threads with anti-seize compound part No. 5613695 or equivalent (new sensor threads are precoated).

7. Installation is the reverse of removal. Tighten sensor to 30 ft.-lb. (41 N•m).

5

CHAPTER SIX

COOLING, HEATING AND AIR CONDITIONING SYSTEMS

The pressurized cooling system consists of a radiator, radiator cap, thermostat, water pump, coolant recovery tank, electric cooling fan, temperature sensor, drive belt and connecting hoses. The crossflow radiator is mounted on a radiator support attached to the frame side rails. The water pump is mounted to the block. A single speed electric fan mounted in the radiator shroud operates when coolant temperature exceeds approximately 238° F or whenever the air conditioner is on.

The heater is a hot water type which circulates coolant through a small radiator (heater core) under the instrument panel.

The air conditioning system is a cycling clutch (intermittent) expansion valve type and uses outside air at all times, except during MAX A/C operation.

This chapter includes service procedures for the radiator, water pump, thermostat, heater and air conditioner. Cooling system flushing procedures are also described.

COOLING SYSTEM

The recommended coolant is a mixture of ethylene glycol antifreeze and low mineral content water, which provides a lower freezing point and higher boiling point than water alone.

The water pump circulates the coolant through the cooling system when the engine is running. When the engine is cold, the coolant is trapped inside the engine water jacket by the thermostat, which is located in the mouth of the hose leading to the radiator inlet tank. The thermostat remains closed until the coolant heats up to operating temperature. It then opens and the coolant flows through the hose into the radiator inlet tank. The coolant passes through the radiator tubes to the outlet tank, where it flows through the radiator outlet hose to the water pump inlet to start the cycle over once again.

The cooling fan draws air through the radiator and removes excess heat from the coolant. Plastic ductwork in front of the radiator is shaped to increase airflow to the radiator core. A shroud attached to the radiator funnels air through the radiator more efficiently.

Hoses route the coolant to the heater core and radiator. A water valve is installed in the heater core inlet hose so that coolant flow to the heater can be shut off if the heater is not required.

COOLING SYSTEM FLUSHING

The recommended coolant is a 50/50 mixture of water and ethylene glycol antifreeze meeting GM specification 1825M (part No. 1052753). The

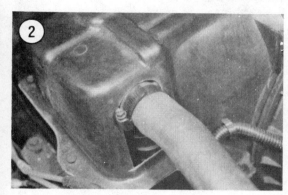

radiator should be drained, flushed and refilled at the intervals specified in Chapter Three.

> *CAUTION*
> *Under no circumstances should a chemical flushing agent be used. Flush the cooling system with clear water only.*

1. Coolant can stain concrete and harm plants. Park the vehicle over a gutter or similar area.

2. Move the heater control lever to HEAT and the temperature lever to WARM.

3. Remove the radiator cap to promote faster draining (**Figure 1**).

4. Open the drain valve at the bottom of the radiator outlet tank.

5. Let the cooling system drain. Close the drain valve.

6. Remove the thermostat as described in this chapter. Temporarily reinstall the thermostat housing and water outlet with the hose connected.

7. Disconnect the top radiator hose from the radiator (**Figure 2**).

8. Disconnect the bottom hose from the radiator.

9. Disconnect the heater inlet and outlet hoses at the water pipes. See **Figure 3** (inlet) and **Figure 4** (outlet).

10. Disconnect the water valve vacuum line (**Figure 5**). Connect a hand vacuum pump and apply sufficient vacuum to open the valve.

11. Connect a garden hose to the heater pipe nearest the front of the engine. This does not have to be a positive fit, as long as most of the water enters the heater pipe. Run water into the heater pipe until clear water flows from the other heater pipe.

12. Insert the garden hose into the top radiator hose fitting. Run water into the fitting until clear

6

water flows from the hose fitting at the bottom of the radiator.

13. Insert the garden hose into the hose fitting at the bottom of the radiator. Run water into the radiator until clear water flows from the top fitting.

14. Insert the garden hose into the top radiator hose. Run water into the hose until clear water flows from the bottom hose. Turn off the water.

15. Disconnect the coolant recovery tank hose (**Figure 6**) from the bottom front of the tank. Remove and empty the tank. Flush the recovery tank first with soapy water, then clean water. Drain the tank and reinstall. Connect the hose.

16. Connect the radiator and heater hoses. Connect the water valve vacuum line. Reinstall the thermostat.

17. Pour 4 quarts of Prestone II or equivalent antifreeze into the radiator. Add sufficient water to bring the coolant level to the top of the filler neck.

18. Install the radiator cap. Fill the recovery tank approximately one-quarter full. This should bring the coolant near the "COLD" mark on the dipstick built into the recovery tank cap.

19. Start the engine and run at a fast idle until the upper radiator hose is hot. Return the engine to normal idle. The recovery tank should be about one-half full, near the "HOT" mark on the dipstick in the tank cap.

20. Allow the radiator to cool for several hours, then recheck the level in the recovery tank. If it is not at the "COLD" mark on the dipstick (about one-quarter full), add coolant as required.

THERMOSTAT

The thermostat blocks coolant flow to the radiator when the engine is cold. As the engine warms up, the thermostat gradually opens, allowing coolant to circulate through the radiator. A 195° F (90° C) thermostat is normally used. The heat range is stamped on the thermostat flange.

Removal and Testing

1. Make sure the engine is cool. Disconnect the negative battery cable. Remove the air cleaner. See Chapter Five.

2. Place a clean container under the radiator drain valve. Remove the radiator cap and open the drain valve. Drain sufficient coolant from the radiator to bring the coolant level below the thermostat housing. If the coolant is clean, save it for reuse.

3. Remove the upper radiator hose from the water outlet (**Figure 7**).

4. Remove the 2 bolts holding the water outlet. Remove the water outlet, gasket, thermostat housing and thermostat. See **Figure 8**.

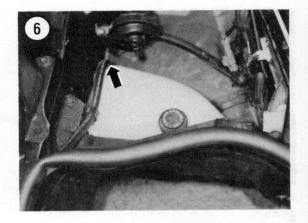

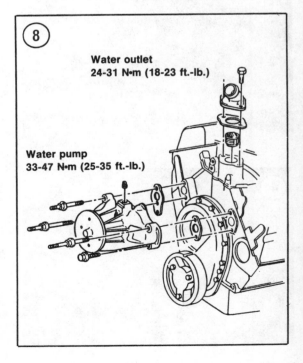

Water outlet
24-31 N•m (18-23 ft.-lb.)

Water pump
33-47 N•m (25-35 ft.-lb.)

5. Pour some of the coolant into a container that can be heated. Submerge the thermostat in this coolant and suspend a thermometer as shown in **Figure 9**.

NOTE
Support the thermostat with wire so it does not touch the sides or bottom of the pan.

6. Heat the coolant 25° F above the temperature stamped on the thermostat flange. The valve should be fully open.

7. Cool the coolant 10° F below the temperature stamped on the thermostat flange. The valve should be completely closed.

8. If the thermostat does not function properly within this temperature range, replace it.

Installation

1. If a new thermostat is being installed, test it as described above.

2. Clean all RTV sealant or gasket residue from the thermostat housing, water outlet and intake manifold mating surfaces with degreaser and a putty knife.

3. Run a 1/8 in. (3 mm) bead of RTV sealant around the thermostat housing sealing surface on the intake manifold.

4. Install the thermostat in the intake manifold. Position the thermostat housing on the intake manifold. Fit water outlet with new gasket on top of thermostat housing. Install attaching bolts and tighten to 18-23 ft.-lb. (24-31 N•m).

5. Install the air cleaner. See Chapter Five.

6. Fill the radiator to the level specified under *Cooling System Flushing* in this chapter.

7. Connect the negative battery cable.

RADIATOR

Removal/Installation

1. Make sure the radiator is cool enough to touch comfortably.

2. Coolant can stain concrete and harm plants. Park the vehicle over a gutter or similar area. Place a clean container under the drain valve.

3. Disconnect the negative battery cable.

4. Remove the radiator cap to promote faster draining (**Figure 1**).

5. Open the drain valve at the lower side of the outlet tank.

6. Remove the upper and lower hose clamps at the radiator. Disconnect the hoses.

7. Disconnect the coolant recovery hose at the radiator filler neck.

WARNING
The air conditioning system contains pressurized refrigerant which can cause frostbite if it touches skin and blindness if it touches the eyes. If discharged near an open flame, the refrigerant forms poisonous gas. Never disconnect air conditioning system lines unless the system has been discharged and evacuated by a professional.

8. Unbolt the accumulator (**Figure 10**) and move to one side without disconnecting the lines.

9. Disconnect the fan motor wire. Remove the shroud and fan assembly attaching bolts (**Figure 11** shows the upper bolts).

6

10. Disconnect and plug the transmission fluid lines at the radiator.

11. Remove the upper support bolts. Remove the upper support.

12. Remove the radiator from the lower support.

13. Installation is the reverse of removal. On automatic transmission models, install the lower cooler line before installing the upper support. Tighten the support and shroud fasteners snugly.

14. Fill the radiator with coolant to the level specified under *Cooling System Flushing* in this chapter.

Radiator Hose Replacement

Replace any hoses that are cracked, brittle, mildewed or very soft and spongy. If a hose is in doubtful condition, but not definitely bad, replace it to be on the safe side. Even though the hoses are easily accessible, this will avoid the necessity of a roadside repair.

> *NOTE*
> *Be sure to use a molded replacement hose. Plain or pleated rubber hoses do not have the same strength as reinforced molded hoses.*

1. Partially drain the cooling system when replacing an upper hose. Completely drain it to replace a lower hose.

2. Loosen the clamp nut at each end of the hose. Twist the hose to break it free of the fitting and take it off.

3. If the hose cannot be twisted free due to rust or corrosion, cut it off with a sharp knife at a point about one inch from the radiator fitting. Use the knife to slit the hose remaining on the fitting lengthwise, then peel the old hose off the fitting.

> *CAUTION*
> *Do not use oil or grease as a lubricant to assist in hose replacement. It may cause the rubber to deteriorate.*

4. New hoses can be installed easily by smearing dishwashing liquid on the fitting and the inside diameter of the hose.

> *CAUTION*
> *To prevent hose or clamp damage, do not overtighten.*

5. Tighten the hose clamps snugly. Recheck them for tightness after operating the vehicle for a few days.

WATER PUMP

A water pump may warn of impending failure by making noise. If the pump seal is defective, coolant may leak from behind the pump pulley. The water

pump can be replaced on all models without discharging the air conditioning system. The pump is serviced as an assembly.

Removal/Installation

1. Disconnect the negative battery cable.

2. Make sure the engine is cool enough to touch comfortably. Drain the cooling system. See *Cooling System Flushing* in this chapter.

3. Hold water pump pulley from turning by depressing the drive belt. Loosen the pump pulley bolts. See **Figure 12** (1984) or **Figure 13** (1985-on).

4. Repeat Step 3 to loosen the air pump pulley bolts. See **Figure 12** (1984) or **Figure 13** (1985-on).

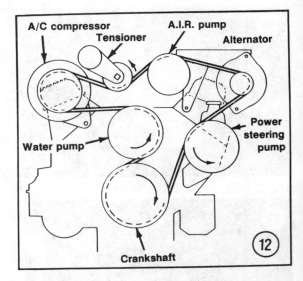

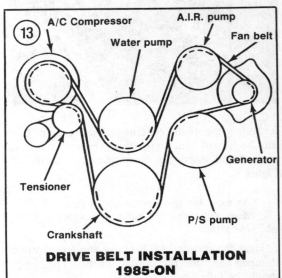

DRIVE BELT INSTALLATION 1985-ON

5. Lift the drive belt tensioner with a 1/2 in. breaker bar and remove the drive belt.

6. Remove the water pump and air pump pulleys.

7. Remove the air management valve adapter (arrow, **Figure 14**).

8. Remove the air pump.

9. Relieve the fuel injection system pressure (Chapter Five). Disconnect the fuel supply and return lines at the throttle body assembly. Cap the lines to prevent leakage. **Figure 15** shows the supply line fitting; **Figure 16** shows the return line fitting.

10. Remove the air conditioner compressor braces and lower mounting bolt.

11. Remove the compressor and idler pulley bracket nuts.

12. Disconnect the compressor wires, then slide mounting bracket forward and remove rear compressor mounting bolt. Remove the compressor.

13. Remove the right and left air injection hoses at the check valve.

14. Remove the air pump injection pipe at the intake manifold and power steering reservoir bracket.

15. Remove the power steering reservoir bracket and top alternator bolt.

16. Remove the lower air pump bracket at the water pump.

17. Remove the lower radiator and heater hoses at the water pump.

18. Remove the water pump mounting bolts. Remove the water pump and gaskets. See **Figure 17**. Discard the gaskets.

19. If a new water pump is to be installed, transfer the heater hose fitting from the old pump.

20. Clean sealing surfaces on engine block and water pump of all gasket residue.

21. Installation is the reverse of removal. Use new gaskets and tighten pump bolts to 100-125 in.-lb. (11-14 N•m).

14

15

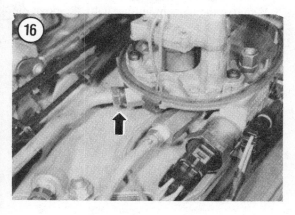

16

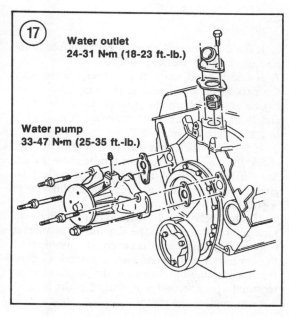

17

Water outlet
24-31 N•m (18-23 ft.-lb.)

Water pump
33-47 N•m (25-35 ft.-lb.)

6

COOLING FAN

The cooling fan is temperature-controlled by a switch located in the right cylinder head near the No. 6 spark plug and dipstick tube (**Figure 18**) and a relay located on the left rear wheelhouse panel (**Figure 19**). In addition, a switch on the air conditioning compressor activates the fan whenever the air conditioner is on.

> *NOTE*
> *Some early production Corvettes may have the air conditioning switch located near the Schrader valve on the accumulator.*

Power is available at all times to the relay contacts. With the ignition switch at RUN, power is sent through the 3 amp fuse in the fuse block cavity marked "C FAN" to the relay coil. When engine temperature reaches approximately 238° F, the fan switch contacts close, completing the relay circuit and operating the fan. When engine temperature drops to about 201° F, the switch opens the fan circuit, shutting the fan off.

> *WARNING*
> *Since it is temperature-controlled, the fan can operate whenever the ignition is ON. Either disconnect the negative battery cable or fan motor connector when working near the fan or exercise caution to prevent personal injury.*

Troubleshooting

1. If fan does not run, check the 3 amp fuse in the fuse block cavity marked "C FAN."
2. If fuse is good, connect a jumper lead between the dark green/white wire at the relay and a good engine ground. Turn the ignition switch to RUN and listen for a click from the relay. If no click is heard, replace the relay.
3. If the relay clicks but the fan still does not run, check the fan motor coolant temperature switch. See Chapter Seven. A malfunctioning switch will give a constant resistance reading during testing regardless of temperature.
4. If the relay and temperature switch are satisfactory, disconnect the fan motor connector. Connect a jumper lead between one terminal on the fan motor and a good engine ground. Connect the other fan motor terminal to the positive battery terminal with a second jumper lead. If the fan does not run, replace the motor.

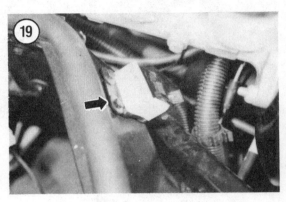

Fan Removal/Installation

1. Disconnect the negative battery cable.
2. Disconnect the fan wire at the motor.
3. Remove the shroud attaching bolts. Remove the shroud with the fan attached.
4. Remove the fan attaching bolts. Remove the fan from the shroud.
5. Installation is the reverse of removal.

Relay Replacement

1. Disconnect the negative battery cable.
2. Disconnect the wiring harness at the relay.
3. Remove the relay mounting bolts. Remove the relay.
4. Installation is the reverse of removal.

DRIVE BELT

The single (serpentine) drive belt's tension is maintained by a spring-loaded tensioner. See **Figure 12** (1984) or **Figure 13** (1985-on). All accessory units are rigidly mounted. The drive belt is removed or installed by lifting the tensioner with a 1/2 in. breaker bar and removing or installing the belt over the accessory pulleys.

Check drive belt tension with a tension gauge positioned between the alternator and air pump. Belt tension should be 120-140 lb. (534-623 N). If

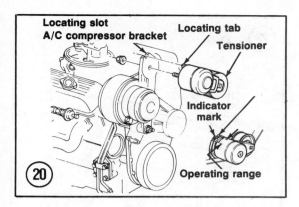

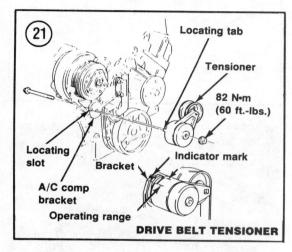

DRIVE BELT TENSIONER

tension is outside this range, check the tensioner to see if the indicator mark on the rear of the unit falls within the slot on the front of the unit which indicates the operating range. See **Figure 20** (1984) or **Figure 21** (1985-on). If the mark is outside the operating range slot, the tensioner is malfunctioning and should be replaced.

HEATER

The Corvette uses a modified blend-type heating system. The temperature of heated air entering the passenger compartment is determined by blending air flowing through heater core passages with cool fresh air which bypasses the heater core. System controls and operation are described in your owner's handbook.

Troubleshooting

1. If the heater does not produce heat, make sure the engine will warm up in a reasonable amount of time. If the thermostat sticks in the open position, the engine will not completely warm up. Since hot engine coolant provides heat for the heater, a defective thermostat may be the problem.
2. If the heater blower does not work, check the 25 amp fuse marked "A/C" in the fuse panel.
3. If the fuse is good, check for a loose connection or a poor ground in the switch wiring.
4. If the heater blower still does not work, remove and test the blower switch and resistor block as described in this chapter.

Blower Switch Testing

Power to the blower motor is provided through the ignition switch, a 25 amp fuse in the fuse block cavity marked "A/C" and the control panel function switch. Blower motor speed is controlled by a separate 2-speed (LO and HI) switch at the left front of the control assembly.
1. Remove the control assembly as described in this chapter.
2. If the problem is in the blower speed, check for continuity between the switch terminal at both switch positions with a test lamp.
3. The lamp should light for each connected pair of terminals. There should be no continuity (lamp should not light) between the switch case and any terminal.

Blower Switch Replacement

1. Remove the control assembly as described in this chapter.
2. Pry the switch knob from the blower switch with a small screwdriver.
3. Remove the switch attaching screws. Remove the switch.
4. Installation is the reverse of removal.

Resistor Block Test

The resistor block is mounted on the evaporator case in the engine compartment.
1. Disconnect the resistor block electrical connector.
2. Remove the resistor block retaining screws. Remove the resistor block.
3. Test the resistor block for an open circuit with a self-powered test lamp. Replace resistor block if open.

Control Panel
Removal/Installation

1. Disconnect the negative battery cable.
2. Remove the instrument cluster bezel. Remove the accessory trim panel above the console. See *Instruments*, Chapter Seven.

6

3. Remove the control panel attaching screws. See **Figure 22**.

4. Pull the control panel out slightly and swivel to one side. Disconnect the electrical connectors, vacuum hoses and temperature control cable.

5. Remove the control assembly.

6. Installation is the reverse of removal.

Temperature Control
Cable Adjustment

The temperature control cable is held in place by self-adjusting retaining clips.

Blower Motor and Fan

The blower motor and fan are removed from the engine compartment.

1. Disconnect the negative battery cable.

2. Remove the rear panel from the front wheel house (passenger side). Move the wheel house seal to one side.

3. Remove the motor cooling tube (A, **Figure 23**).

4. Remove the air conditioning high-speed blower relay (B, **Figure 23**).

5. Disconnect the electrical connectors (C, **Figure 23**).

6. Remove the blower motor attaching screws. Remove the motor and fan assembly.

7. Installation is the reverse of removal.

AIR CONDITIONING

This section covers the maintenance and minor repairs that can prevent or correct common air conditioning problems. Major repairs require special training and equipment and should be left to a dealer or air conditioning expert.

System Operation

There are 5 basic components common to the air conditioning system.

   a. Compressor.
   b. Condenser.
   c. Expansion valve.
   d. Evaporator.
   e. Accumulator/drier.

For practical purposes, the cycle begins at the compressor. See **Figure 24**. The refrigerant enters the low-pressure side of the compressor in a warm low-pressure vapor state. It is compressed to a high-pressure hot vapor and pumped out of the high-pressure side to the condenser.

Air flow through the condenser removes heat from the refrigerant and transfers the heat to the outside air. As the heat is removed, the refrigerant condenses to a warm high-pressure liquid.

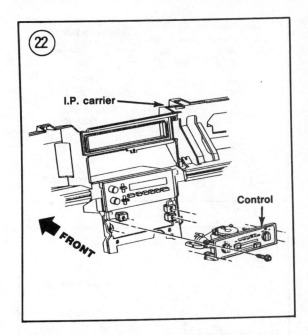

The refrigerant then flows through the orifice in the expansion valve to the evaporator. As the refrigerant leave the expansion valve, it changes from a warm high-pressure liquid to a cold, low-pressure liquid.

In the evaporator, the refrigerant removes heat from the passenger compartment air that is blown across the evaporator's fins and tubes. This changes the refrigerant from a cold, low-pressure liquid back to a warm, low-pressure vapor. This vapor passes into the accumulator/drier where moisture is removed and impurities are filtered out. The low-pressure vapor returns to the compressor with a small amount of low-pressure liquid that did not boil off completely and the cycle begins again.

GET TO KNOW
YOUR VEHICLE'S SYSTEM

Figure 24 shows the major components of the air conditioning system. Refer to it to locate each of the following components in turn:

   a. Compressor.
   b. Condenser.
   c. Expansion valve.
   d. Evaporator.
   e. Accumulator/drier.

Compressor

The compressor is located on the drive belt end of the engine, like the alternator, and is driven by the serpentine belt. The large pulley on the front of the compressor contains an electromagnetic clutch. This activates and operates the compressor when the air conditioning is switched on.

Condenser

The condenser is mounted in front of the radiator. Air passing through the condenser tubes and fins removes heat from the refrigerant in the same manner it removes heat from the engine coolant as it passes through the radiator. The radiator cooling fan pulls air through the condenser.

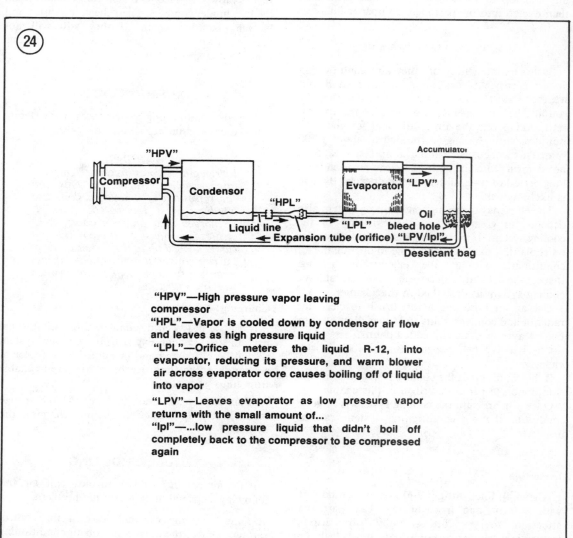

24

"HPV"—High pressure vapor leaving compressor

"HPL"—Vapor is cooled down by condensor air flow and leaves as high pressure liquid

"LPL"—Orifice meters the liquid R-12, into evaporator, reducing its pressure, and warm blower air across evaporator core causes boiling off of liquid into vapor

"LPV"—Leaves evaporator as low pressure vapor returns with the small amount of...

"lpl"—...low pressure liquid that didn't boil off completely back to the compressor to be compressed again

Accumulator/Drier

The accumulator/drier is a small tank-like unit mounted at the right front of the engine near the air pump.

Expansion Valve

The expansion valve is located in the line between the condenser and the evaporator. It meters refrigerant into the evaporator.

Evaporator

The evaporator is mounted on the firewall in the engine compartment. Warm air is blown across the fins and tubes, where it is cooled and dried and then ducted into the passenger compartment.

ROUTINE MAINTENANCE

Basic maintenance of the air conditioning system is easy. At least once a month, even in cold weather, start your engine, turn on the air conditioner and operate it at each of the control settings. Operate the air conditioner for about 10 minutes, with the engine running at about 1,500 rpm. This will ensure that the compressor seal does not deform from sitting in the same position for a long period of time. If deformation occurs, the seal is likely to leak.

The efficiency of the air conditioning system also depends in great part on the efficiency of the cooling system. If the cooling system is dirty or low on coolant, it may be impossible to operate the air conditioner without the engine overheating. Inspect the coolant. If necessary, flush and refill the cooling system as described in this chapter.

Use an air hose and a soft brush to clean the radiator and condenser fins and tubes. Remove any bugs, leaves or other imbedded debris.

Check drive belt tension as described in this chapter.

If the condition of the cooling system thermostat is in doubt, test it as described in this chapter.

Once you are sure the cooling system is in good condition, the air conditioning system can be inspected.

Inspection

1. Clean all lines, fittings and system components with solvent and a clean rag. Pay particular attention to the fittings; oily dirt around connections almost certainly indicates a leak. Oil from the compressor will migrate through the system to the leak. Carefully tighten the connection, but do not overtighten and strip the threads. If the leak persists, it will soon be apparent as oily dirt will continue to accumulate.

2. Clean the condenser fins and tubes with a soft brush and an air hose or with a high-pressure stream of water from a garden hose. Remove any bugs, leaves or other imbedded debris. Carefully straighten any bent fins with a screwdriver, taking care not to puncture or dent the tubes.

3. Start the engine and check the operation of the blower motor and the compressor clutch by turning the controls on and off. If either the blower or clutch fails to operate, shut off the engine and check the air conditioner fuse. See Chapter Seven. If it is blown, replace it. If not, remove and clean the fuse holder contacts. Then check the clutch and blower operation again. If they still will not operate, take the vehicle to a dealer or air conditioning specialist.

REFRIGERANT

The air conditioning system uses a refrigerant called dichlorodifluoromethane or R-12.

> *WARNING*
> *Refrigerant creates freezing temperatures when it evaporates. This can cause frostbite if it touches skin, and blindness if it touches the eyes. If discharged near an open flame, R-12 creates poisonous gas. If the refrigerant can is hooked up to the pressure side of the compressor, it may explode. Always wear safety goggles and gloves when working with R-12.*

Charging

If a hose has been disconnected or any internal part of the system exposed to air, the system should be evacuated and recharged by a dealer or air conditioning shop. Recharge kits are available from auto parts stores.

Carefully read and understand the gauge manufacturer's instructions before charging the system.

TROUBLESHOOTING

If the air conditioner fails to blow cold air, the following steps will help locate the problem.

1. First, stop the car and look at the control settings. One of the most common air conditioning

problems occurs when the temperature is set for maximum cold and the blower is set on LO. This promotes ice buildup on the evaporator fins and tubes, particularly in humid weather. Eventually, the evaporator will ice over completely and restrict air flow. Turn the blower on HI and place a hand over an air outlet. If the blower is running but there is little or no air flowing through the outlet, the evaporator is probably iced up. Leave the blower on HI and turn the temperature control off or to its warmest setting and wait. It will take 10-15 minutes for the ice to start melting.

2. If the blower is not running, the fuse may be blown, there may be a loose wiring connection or the motor may be burned out. First, check the fuse panel for a blown or incorrectly seated fuse, then check the wiring for loose connections.

3. Shut off the engine and inspect the serpentine drive belt. See Chapter Three.

4. Start the engine. Check the compressor clutch by turning the air conditioner on and off. If the clutch does not activate, its fuse may be blown or the evaporator temperature-limiting switches may be defective. If the fuse is defective, replace it. If the fuse is not the problem, have the system checked by a dealer or an air conditioning specialist.

5. If the system appears to be operating as it should, but air flow into the passenger compartment is not cold, check the condenser for debris that could block air flow. Recheck the cooling system as described in this chapter. If the preceding steps have not solved the problem, take the car to a dealer or air conditioning shop for service.

6

ELECTRICAL SYSTEMS

This chapter provides service procedures for the battery, charging system, starter, ignition system, lights, switches, turn signal indicators, horn, windshield wipers and washer, fuses and fusible links. Engine compartment wiring harness diagrams and **Table 1** and **Table 2** are at the end of the chapter.

BATTERY

All Corvettes are equipped with a sealed battery which requires no maintenance (**Figure 1**). This battery incorporates a visual test indicator (**Figure 2**). This test indicator is a built-in hydrometer in one cell. It provides visual information of battery condition for testing only and should not be used as a basis of determining whether the battery is properly charged or discharged, good or bad.

Using the Test Indicator

Refer to **Figure 3**. Make sure the battery is level and the test indicator sight glass is clean. A penlight is useful under dim lighting conditions to determine the indicator color. Look down into the

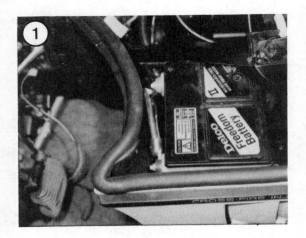

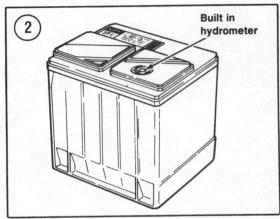

Built in hydrometer

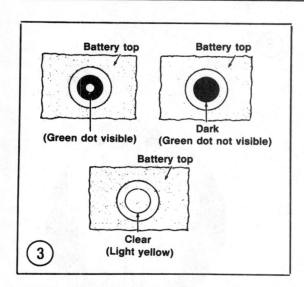

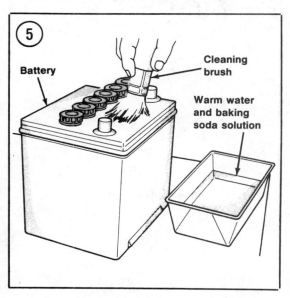

sight glass. If the dot appears green in color, the battery has a sufficient charge for testing. If it appears dark or black, charge the battery before testing. A clear or light yellow appearance indicates that the battery should be replaced and the charging system checked.

Care and Inspection

1. Disconnect both battery cables (negative first, then positive). Remove the battery hold-down clamp (**Figure 4**).

2. Attach a battery carry strap to the terminal posts. Remove the battery from the engine compartment.

3. Check the entire battery case for cracks. If the battery has removable filler caps, cover the vent holes in each cap with a small piece of masking tape.

CAUTION
Keep cleaning solution out of the battery cells in Step 4 or the electrolyte will be seriously weakened.

4. Clean the top of the battery with a stiff bristle brush using baking soda and water solution (**Figure 5**). Rinse the battery case with clear water and wipe dry with a clean cloth or paper towel.

5. Inspect the battery tray in the engine compartment for corrosion and clean if necessary with the baking soda and water solution.

6. Remove the masking tape from the filler cap vent holes. Position the battery on the battery tray and install the hold-down clamp. Tighten the clamp bolt to 9 ft.-lb. (12 N•m).

7. Clean the battery cable clamps with a stiff wire brush or one of the many tools made for this purpose. The same tool is used for cleaning the battery posts.

8. Reconnect the positive battery cable, then the negative cable.

CAUTION
Be sure the battery cables are connected to their proper terminals. Connecting the battery backwards will reverse the polarity and can damage the alternator.

9. Tighten the battery cable connections to 9 ft.-lb. (12 N•m) and coat with a petroleum jelly such as Vaseline or a light mineral grease.

10. If the battery has removable filler caps, check the electrolyte level. Top up with distilled water, if necessary.

Testing

This procedure applies to batteries with removable filler caps. Testing sealed batteries requires special equipment, but any good service station or your dealer can make the test for a nominal fee.

Hydrometer testing is the best way to check battery condition. Use a hydrometer with numbered gradations from 1.100-1.300 rather than one with just color-coded bands. To use the hydrometer, squeeze the rubber ball, insert the tip in a cell and release the ball (**Figure 6**).

Draw enough electrolyte to float the weighted float inside the hydrometer. Note the number in line with the surface of the electrolyte. This is the specific gravity for the cell. Return the electrolyte to the cell from which it came.

The specific gravity of the electrolyte in each battery cell is an excellent indicator of that cell's condition. A fully charged cell will read 1.260 or more at 68° F (20° C). If the cells test below 1.200, the battery must be recharged. Charging is also necessary if the specific gravity varies more than 0.025 from cell to cell.

> *NOTE*
> *If a temperature-compensated hydro-meter is not used, add 0.004 to the specified gravity reading for every 10° above 80° F (25° C). For every 10° below 80° F (25° C), subtract 0.004.*

Charging

The battery does not have to be removed from the car for charging. Just make certain that the area is well-ventilated and that there is no chance of sparks or flames occurring near the battery.

> *WARNING*
> *Charging batteries give off highly explosive hydrogen gas. If this gas explodes, it may spray battery acid over a wide area.*

Disconnect the negative battery cable first, then the positive cable. Install a pair of screw-in battery posts or a charging adapter strap (**Figure 7**) to provide an adequate conductive surface for the charger leads.

On unsealed batteries, make sure the electrolyte is fully topped up. Remove the vent caps and place a folded paper towel over the vent openings to catch any electrolyte that may spew as the battery charges.

Connect the charger to the battery—negative to negative, positive to positive. If the charger output is variable, select a low setting (5-10 amps), set the

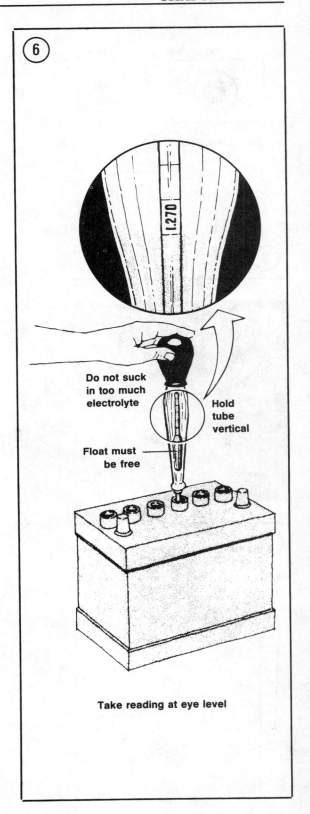

(6)

1.270

Do not suck in too much electrolyte

Hold tube vertical

Float must be free

Take reading at eye level

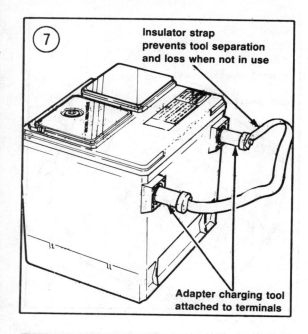

⑦

Insulator strap prevents tool separation and loss when not in use

Adapter charging tool attached to terminals

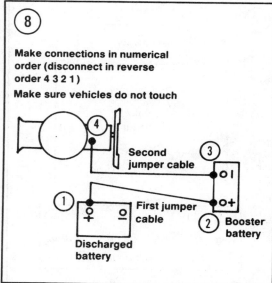

⑧

Make connections in numerical order (disconnect in reverse order 4 3 2 1)

Make sure vehicles do not touch

④

Second jumper cable

③

O I

O +

①

First jumper cable

② Booster battery

Discharged battery

voltage regulator to 12 volts and plug the charger in. If the battery is severely discharged, allow it to charge for at least 8 hours. Batteries that are not as badly discharged require less charging time. **Table 1** shows approximate state of charge according to specific gravity. On unsealed batteries, check charging progress with the hydrometer.

Jump Starting

If the battery becomes severely discharged on the road, it is possible to start and run a vehicle by jump starting it from another battery. If the proper procedure is not followed, however, jump starting can be dangerous. Check the electrolyte level before jump starting any battery. If is is not visible or if it appears to be frozen, *do not* attempt to jump start the vehicle, as the battery may explode or rupture. *Do not* jump start sealed batteries when the temperature is 32° F (0° C) or lower.

WARNING
Use extreme caution when connecting a booster battery to one that is discharged to avoid personal injury or damage to the vehicle.

1. Position the 2 cars so that the jumper cables will reach between the batteries, but the cars do not touch.
2. Connect the jumper cables in the order and sequence shown in **Figure 8**.

WARNING
An electrical arc may occur when the final connection is made. This could cause an explosion if it occurs near the battery. For this reason, the final connection should be made to the alternator mounting bracket and not the battery itself.

3. Check that all jumper cables are out of the way of moving parts on both engines.
4. Start the car with the good battery and run the engine at a moderate speed.
5. Start the car with the discharged battery. Once the engine starts, run it at a moderate speed.

CAUTION
Racing the engine may cause damage to the electrical system.

6. Remove the jumper cables in the exact reverse order of that shown in **Figure 8**. Begin at point No. 4, then 3, 2 and 1.

1984-1985 CHARGING SYSTEM

An SI charging system with integral regulator is used on 1984-1985 models. This consists of the battery, a 17 SI alternator with integral voltage regulator, digital charge indicator display and wiring. The Delcotron alternator has a rated output of 70 amps. The integral solid-state voltage regulator is serviced by replacement only.

Charging System Test

A voltmeter with a 0-20 volt scale and an engine tachometer are required for an accurate charging system test.

7

1. Check the serpentine belt tension. See Chapter Three.
2. Check the battery terminals and cables for corrosion or loose connections. Clean and tighten as necessary.
3. Check all wiring connections between the alternator and engine.
4. Connect the positive voltmeter lead to the positive battery cable clamp. Connect the negative voltmeter lead to the negative battery cable clamp. Make sure the ignition and all accessories are off.
5. Record the battery voltage displayed on the voltmeter scale. This is the base voltage.
6. Connect a tachometer to the engine according to the manufacturer's instructions.
7. Start the engine and bring its speed up to about 1,500 rpm. The voltmeter reading should increase from that recorded in Step 5, but not by more than 2 volts.
8. If the voltage does not increase, perform the *Undercharge Test*. If the voltage increase is greater than 2 volts, remove the alternator and have it checked by a dealer or an automotive electrical shop for grounded or shorted field windings.

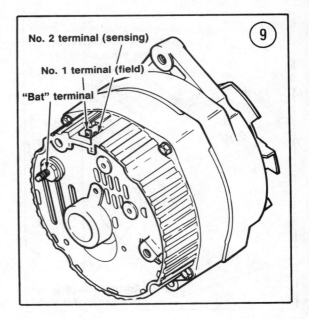

Undercharge Test

A voltmeter with a 0-20 volt scale, an ammeter and a carbon pile are required for this procedure. Refer to **Figure 9** for test points.
1. Turn the ignition switch ON. Make sure all electrical harness leads are properly connected.
2. Connect the negative voltmeter lead to a good engine ground. Connect the positive voltmeter first to the alternator battery (BAT) terminal, then to the alternator No. 1 terminal and finally, to the alternator No. 2 terminal (**Figure 9**).
3. Read the voltmeter as each connection in Step 2 is made. A zero reading at any of the connections indicates an open circuit.
4. Disconnect the voltmeter. Disconnect the negative battery cable.
5. Disconnect the alternator wiring connector at the BAT terminal. Connect an ammeter between the BAT terminal and the wiring connector.
6. Reconnect the negative battery cable. Turn on all accessories.
7. Connect a carbon pile across the battery posts.
8. Start the engine and run at 2,000 rpm. Adjust the carbon pile to obtain the maximum current output.
9. If the reading is within 10 amps of the alternator's rated output, the unit is satisfactory.
10. If the ammeter reading is not within 10 amps of the rated output, remove the alternator and have

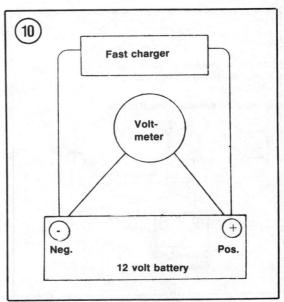

it checked by your dealer or an automotive electrical shop.

Regulator Test

Connect a fast charger and a voltmeter to the battery. See **Figure 10**. Turn on the ignition and increase the charge rate slowly. If the instrument panel digital display does not dim at the voltage regulator setting (13.5-16.0 volts), have the regulator replaced by a dealer or an automotive electrical shop.

1986 CHARGING SYSTEM

A CS charging system with integral regulator is used on 1986 and later models. This consists of the battery, a CS-130 or CS-144 alternator with integral voltage regulator, digital charge indicator display and wiring. Unlike other voltage regulators, the CS integral solid-state regulator switches the field current at a fixed frequency, varying the current duty cycle (percentage of on-time to off-time) to control the average field current and regulate voltage. CS alternators have no test hole to ground the regulator for full-field testing. The regulator cannot be tested with an ohmmeter; a special tester is required. The indicator lamp in a CS charging system functions differently than in an SI system. Any defect causes it to light at full illumination, and the lamp will also light when charging voltage is too high or too low.

Charging System Test

The following general test procedure is recommended by Delco-Remy for the CS Delcotron system. If the vehicle does not have an indicator lamp, omit Steps 3-5.

1. Test the battery and charge it, if necessary, before testing the charging system.
2. Inspect the drive belt and all circuit wiring. Correct any problems noted.
3. Turn on the ignition but do not start the engine. The indicator lamp should light. If it does, proceed with Step 5.
4. If the indicator lamp does not light in Step 3, disconnect the harness connector at the regulator terminals and ground the "L" terminal in the harness with a jumper wire.
   a. If the lamp now lights, remove the Delcotron for service.

b. If the lamp does not light, there is an open circuit between the ignition switch and the grounded "L" terminal in the harness.
   c. Reconnect the harness connector.

5. Start and run the engine at approximately 2,000 rpm. If the lamp does not turn off, disconnect the Delcotron harness connector.
   a. If the lamp then stays off, remove the Delcotron for service.
   b. If the lamp remains on, there is a grounded "L" terminal wire in the harness.

6. If the indicator lamp lights during normal operation, or if the battery is consistently under- or overcharged, proceed as follows:
   a. Disconnect the harness at the Delcotron.
   b. Connect a voltmeter between the "L" terminal in the harness connector and ground. If the regulator has an "I" terminal, connect it to the positive voltmeter lead with a jumper wire.
   c. Turn the ignition on, but do not start the engine. If the voltmeter shows no voltage, look for an open circuit in the harness.
   d. Reconnect the Delcotron harness and run the engine at approximately 2,000 rpm with all accessories off.
   e. Connect the voltmeter across the battery terminals to measure battery voltage. If the reading exceeds 16 volts, the regulator is defective.

7. Connect an ammeter in the Delcotron output circuit (BAT terminal) and use a carbon pile to load the battery for maximum charging current at approximately 13 volts. If charging current is not within 15 amps of the Delcotron's rated output, repair or replace the Delcotron.

Alternator Removal/Installation

1. Disconnect the negative battery cable.
2. Remove the electrical connectors from the rear of the alternator (A, **Figure 11**).
3. Loosen alternator mounting and brace bolts (B, **Figure 11**).
4. Lift or rotate the drive belt tensioner with a 1/2 in. breaker bar and remove the belt from the alternator pulley.
5. Remove alternator mounting and brace bolts (B, **Figure 11**).
6. Remove the alternator.
7. Installation is the reverse of removal. Tighten the mounting and brace bolts to 25 ft.-lb. (34 N•m).

STARTER

The Delco 10MT starter is used. The starter solenoid is enclosed in the drive housing to protect it from exposure to dirt and adverse weather conditions.

This section includes on-car testing of the starter, starter and solenoid replacement and starter brush replacement. Complete starter overhaul is not possible. Starter brushes, however, can be replaced.

On-car Testing

Two of these procedures require a pair of jumper cables and a fully charged 12 volt battery to be used as a booster. Use the jumper cables as outlined under *Jump Starting* in this chapter, following all of the precautions noted.

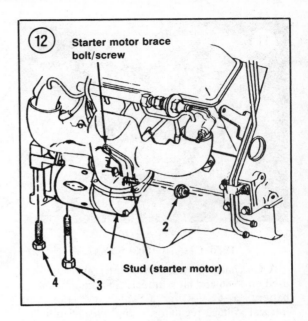

Slow cranking starter

1. Connect the jumper cables. Listen to the starter cranking speed as the engine is started. If the cranking speed sounds normal, check the battery for loose or corroded connections or a low charge. Clean and tighten the connections as required. Recharge the battery if necessary.
2. If cranking speed does not sound normal, clean and tighten all starter solenoid connections and the battery ground on the engine.
3. Repeat Step 1. If the cranking speed is still too slow, replace the starter.

Starter solenoid clicks, starter does not start

1. Clean and tighten all starter and solenoid connections. Make sure the terminal eyelets are securely fastened to the wire strands and are not corroded.
2. Connect the jumper cables. If the starter still does not crank, replace it.

Starter solenoid chatters (no click), starter does not start

1. Place the transmission in NEUTRAL or PARK.
2. Remove the purple wire at the solenoid. Connect a jumper wire between this solenoid connector and the positive battery post.
3. Try starting the engine. If it starts, check the ignition switch, the neutral start switch or the starting circuit wiring for loose connections. If the engine does not start, replace the solenoid.

Starter spins but does not crank

Remove the starter. Check the armature shaft for corrosion. If there is none, the starter drive mechanism is slipping. Replace the starter with a new or rebuilt unit.

Starter Solenoid Replacement

1. Disconnect the negative battery cable.
2. Securely block the rear wheels. Raise the front of the car and place it on jackstands.
3. Remove the plastic protective cover from the solenoid electrical connectors, if so equipped.
4. Disconnect the field strap at the starter from the motor terminal.
5. Remove the solenoid-to-drive housing screws and the motor terminal bolt.
6. Rotate the solenoid 90° and remove from the drive housing with the plunger return or torsion spring.
7. Installation is the reverse of removal.

Starter Removal/Installation

Refer to **Figure 12** for this procedure.
1. Disconnect the negative battery cable.
2. Set the parking brake and place the transmission in PARK or 1st gear. Raise the front of the car and place it on jackstands.
3. Remove the plastic protective cover from the solenoid electrical connectors, if so equipped. Disconnect the starter cable and solenoid wires.
4. Remove the starter motor brace nut.
5. Remove the flywheel cover.

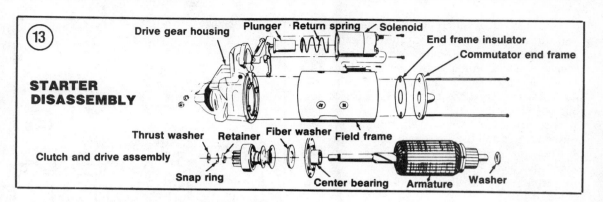

⑬ STARTER DISASSEMBLY

Drive gear housing — Plunger — Return spring — Solenoid — End frame insulator — Commutator end frame — Thrust washer — Retainer — Fiber washer — Field frame — Clutch and drive assembly — Snap ring — Center bearing — Armature — Washer

⑭

6. Remove the starter mounting bolts. Remove the starter.

7. Installation is the reverse of removal. Reinstall any shims that were removed to assure proper pinion-to-flywheel mesh. Tighten the mounting bolts to 26-37 ft.-lb. (36-50 N•m).

Starter Brush Replacement

Brush replacement requires partial disassembly of the starter. Refer to **Figure 13** for this procedure.

1. Remove the 2 through bolts, commutator end frame and insulator washer.

2. Separate the field frame from the drive housing. Remove the armature and washer.

3. Remove the brush holder pivot pin.

4. Remove the brush spring.

5. Check all brushes for length and condition. Replace all if any are worn to 1/4 in. or less in length.

6. Reverse Steps 1-4 to assemble the starter.

IGNITION SYSTEM

The ignition system consists of the battery, a breakerless distributor, ignition coil, ignition switch, ignition module, spark plugs and connecting primary and secondary wiring.

A High Energy Ignition (HEI) distributor with Electronic Spark Timing (EST) is used. All changes in ignition timing are controlled by an Electronic Control Module (ECM) based on data received from various engine sensors. A back-up spark advance system is provided to signal the ignition module in the distributor if the ECM should fail.

A magnetic pick-up assembly in the HEI distributor contains a permanent magnet, a pole piece with internal teeth and a pick-up coil. A timer core with external teeth rotates inside the pole piece. When the timer core teeth align with the pole piece teeth, a voltage is induced in the pick-up coil. This voltage signal is sent to an electronic module in the distributor. The module breaks the coil primary circuit, inducing a high voltage in the ignition coil secondary windings. This high voltage is sent to the distributor where it is directed to the appropriate spark plug by the rotor.

A radio suppression capacitor is located in the coil wire harness.

Distributor Removal/Installation

1. Disconnect the negative battery cable.

2. 1984—remove the air cleaner cover.

3. 1985-on—remove the distributor shield or cover.

4. Turn the engine over by hand until the No. 1 cylinder is at top dead center on its compression stroke. The 0 degree mark on the timing tab will align with the notch scribed on the pulley and the distributor rotor will point to the No. 1 terminal in the distributor cap.

5. Depress the wiring harness latches (A, **Figure 14**) and remove harness retainer from distributor cap.

7

6. Disconnect the battery feed and tachometer lead wires from the distributor cap (B, **Figure 14**).

7. Rotate the 4 distributor cap latches 90° counterclockwise with a screwdriver (C, **Figure 14** shows the 2 front latches; the other 2 latches are at the rear of the cap). Remove the cap and place it to one side out of the way.

8. Disconnect the 3-terminal distributor-to-ECM wiring harness and the 4-terminal EST connector.

9. Mark the position of the distributor housing and engine block. Note the rotor position.

10. Remove the distributor hold-down bolt and clamp.

> *NOTE*
> *The oil pump drive shaft may come out with the distributor. Be sure to reinstall it when you reinstall the distributor.*

11. Pull upward on the distributor with a rotating motion. As the drive gear disengages from the camshaft drive gear, the rotor will move slightly.

12. Installation is the reverse of removal. If the engine has been turned over with the distributor out, remove the No. 1 spark plug and place a finger over the plug hole as you slowly turn the engine over until compression is felt. At this point, the timing marks and distributor rotor will be positioned as in Step 2. Align the distributor and engine block marks made in Step 9. When the distributor engages the camshaft drive gear, the rotor will turn slightly and the distributor will seat fully.

Ignition Coil Replacement

The coil is mounted in the distributor cap. Disconnect the distributor-to-cap wiring connector. Remove the cap. Release the 2 spark plug wiring harness latches and separate the wiring harness retainer from the distributor cap. Remove the coil cover attaching screws and cover. Remove the coil attaching screws. Lift coil and leads from distributor cap. See **Figure 15**.

Ignition Module Replacement

The module is located inside the distributor. See **Figure 16**. Replacement can be made with the distributor in the engine but module service is far easier if the distributor is removed from the engine.

1. Disconnect the negative battery cable.

2. Remove the distributor as described in this chapter.

3. Remove the distributor cap.

4. Remove the distributor rotor attaching screws. Remove the rotor.

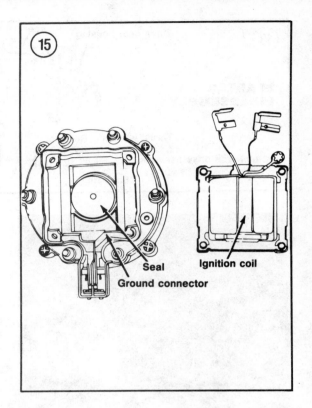

Seal
Ground connector
Ignition coil

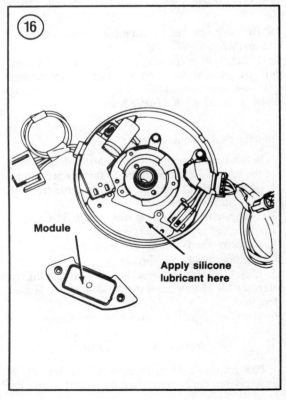

Module
Apply silicone lubricant here

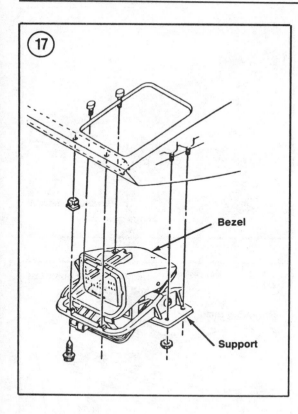

Bezel

Support

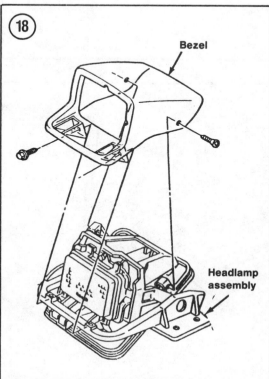

Bezel

Headlamp
assembly

5. Disconnect the wiring connectors at each end of the module. Remove the 2 module screws. Remove the module.

NOTE
The module base which mates against the distributor base is covered with silicone grease to protect the module from heat. Apply the packet of grease accompanying the new module to its base before installation.

6. Wipe the distributor base and module with a clean, dry cloth. Apply silicone grease to the distributor and module base before installing the new module.

7. Installation is the reverse of removal.

LIGHTING SYSTEM

Headlight Replacement

Concealed rectangular combination high/low beam halogen lamps are standard equipment on the Corvette. Always replace a burned-out headlight with another of the same type. While halogen and ordinary sealed beam lamps are physically interchangeable, the wiring circuitry is different.

The electrically-operated concealed headlights use a permanent magnet motor to raise and lower the headlamp assembly. If an electrical failure occurs in the circuit, the headlight can be raised or lowered manually by the knob on the motor.

1. Open the hood. Move the headlamp switch to bring the lights into the raised position.
2. Disconnect the negative battery cable.
3. Remove the fasteners holding the headlamp assembly to the hood. See **Figure 17**.
4. Disconnect headlamp and motor connectors.
5. Remove headlamp assembly from hood.
6. Remove headlight bezel attaching screws (**Figure 18**).
7. Using a cotter pin remover or other hooked tool, pull the retaining spring to one side and release the headlight.
8. Rotate the right headlight clockwise (or left headlight counterclockwise) to release it from the aiming pins.
9. Disconnect the electrical harness connector.
10. Remove the retaining ring.
11. Install the new lamp in the retaining ring. Reverse Steps 1-9 to complete installation. Check operation of the lights. Have headlight aim checked by a dealer or official lamp adjusting station.

7

Front Park/Turn Signal/Fog Lamp

1. Open the hood. Reach behind the lamp assembly and remove the twist-lock socket.
2. Depress the bulb in the socket, rotate counterclockwise and remove.
3. If the lamp assembly is to be replaced, remove the 2 screws (**Figure 19**) and remove assembly.
4. Installation is the reverse of removal.

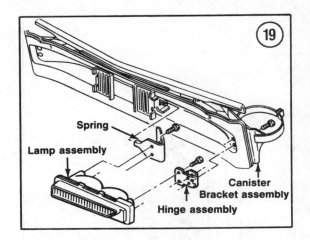

Side Marker/Cornering Lamp

1. Reach under the front fender and rotate bulb socket counterclockwise to remove from the housing.
2. Depress the bulb in the socket, rotate counterclockwise and remove.
3. If the lamp assembly is to be replaced, remove the 2 screws (**Figure 20**) and remove assembly.
4. Installation is the reverse of removal.

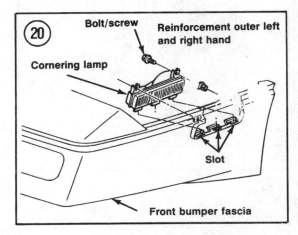

Rear Lamp Assembly Service

All rear lamp bulbs are replaced by removing the rear trim panel screws and removing the panel. Depress and turn the individual sockets counterclockwise to remove them from the lamp assembly. See **Figure 21**. Installation is the reverse of removal.

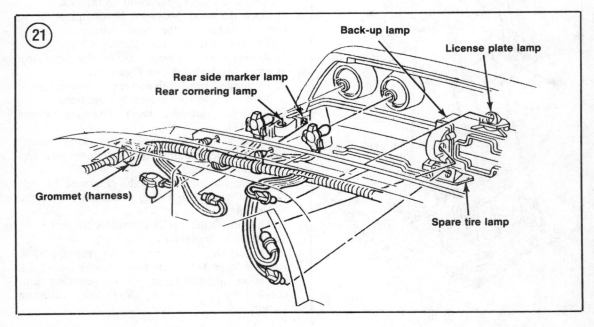

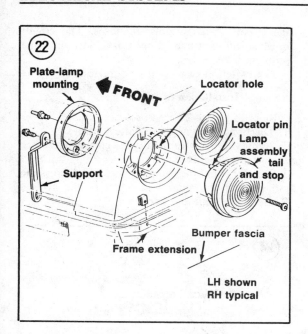

22

Plate-lamp mounting

FRONT

Locator hole

Locator pin

Lamp assembly tail and stop

Support

Bumper fascia

Frame extension

LH shown
RH typical

To replace the stop or tail lamp assembly, remove the fasteners (**Figure 22**) and pull the lamp assembly from the mounting plate. Installation is the reverse of removal.

Instrument Lights

The instrument cluster bezel must be removed to replace any lamp. See *Instruments* in this chapter.

IGNITION SWITCH

A blade-type terminal switch with one multiple connector is used. The switch is attached to the steering column with a stud and a screw. The dimmer light switch is attached in such a way that it must be removed in order to remove the ignition switch.

Removal

Refer to **Figure 23** for this procedure.
1. Disconnect the negative battery cable.

7

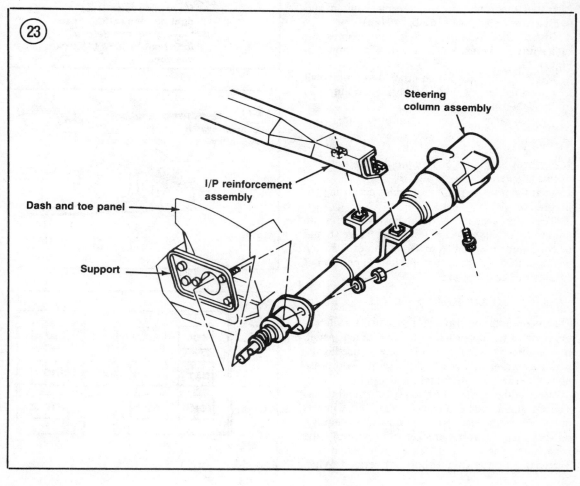

23

Steering column assembly

I/P reinforcement assembly

Dash and toe panel

Support

2. Remove the lower steering column attaching bolt.
3. Remove the steering column trim cover.
4. Remove the support bracket bolts. Lower the steering column.
5. Disconnect the ignition and dimmer switch connectors.
6. Remove the dimmer switch fasteners. Disengage the switch from its actuator rod and remove.
7. Remove the ignition switch fasteners. Disengage the switch from its actuator rod and remove from the steering column.

Installation

1A. With key release feature—position ignition switch slider to the extreme right position as shown in **Figure 24**.
1B. Without key release feature—position ignition switch slider to the extreme right position (**Figure 24**), then move it 2 detents to the left.
2. Install the actuator rod in the switch slider hole.
3. Install the switch to the steering column and tighten lower stud to 35 in.-lb. (4 N•m).
4. Install the dimmer switch and depress it sufficiently to insert a 3/32 in. drill as shown in **Figure 25**.
5. Move the dimmer switch upward to remove all lash, then tighten the attaching screw and nut to 35 in.-lb. (4 N•m).
6. Reverse Steps 1-5 of *Removal* procedure.

Testing

1. Perform Steps 1-5 of *Ignition Switch Removal* in this chapter.
2. Identify the switch terminals according to **Figure 26**.
3. Test the switch at each position with an ohmmeter or self-powered test lamp. There should be continuity as specified in **Table 2** in each switch position. Replace the switch if it fails to perform as specified in any position.

HEADLIGHT SWITCH

The combination 3-position headlight switch is mounted in the upper left of the instrument panel. It controls circuits to the headlights, parking/marker and rear light assemblies, license plate, interior and instrument panel lights.

The headlight switch has power to it at all times. The headlights come on only when the switch is pulled out to the last detent. The switch contains a self-resetting circuit breaker to protect the headlights. The circuit breaker opens when it is overheated from a circuit short or overload. When

the circuit breaker cools, it closes. The circuit breaker will continue to open and close until the problem is corrected.

The switch must be removed for testing.

Removal/Installation

Refer to **Figure 27** for this procedure.
1. Disconnect the negative battery cable.
2. Remove the instrument panel cluster bezel. See *Instruments* in this chapter.
3. Reach behind instrument panel and depress the tab holding the shaft and knob in the switch. Remove the shaft and knob.

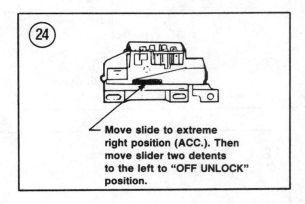

24

Move slide to extreme right position (ACC.). Then move slider two detents to the left to "OFF UNLOCK" position.

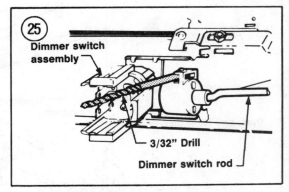

25

Dimmer switch assembly

3/32" Drill

Dimmer switch rod

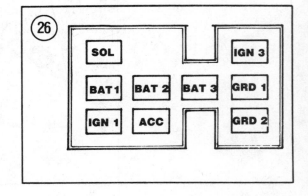

26

SOL			IGN 3
BAT 1	BAT 2	BAT 3	GRD 1
IGN 1	ACC		GRD 2

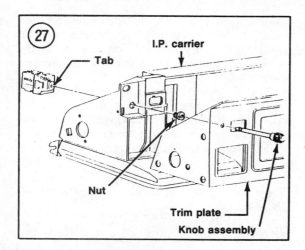

27

Tab

I.P. carrier

Nut

Trim plate

Knob assembly

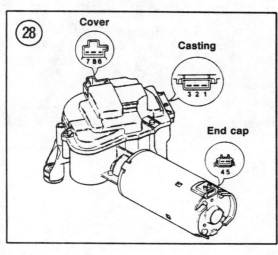

28

Cover

7 8 6

Casting

3 2 1

End cap

4 5

4. Remove the trim plate from the instrument panel carrier.

5. Remove the switch nut.

6. Carefully pull switch from behind instrument panel carrier and disconnect from the wiring harness. Remove the switch.

7. Installation is the reverse of removal.

Testing

1. Remove the switch as described in this chapter, but do not disconnect the wiring harness. Lower the switch as far as possible under the instrument panel.

2. Check the red and yellow wire terminals at the switch with a test light. If the bulb lights at the red but not the yellow wire terminal, replace the switch.

WIPER/WASHER SWITCH

The wiper/washer switch is mounted in the left door armrest under the trim panel escutcheon plate. The switch test is performed at the wiper motor wiring harnesses. Wiper/washer switch removal is required only if the switch is defective.

Testing

1. Disconnect the 3 wiring harnesses from the wiper motor. See **Figure 28**.

2. Turn the ignition switch ON.

3. Probe terminals 1-8 of the 3 harnesses with a digital voltmeter. Refer to **Figure 29** for switch position and test results. Replace the wiper/washer switch if it fails to perform as specified in any position.

7

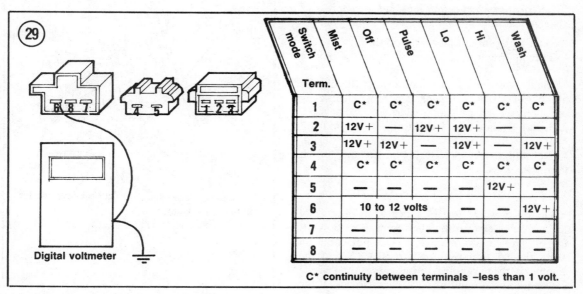

29

Digital voltmeter

Switch mode / Term.	Mist	Off	Pulse	Lo	Hi	Wash
1	C*	C*	C*	C*	C*	C*
2	12V+	—	12V+	12V+	—	—
3	12V+	12V+	—	12V+	—	12V+
4	C*	C*	C*	C*	C*	C*
5	—	—	—	—	12V+	—
6	10 to 12 volts			—	—	12V+
7	—	—	—	—	—	—
8	—	—	—	—	—	—

C* continuity between terminals –less than 1 volt.

Removal/Installation

1. Disconnect the negative battery cable.
2. Remove the trim panel escutcheon plate screws.
3. Pull the escutcheon plate out far enough to disconnect the electrical connectors. Remove the switch from the plate.
4. Installation is the reverse of removal.

COOLANT TEMPERATURE SWITCH

The coolant temperature switch is mounted in the engine block at a point behind the alternator between the exhaust manifold and air injection check valve (arrow, **Figure 30**). A second coolant temperature switch in the right cylinder head controls the cooling fan motor. See Chapter Six.

Testing

1. Remove temperature switch as described in this chapter.
2. Measure the resistance across the terminals with an ohmmeter. The resistance should be approximately 350 ohms at a temperature of 100° F.
3. Place the switch in a pan of coolant and heat the pan until the coolant comes to a rapid boil.
4. Repeat Step 2. The resistance should drop considerably at a temperature of about 260° F, indicating that the switch has closed.
5. Replace the switch if it does not meet the specifications in Step 2 and Step 4.

Replacement

> *NOTE*
> *Remove the radiator cap to relieve any pressure when installing a new coolant temperature switch.*

Refer to **Figure 30** for this procedure.
1. Disconnect electrical lead at switch. Remove the switch.
2. Wrap a piece of Teflon tape around the threads of the new switch. Teflon paste or other electrically conductive water-resistant sealers can also be used.
3. Install the new switch and torque to 72 in.-lb. (7 N•m).
4. Reconnect the electrical lead to the switch terminal.

OIL PRESSURE SWITCH

The oil pressure switch is located at the rear of the engine block near the distributor (**Figure 31**). If the oil pressure warning light does not come on when the ignition is turned to START and the engine is not running, disconnect the wiring connector and ground it to the engine block. If the

warning light comes on, replace the oil pressure switch. If the warning light still does not come on, check for a burned-out bulb or an open in the wiring between the bulb and the oil pressure switch.

If the oil pressure warning light remains on with the engine running, check the oil level in the crankcase. If the level is satisfactory, check the switch wiring for a short. If none is found, replace the oil pressure switch.

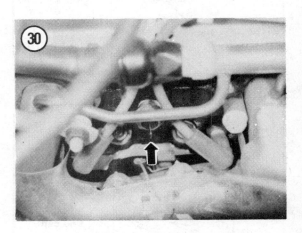

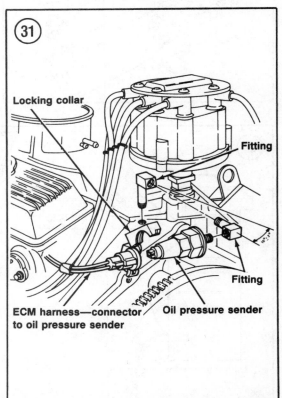

Locking collar

Fitting

Fitting

ECM harness—connector to oil pressure sender

Oil pressure sender

INSTRUMENTS

The Corvette instrument cluster is an electronic microprocessor-controlled liquid crystal display (LCD) unit. If any cluster function or display is incorrect or does not work, the entire cluster is replaced as an assembly.

Instrument Cluster
Removal/Installation

Refer to **Figure 32** and **Figure 33** for this procedure.
1. Disconnect the negative battery cable.
2. Remove the spring-loaded light switch knob.
3. Remove the steering column trim cover.
4. Remove the 2 steering column bracket bolts. Lower the steering column.
5. Remove cluster bezel screws at front and left side.

6. Remove the cluster bezel from the instrument panel.
7. Remove the 4 screws holding the cluster to the instrument panel (**Figure 33**).
8. Pull the cluster forward far enough to disconnect the wiring connectors at the rear of the cluster.
9. Remove the cluster from the instrument panel.
10. Installation is the reverse of removal.

HORN

Dual horns are standard on the Corvette. A relay in the circuit reduces the length of heavy gauge wire required to operate the horns, providing higher voltage for horn operation. Typical horn location is shown in **Figure 34**. The horn relay is located in the multi-use relay center behind the instrument panel warning light/function switch panel.

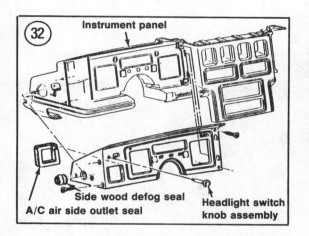

32 Instrument panel

A/C air side outlet seal — Side wood defog seal — Headlight switch knob assembly

34

7

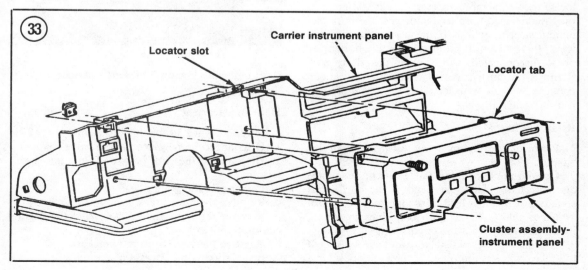

33 Locator slot — Carrier instrument panel — Locator tab — Cluster assembly-instrument panel

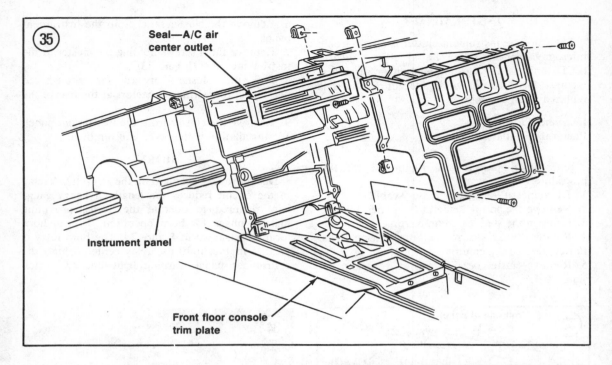

(35) Seal—A/C air center outlet

Instrument panel

Front floor console trim plate

Testing

Voltage is applied to the horn relay at all times. Depressing the horn pad grounds the relay coil and closes its contacts. If the horn does not sound, check the 15A fuse in the fuse block cavity marked "CTSY/CLK," then check the horn ground lead. If corroded or loose, clean or tighten as required.

If the horn still does not sound, disconnect the horn lead. Connect a jumper wire between the positive battery terminal and the horn. The horn should sound if its ground is good. If this does not locate the problem, connect a 12-volt test lamp to the disconnected horn lead and press the horn pad on the steering wheel. If the horn still does not work, the problem is either a defective horn relay or a disconnected wire under the horn pad. Remove the horn pad and check for bent metal contacts or a disconnected wire. If none are found, test the relay.

Relay Testing

1. Perform Steps 2-4 of *Relay Replacement* in this chapter.
2. Ground the horn relay coil. If the horn sounds, disconnect the black relay lead. If the horn stops sounding with the lead disconnected, the horn switch is faulty. If the horn continues to sound, isolate the relay from the circuit.
3. Use a self-powered test lamp and check to see if the relay contacts are open. If they are, look for a

(36)

short in the black wire. If they are not open, replace the relay.

Horn Replacement

Refer to **Figure 34** for this procedure.
1. Disconnect the negative battery cable.
2. Disconnect the horn wire from the horn terminal.
3. Disconnect the ground lead.
4. Remove the horn bracket mounting screw.
5. Remove the horn and bracket from the engine compartment.
6. Remove the horn from the bracket.
7. Installation is the reverse of removal.

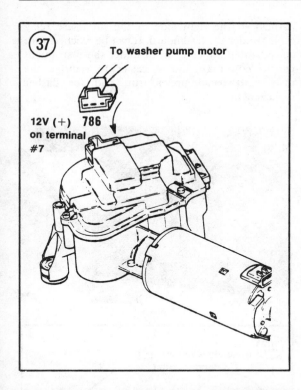

37

To washer pump motor

12V (+) **786**
on terminal
#7

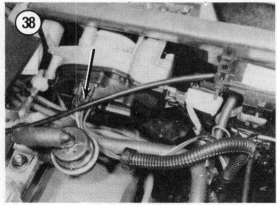

38

Relay Replacement

1. Disconnect the negative battery cable.
2. Remove the instrument panel cluster bezel. See *Instruments* in this chapter.
3. Remove the instrument panel accessory trim plate assembly (**Figure 35**).
4. Remove the screws holding the warning light/function switch panel (**Figure 36**). Remove the panel.
5. Reach inside the multi-use relay center and remove the horn relay. It is located just to the right of the hazard flasher.
6. Installation is the reverse of removal.

WINDSHIELD WIPERS AND WASHER

The windshield wiper system uses a pulse-type wiper motor, a washer pump installed under the washer reservoir and a wiper switch mounted in the trim panel of the door on the driver's side. Wiper/washer operation is controlled by a printed circuit board attached to the wiper motor cover.

Wiper Troubleshooting

1. If the wipers do not work, check the 25 amp fuse in the fuse block cavity marked "WPR."
2. If the wipers do not work with a good fuse, check the wiper/washer switch operation as described in this chapter.
3. If the wiper/washer switch is good, the most likely problem is in the printed circuit board in the wiper cover.

Washer Pump Troubleshooting

1. If the washer does not pump water, make sure the reservoir is filled with fluid.
2. Remove the pump electrical connector from the wiper motor cover and apply 12 volts to terminal 7 of the connector. See **Figure 37**.
3. If the washer still does not pump water, replace the washer pump.
4. If the washer pump operates and pumps water,

Wiper Motor Replacement

CAUTION
Wiper motors contain ceramic permanent magnets. Handle the motor carefully and do not tap with a hammer or the magnets may be damaged.

1. Remove the wiper arms.
2. Remove the air inlet screen.
3. Turn ignition ON and start motor with wiper switch. Let the motor crank arm rotate until it reaches a position between 4 and 5 o'clock as seen from the passenger compartment. Turn ignition switch OFF at this point to stop motor.
4. Disconnect negative battery cable.
5. Disconnect upper electrical connectors from motor (**Figure 38**).
6. Remove motor mounting bolts. Lift motor up and disconnect lower electrical connector. Remove motor.
7. Installation is the reverse of removal.

FUSES

The fuse block contains mini-fuses and circuit breakers for the power window and power door locks. It is located under a cover in the right-hand

7

end of the instrument panel (**Figure 39**). To gain access to the fuse block, rotate the cover screw with a coin and remove the cover (**Figure 40**).

Fuse and circuit breaker information is shown in **Figure 41** (1984-1985) and **Figure 42** (1986-on).

A multi-use relay center (**Figure 43**) located behind the center of the instrument panel warning light/function switch display contains the horn relay, door lock relay, hazard flasher, seat belt alarm module and a 10 amp mini-fuse for the theft deterrent system.

Mini-fuses are identified by a numbered ampere value and a color code. Some colors make it difficult to determine whether the fuse is good or bad. Terminals on each side of the fuse permit testing with a test light or voltmeter without removing it from the fuse block. **Figure 44** shows a blown fuse, test points and mini-fuse color codes.

To replace, pull out the old mini-fuse. Be sure to install a new one of the same color. Whenever a fuse blows, find out the cause before replacing it. Usually, the trouble is a short circuit in the wiring. This may be caused by worn-through insulation or by a wire that works its way loose and touches metal. Carry several spare fuses of the proper amperage values in the glove compartment.

FUSIBLE LINKS

These are short lengths of wire smaller in gauge than the wire in the circuit. They are covered with a thick non-flammable insulation and are intended to burn out if an overload occurs, thus protecting the wiring harness and accessories. Two red fusible links are used at the battery positive cable, 2 red and 1 brown fusible links are located at the starter motor and each headlight relay is protected by a red fusible link. Additional fusible link location is shown in **Figure 45**.

> *CAUTION*
> *Always replace a burned fusible link with a replacement bearing the same color code or wire gauge. Never use ordinary wire, as this can cause an overload, an electrical fire and complete loss of the car.*

Burned out fusible links can usually be detected by melted or burned insulation. When the link appears to be good but the accessory or system does not work, check the circuit for continuity with an ohmmeter or a self-powered test lamp.

TURN SIGNALS

The turn signal flasher is a bright yellow assembly taped to the instrument panel wire

harness to the right side of the multi-use relay center under the dashboard. It can be reached with considerable difficulty from under the instrument panel. You may find it easier to remove the instrument panel upper trim pad for flasher replacement.

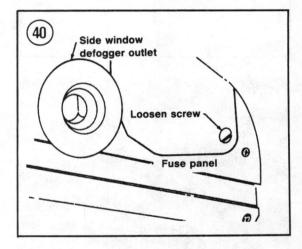

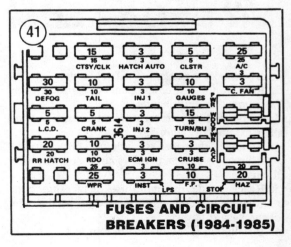

FUSES AND CIRCUIT BREAKERS (1984-1985)

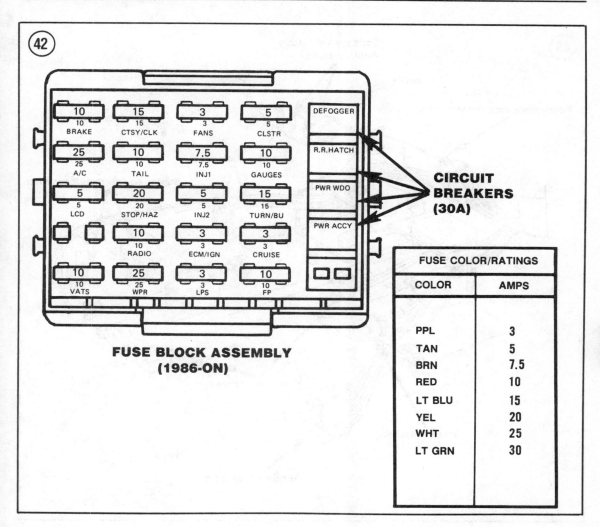

**FUSE BLOCK ASSEMBLY
(1986-ON)**

FUSE COLOR/RATINGS	
COLOR	AMPS
PPL	3
TAN	5
BRN	7.5
RED	10
LT BLU	15
YEL	20
WHT	25
LT GRN	30

Testing

1. *One side flashes later than the other, or only one side operates.* Check for a burned-out bulb. Clean socket of any corrosion. Check for a badly grounded bulb. Check for breaks in the wiring.

2. *Turn signals do not work at all.* Check the 15 amp fuse in the fuse block cavity marked "TURN B/U" by operating the back-up lights. If the fuse is good, check the wiring for a break or poor connection. If the wiring is good, install a new flasher unit.

3. *Lights flash slowly or stay on* . Make sure the battery is fully charged. Check the fuse in the "TURN B/U" cavity for a poor contact. Check for a break or poor connection in the wiring. If none of these problems are found, replace the flasher.

4. *Lights flash too quickly.* Check for a burned-out bulb or disconnected wire. If none are found, replace the flasher.

HAZARD FLASHER

The hazard flasher is located to the left of the horn relay in the multi-use center located behind the instrument panel warning light/function switch display. To replace the flasher, see *Horn Relay Replacement* in this chapter.

Testing

1. Check the 20 amp fuse in the fuse block cavity marked "STOP/HAZ" by operating the stop lights.
2. If the fuse is good and the turn signals operate on both sides, replace the hazard flasher.

WIRING HARNESSES

Engine compartment wiring harnesses are shown in **Figures 46-56**.

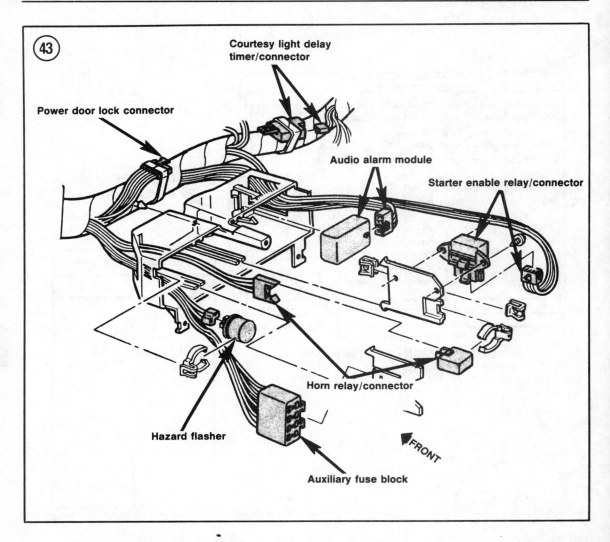

(43)

Courtesy light delay timer/connector

Power door lock connector

Audio alarm module

Starter enable relay/connector

Horn relay/connector

Hazard flasher

FRONT

Auxiliary fuse block

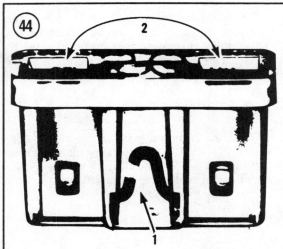

(44)

2

1

To test for blown mini-fuse:
1. Pull fuse out and check visually.
2. With the circuit activated, use a test light across the points shown.

Multi-fuse color codes

Rating	Color
5 amp	Tan
10 amp	Red
20 amp	Yellow
25 amp	White

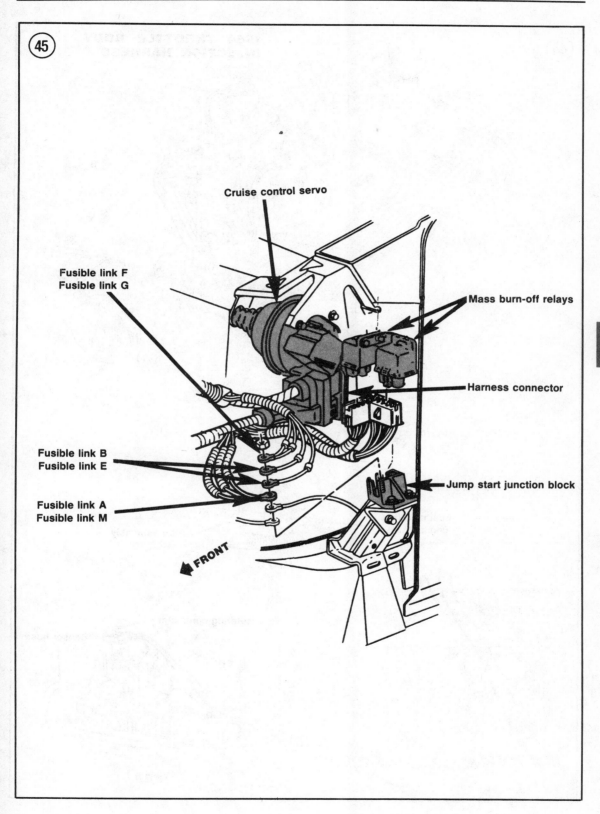

Cruise control servo

Fusible link F
Fusible link G

Mass burn-off relays

7

Harness connector

Fusible link B
Fusible link E

Fusible link A
Fusible link M

Jump start junction block

FRONT

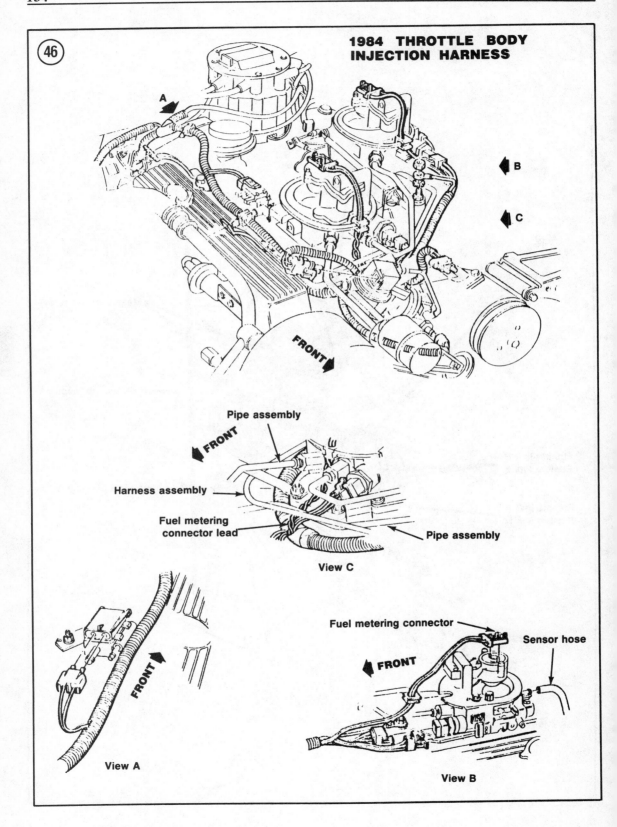

46

1984 THROTTLE BODY INJECTION HARNESS

A

B

C

FRONT

Pipe assembly

FRONT

Harness assembly

Fuel metering connector lead

Pipe assembly

View C

FRONT

View A

Fuel metering connector

Sensor hose

FRONT

View B

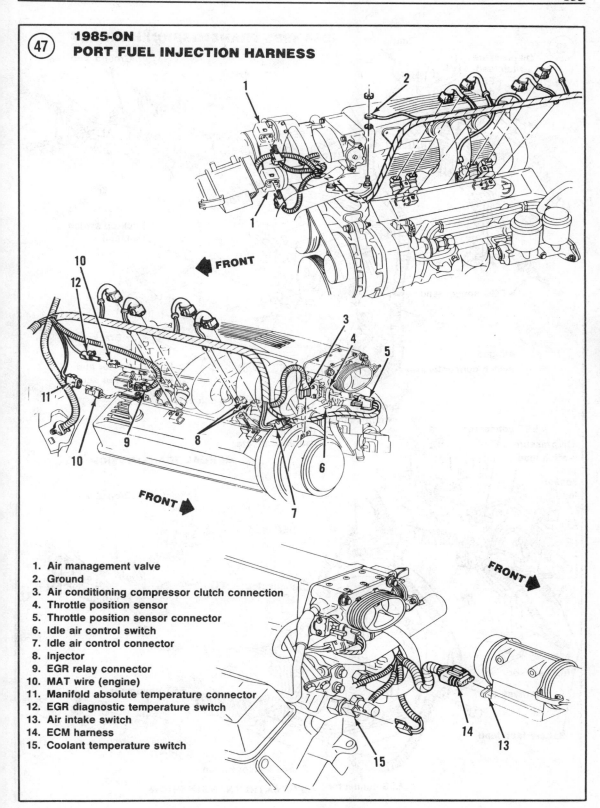

47 **1985-ON**
PORT FUEL INJECTION HARNESS

FRONT

FRONT

FRONT

7

1. Air management valve
2. Ground
3. Air conditioning compressor clutch connection
4. Throttle position sensor
5. Throttle position sensor connector
6. Idle air control switch
7. Idle air control connector
8. Injector
9. EGR relay connector
10. MAT wire (engine)
11. Manifold absolute temperature connector
12. EGR diagnostic temperature switch
13. Air intake switch
14. ECM harness
15. Coolant temperature switch

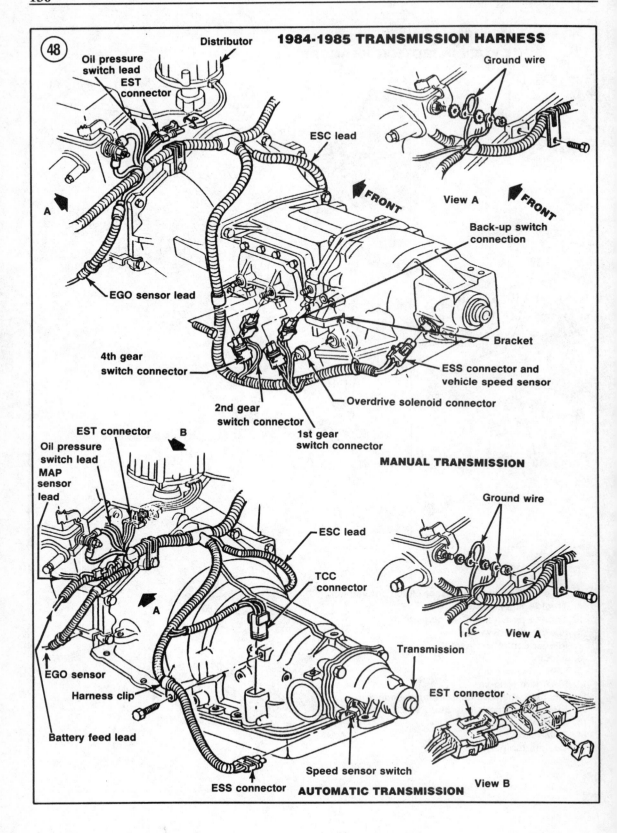

48

1984-1985 TRANSMISSION HARNESS

Distributor

Oil pressure switch lead

EST connector

Ground wire

ESC lead

FRONT

View A

FRONT

A

Back-up switch connection

EGO sensor lead

Bracket

4th gear switch connector

ESS connector and vehicle speed sensor

Overdrive solenoid connector

2nd gear switch connector

1st gear switch connector

MANUAL TRANSMISSION

EST connector

B

Oil pressure switch lead

MAP sensor lead

Ground wire

ESC lead

TCC connector

A

View A

EGO sensor

Harness clip

Transmission

Battery feed lead

EST connector

Speed sensor switch

ESS connector

AUTOMATIC TRANSMISSION

View B

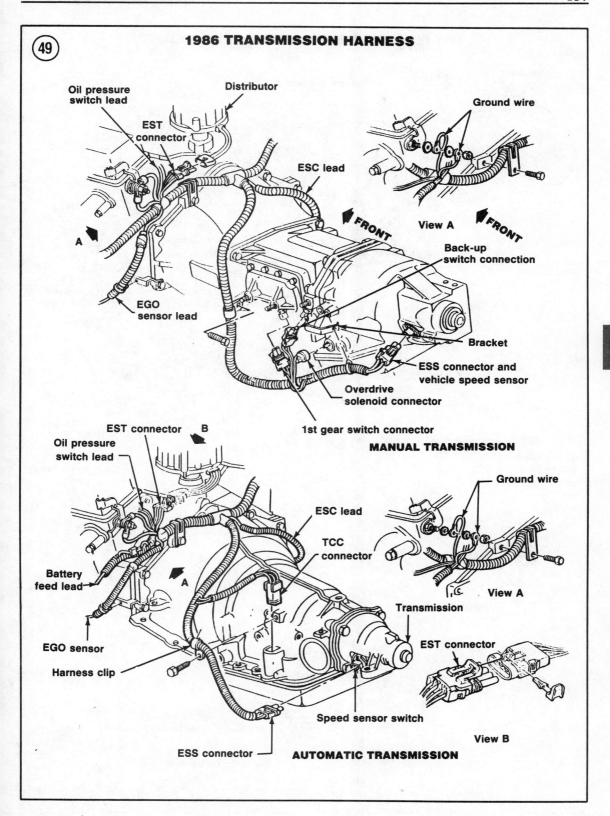

1986 TRANSMISSION HARNESS

Oil pressure switch lead

Distributor

Ground wire

EST connector

ESC lead

A

EGO sensor lead

FRONT

View A

FRONT

Back-up switch connection

Bracket

ESS connector and vehicle speed sensor

Overdrive solenoid connector

1st gear switch connector

MANUAL TRANSMISSION

EST connector B

Oil pressure switch lead

ESC lead

TCC connector

Ground wire

Battery feed lead

A

View A

Transmission

EGO sensor

EST connector

Harness clip

Speed sensor switch

ESS connector

View B

AUTOMATIC TRANSMISSION

7

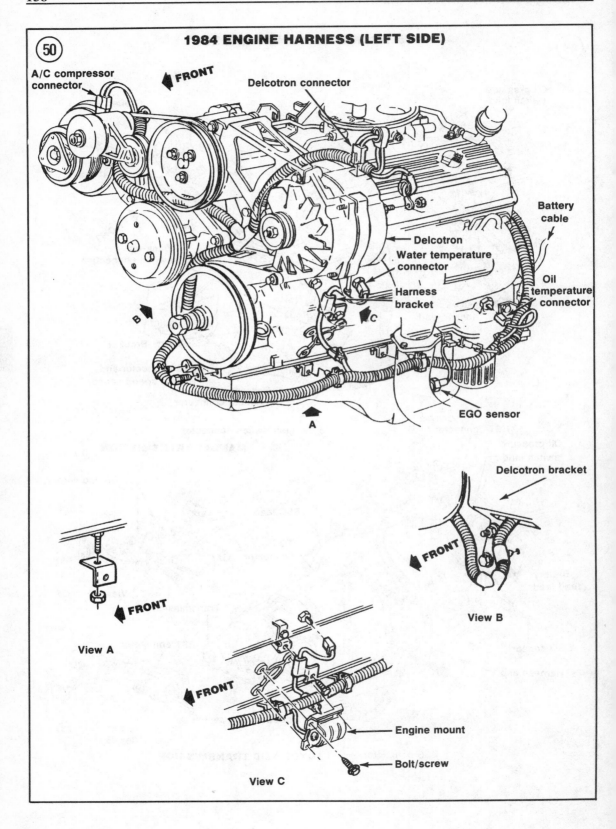

50

1984 ENGINE HARNESS (LEFT SIDE)

A/C compressor connector

FRONT

Delcotron connector

Battery cable

Delcotron

Water temperature connector

Oil temperature connector

Harness bracket

B

C

A

EGO sensor

Delcotron bracket

FRONT

View B

FRONT

View A

FRONT

Engine mount

Bolt/screw

View C

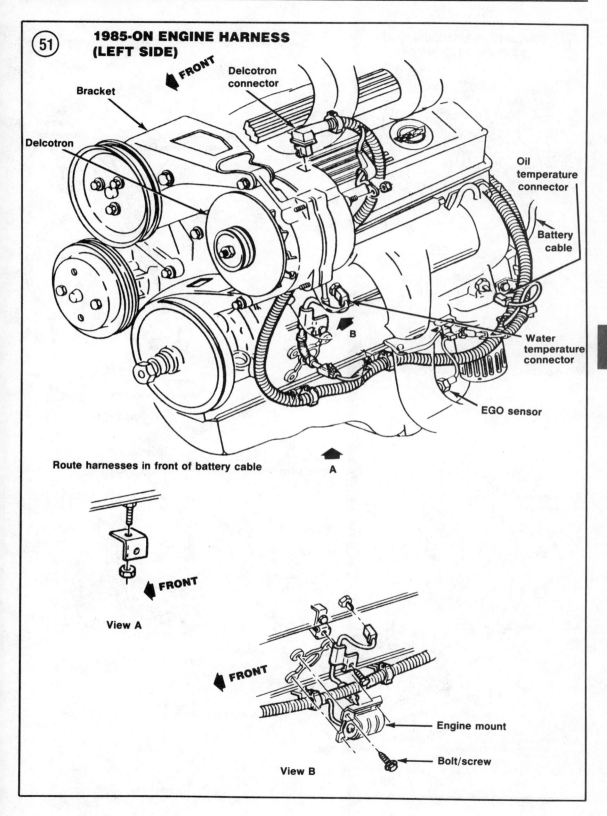

51 **1985-ON ENGINE HARNESS (LEFT SIDE)**

FRONT

Bracket

Delcotron connector

Delcotron

Oil temperature connector

Battery cable

B

A

Water temperature connector

EGO sensor

Route harnesses in front of battery cable

FRONT

View A

FRONT

Engine mount

Bolt/screw

View B

7

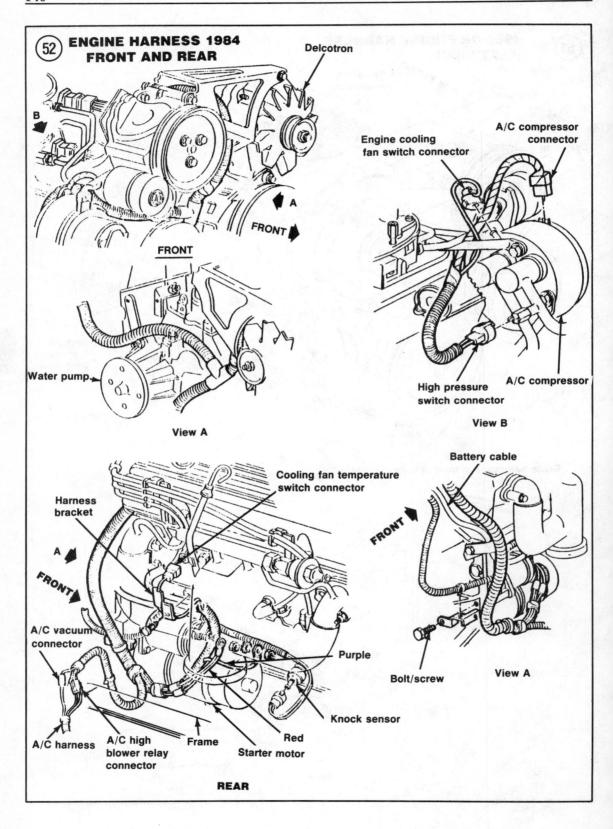

(52) **ENGINE HARNESS 1984
FRONT AND REAR**

Delcotron

Engine cooling
fan switch connector

A/C compressor
connector

B

A

FRONT

FRONT

Water pump

A/C compressor

High pressure
switch connector

View A

View B

Cooling fan temperature
switch connector

Battery cable

Harness
bracket

A

FRONT

FRONT

A/C vacuum
connector

Purple

Bolt/screw

View A

A/C harness

A/C high
blower relay
connector

Frame

Knock sensor

Red

Starter motor

REAR

1984 HARNESS PLENUM AND RELAY WIRING

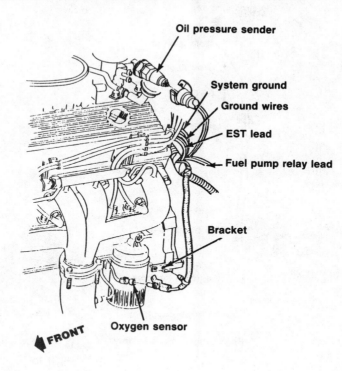

Oil pressure sender

System ground

Ground wires

EST lead

Fuel pump relay lead

Bracket

Oxygen sensor

FRONT

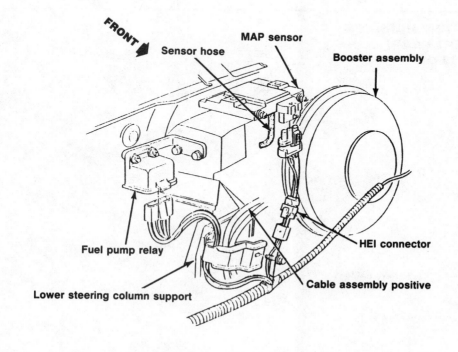

FRONT

Sensor hose

MAP sensor

Booster assembly

Fuel pump relay

HEI connector

Lower steering column support

Cable assembly positive

7

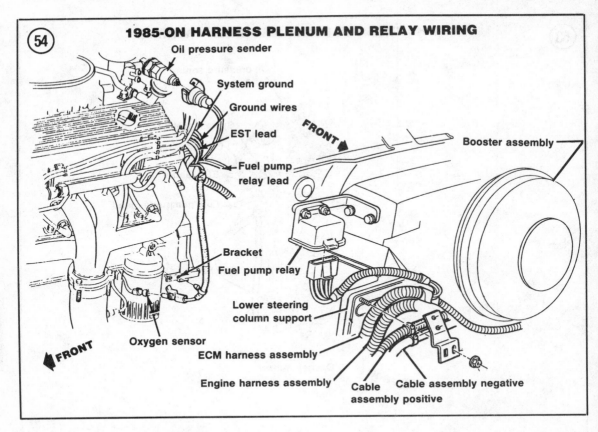

54 **1985-ON HARNESS PLENUM AND RELAY WIRING**

Oil pressure sender

System ground

Ground wires

EST lead

FRONT

Fuel pump relay lead

Booster assembly

Bracket

Fuel pump relay

Lower steering column support

Oxygen sensor

FRONT

ECM harness assembly

Engine harness assembly

Cable assembly positive

Cable assembly negative

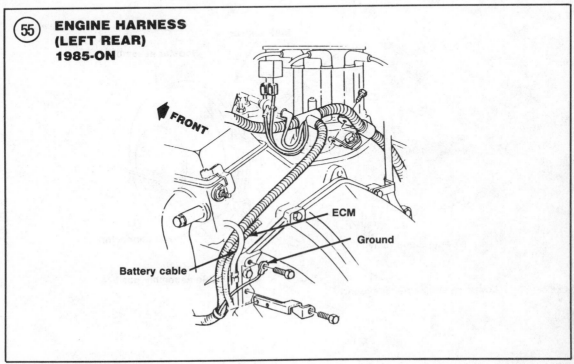

55 **ENGINE HARNESS (LEFT REAR) 1985-ON**

FRONT

ECM

Ground

Battery cable

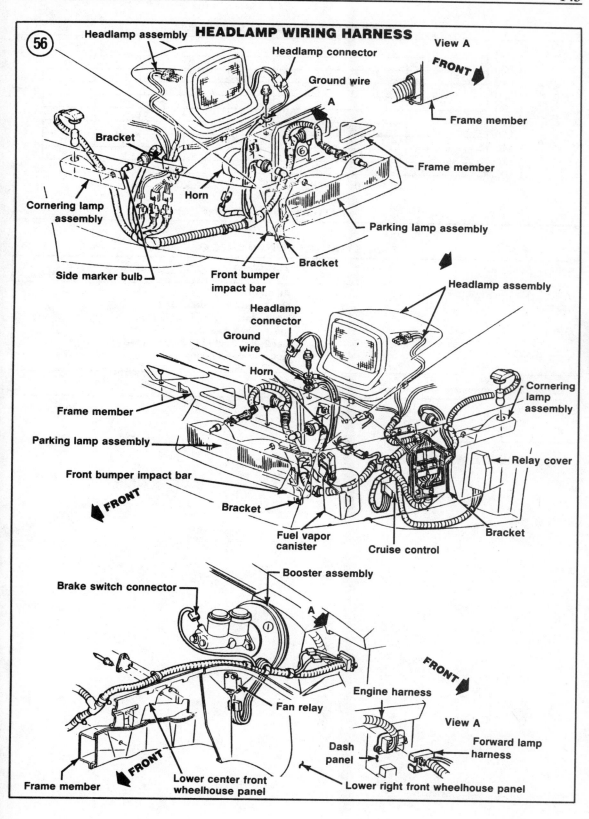

HEADLAMP WIRING HARNESS

56

Headlamp assembly

Headlamp connector

Ground wire

A

View A

FRONT

Frame member

Bracket

Horn

Frame member

Cornering lamp assembly

Parking lamp assembly

Side marker bulb

Front bumper impact bar

Bracket

Headlamp connector

Ground wire

Horn

Headlamp assembly

Cornering lamp assembly

Frame member

Parking lamp assembly

Relay cover

Front bumper impact bar

FRONT

Bracket

Fuel vapor canister

Cruise control

Bracket

7

Brake switch connector

Booster assembly

A

Engine harness

FRONT

Fan relay

View A

Dash panel

Forward lamp harness

Frame member

FRONT

Lower center front wheelhouse panel

Lower right front wheelhouse panel

Table 1 STATE CHARGE OF BATTERY

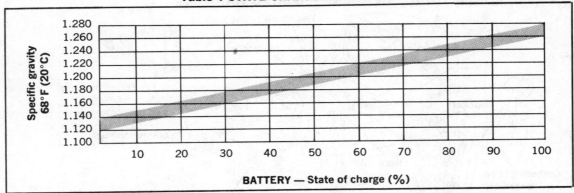

BATTERY — State of charge (%)

Table 2 IGNITION SWITCH CHECK*

Switch position	Terminals
OFF	All open
START	Grd 1 and Grd 2 grounded
	Ign 1, Bat 1 and Sol connected
RUN	Ign 1, Bat 1 and Acc connected
	Bat 2, Bat 3 and Ign 3 connected
ACCESSORY	Acc and Bat 2 connected

* Bat 1, 2 and 3 terminals are common.

CHAPTER EIGHT

CLUTCH AND TRANSMISSION

The Corvette is available either with a 4-speed manual transmission and automatic overdrive or with a 4-speed automatic transmission and lock-up converter.

Power is transmitted from the engine to the transmission, then to the differential where it is sent to the axle drive shafts which turn the wheel hubs. Manual transmissions are connected to the engine by the clutch; automatic transmissions are connected to the engine by a torque converter.

This chapter provides inspection, repair and replacement procedures for the clutch, as well as inspection, adjustment and replacement procedures for the manual overdrive and the automatic transmission. Transmission repair requires special skills and tools and should be left to a dealer or other qualified shop. The inspection procedures will tell you if repairs are necessary.

Tightening torques are provided in **Table 1** at the end of the chapter.

CLUTCH

Manual transmission models use a single dry disc driven plate type clutch. The steel cover assembly containing the pressure plate, release levers and springs is bolted to the flywheel. The clutch operates through a hydraulic system consisting of a master clutch cylinder, a slave cylinder and interconnecting hydraulic lines.

The major clutch components used are the driven plate, clutch cover, clutch housing, throwout lever and bearing and clutch pedal. See **Figure 1**.

The master clutch cylinder furnishes hydraulic fluid to operate a slave cylinder mounted on the clutch housing. (**Figure 2**). Hydraulic fluid transmits pedal pressure to the clutch throwout lever. The throwout lever moves the throwout bearing into contact with the clutch cover release fingers to disengage the clutch.

Clutch Removal

1. Remove transmission as described in this chapter.

NOTE
Do not disconnect hydraulic line from slave cylinder in Step 2.

2. Remove slave cylinder attaching bolts. Remove slave cylinder and move out of the way.
3. Remove flywheel housing.
4. Disconnect clutch fork from ball stud. Remove fork from dust boot.
5. Install a dummy shaft to support the clutch assembly during removal.

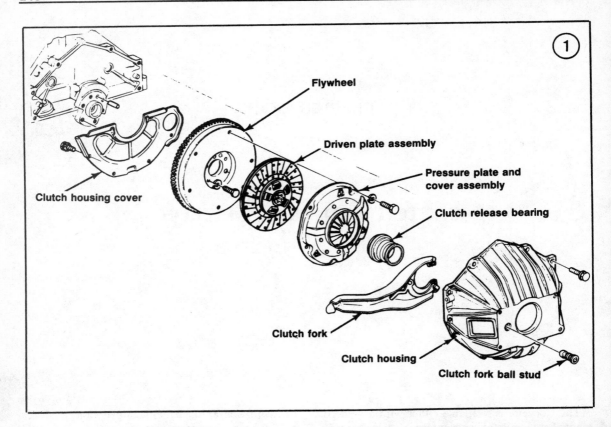

①

Flywheel

Driven plate assembly

Pressure plate and cover assembly

Clutch release bearing

Clutch housing cover

Clutch fork

Clutch housing

Clutch fork ball stud

6. Scribe a mark on the clutch cover and flywheel for reinstallation alignment.

> *CAUTION*
> *Loosen cover bolts as specified in Step 7 to prevent possible warping of the stamped steel cover.*

7. Loosen cover bolts one turn at a time in a diagonal pattern to relieve spring tension.

> *NOTE*
> *Note which side of driven plate faces flywheel. Paint identifying marks on the plate to assist in proper realignment during reinstallation.*

8. Remove cover bolts. Remove cover and driven plate from flywheel.

Clutch Disc Inspection

Check the clutch disc (**Figure 3**) for the following:
  a. Oil or grease on the facings.
  b. Glazed or warped facings.
  c. Loose or missing rivets.
  d. Facings worn to within 1/16 in. (2 mm) of any rivet.
  e. Broken torsional springs.

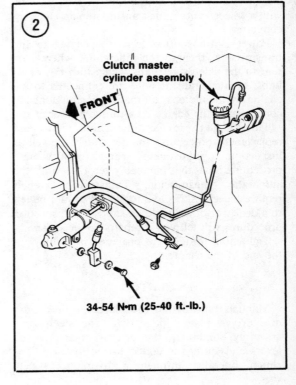

②

Clutch master cylinder assembly

FRONT

34-54 N•m (25-40 ft.-lb.)

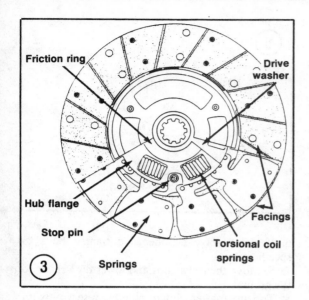

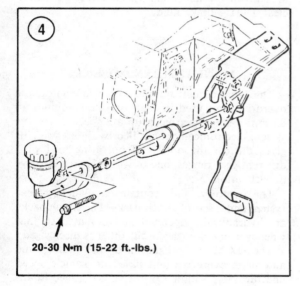

20-30 N•m (15-22 ft.-lbs.)

f. Loose fit or rough movement on the transmission input shaft splines.

Small amounts of oil and grease may be removed with aerosol brake cleaner and the facings dressed with a wire brush. However, if the facings are soaked with oil or grease, the clutch driven plate must be replaced. The driven plate must also be replaced if any of the other defects is present or if the facings are partially worn and a new clutch cover is being installed.

Clutch Cover Inspection

1. Check the clutch cover for:
   a. Scoring.
   b. Burn marks.
   c. Cracks.
2. Check the diaphragm springs for wear or damage at .the release bearing contact surface. Check for bent or broken spring fingers. Replace the cover if these are found.
3. If the clutch trouble is still not apparent, take the cover and clutch disc to a competent machine shop. Have the assembly checked for runout and the diaphragm springs checked for correct finger height. Do not attempt to dismantle the cover or readjust the fingers yourself without the proper tools and experience.

Clutch Installation

1. Make sure your hands are clean and free of oil or grease.
2. Make sure the clutch plate facings, cover and flywheel are free of oil, grease and other foreign material.
3. Install an alignment or dummy shaft in clutch plate hub. Mount hub and tool to flywheel with damper springs on disc facing the transmission.
4. Install clutch cover on flywheel over clutch plate and alignment shaft. Align cover according to reference marks scribed before disassembly.
5. Install cover bolts finger-tight. Tighten bolts evenly in a diagonal pattern to specifications (**Table 1**). Remove the dummy shaft.
6. Install throwout bearing in throwout lever, if removed, and center over clutch cover release fingers.
7. Lubricate ball socket and fork fingers at release bearing with graphite grease, then reinstall fork on ball stud.
8. Lubricate recess on inside of release bearing collar and clutch fork groove with graphite grease.
9. Install flywheel housing.
10. Install slave cylinder and tighten bolts to specifications (**Table 1**).
11. Connect clutch fork pushrod and lubricate pushrod ends.
12. Adjust shift linkage as described in this chapter.

Clutch Adjustment

The hydraulic clutch mechanism is self-adjusting. Free play adjustments are not necessary and cannot be made.

Clutch Master Cylinder
Removal/Installation

Refer to **Figure 4** for this procedure.
1. Disconnect the negative battery cable.

2. Remove the hush panel from underneath the dash.

3. Disconnect the pushrod from the clutch pedal.

4. Disconnect the hydraulic line at the master cylinder. It is best to use a flarenut wrench to loosen and remove the fitting, as it can be damaged by use of an open-end wrench.

5. Cap the hydraulic line and cylinder opening.

6. Remove bolts holding master cylinder at front of dash in engine compartment. Remove cylinder.

7. Installation is the reverse of removal. Tighten cylinder attaching nuts to specifications (**Table 1**). Fill the master cylinder reservoir to the level indicated on reservoir side with clean DOT 3 brake fluid. Bleed the hydraulic system as described in this chapter.

Clutch Slave Cylinder
Removal/Installation

Refer to **Figure 2** and **Figure 5** for this procedure.

1. Securely block the wheels that remain on the ground. Raise the vehicle on a jack and place it on jackstands.

2. Disconnect the hydraulic line at the slave cylinder.

3. Remove the cylinder attaching bolts. Remove the cylinder and pushrod.

4. Installation is the reverse of removal. Lubricate leading end of cylinder with Girling rubber lube or equivalent. Bleed the hydraulic system as described in this chapter.

Clutch Hydraulic System Bleeding

1. Fill master clutch cylinder with clean DOT 3 brake fluid.

2. Securely block the wheels that remain on the ground. Raise the vehicle with a jack and place it on jackstands.

3. Remove the slave cylinder attaching bolts. Hold cylinder at a 45 degree angle with bleed screw at highest point.

4. Connect a rubber hose to the slave cylinder bleed screw. Put the other end of the hose in a container 1/2 full of clean DOT 3 brake fluid. Make sure hose remains submerged in the brake fluid.

> *NOTE*
> *Do not let the clutch cylinder reservoir run dry in Step 5.*

5. Have a helper depress and hold the clutch pedal to the floor. Loosen the bleed screw. Tighten bleed screw and have the helper release the pedal. Repeat this operation until the fluid entering the container is free of air bubbles.

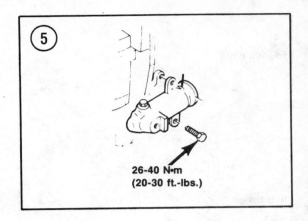

26-40 N·m
(20-30 ft.-lbs.)

6. Reinstall slave cylinder and tighten bolts to specifications.

7. Remove the jackstands and lower the vehicle to the ground.

8. Top up master clutch cylinder reservoir with clean DOT 3 brake fluid.

MANUAL TRANSMISSION

The 4-speed manual transmission and automatic overdrive unit used in the Corvette combines an 83 mm 4-speed gearbox with a 2-speed overdrive system electronically controlled by the ECM. This gives the car the option of operating in 1 of 7 different gear ranges, one of which is an overdrive (0.69:1 ratio).

The overdrive unit contains a planetary gear system and 2 sets of clutch packs. The clutch packs are hydraulically operated and designed so that whenever one is engaged, the other is disengaged.

The ECM is programmed to control the automatic overdrive unit based on vehicle speed and throttle position. Overdrive is engaged in 4th gear or whenever vehicle speed exceeds 110 mph. Rapid acceleration returns the unit to direct drive (1:1 ratio). If desired, the driver can lock out the overdrive operation by means of a switch on the console.

The transmission uses a floor mounted shift control with 3 linkage rods to shift the gears and a cable to provide a park-lock function. In addition, a throttle valve (TV) cable is used to control the hydraulic function. Hydraulic fluid used to operate the overdrive unit is carried to an oil cooler in the radiator by steel lines.

Transmission overhaul should be referred to a dealer or qualified specialist. You can save money by removing and installing the unit yourself.

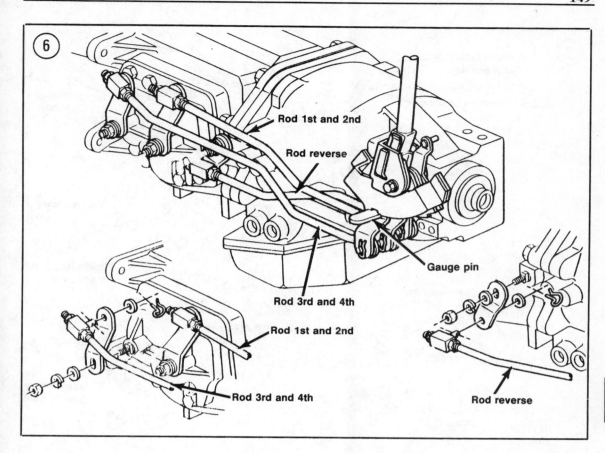

Rod 1st and 2nd

Rod reverse

Gauge pin

Rod 3rd and 4th

Rod 1st and 2nd

Rod 3rd and 4th

Rod reverse

8

Shift Linkage Adjustment

Refer to **Figure 6** for this procedure.
1. Disconnect the negative battery cable.
2. Remove the left seat from the passenger compartment.
3. Remove the shift knob.
4. Remove the console cover.
5. Remove the glove box lock in the console.
6. Remove the console left side panel.
7. Place the shift lever in NEUTRAL.
8. Raise the vehicle and place it on jackstands.
9. Remove the shifter cover and loosen the adjusting nuts on the shifter rods.
10. Make sure the transmission is in NEUTRAL, then install the alignment or gauge pin in the shifter as shown in **Figure 6**.
11. Equalize each shift lever swivel, then finger-tighten the front and rear adjusting nuts on one lever at the same time.
12. Repeat Step 12 for each of the 2 remaining levers, then torque all nuts to specifications.
13. Shift the transmission through the gear range to check for shift effort and accuracy. If necessary, repeat Steps 11-13.

14. Reverse Steps 1-10 to reinstall the components removed.

Shifter Assembly
Removal/Installation

1. Perform Steps 1-9 of *Shift Linkage Adjustment* in this chapter.
2. Remove shift rod adjust nuts from each shift rod and disconnect the rods from the shift cover.
3. Disconnect the park-lock cable at the shifter assembly (**Figure 7**).
4. Remove the shifter cross bolt.
5. Remove the shifter mounting bracket.
6. Remove the bolt holding the shifter assembly to the body panel. Remove the shifter assembly.
7. Installation is the reverse of removal.

Park-lock Cable Adjustment

Refer to **Figure 7** for this procedure.
1. Perform Steps 1-6 of *Shift Linkage Adjustment* in this chapter, then remove the shifter cover.
2. Lift up on the adjusting key at the cable connection to the shifter assembly. Release the cable.

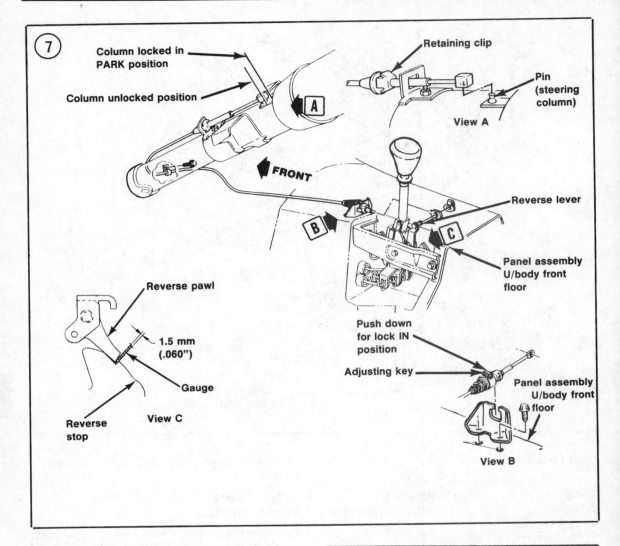

(7) Column locked in PARK position

Column unlocked position

Retaining clip

A

FRONT

Pin (steering column)

View A

Reverse lever

B

C

Panel assembly U/body front floor

Reverse pawl

1.5 mm (.060")

Gauge

Reverse stop

View C

Push down for lock IN position

Adjusting key

Panel assembly U/body front floor

View B

3. Position the steering column lock lever in the park-lock position.

4. Shift the transmission into REVERSE.

5. Depress the adjusting key at the cable connection to the shifter assembly to set the cable adjustment.

6. Install shifter cover and reverse Steps 1-6 of *Shift Linkage Adjustment.*

Throttle Valve (TV)
Cable Adjustment

Refer to **Figure 8** (1984) or **Figure 9** (1985-on) for this procedure.

1. 1984—remove the air cleaner cover.

2. Depress and hold the metal lock tab on the TV cable slider. See **Figure 10**.

3. Move the slider through the fitting away from the throttle body lever until it stops against the fitting.

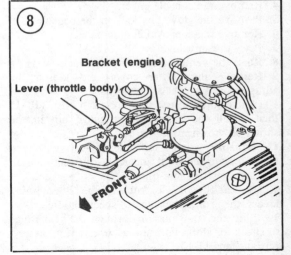

(8)

Bracket (engine)

Lever (throttle body)

FRONT

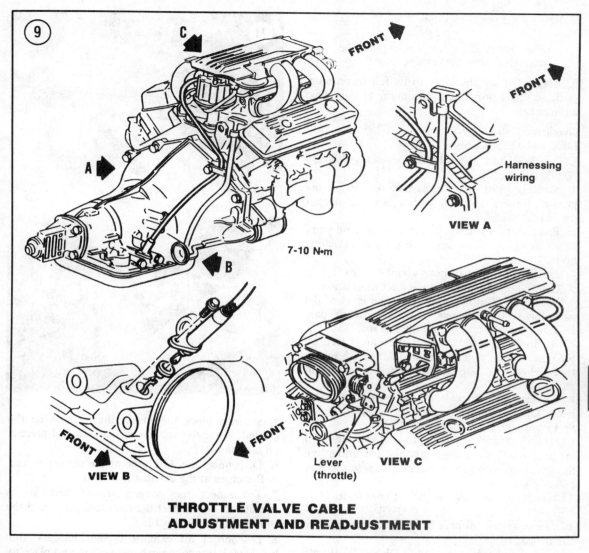

⑨

C

FRONT

FRONT

A

B

7-10 N•m

Harnessing wiring

VIEW A

FRONT

FRONT

VIEW B

Lever (throttle)

VIEW C

THROTTLE VALVE CABLE ADJUSTMENT AND READJUSTMENT

8

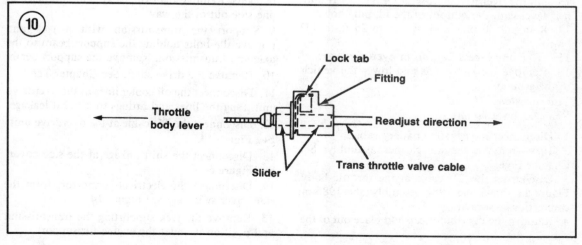

⑩

Lock tab

Fitting

Throttle body lever

Readjust direction

Slider

Trans throttle valve cable

4. Release the metal lock tab.

NOTE
The metal lock tab must not be depressed while performing Step 5.

5. Rotate the throttle lever to its full travel stop position. This provides a minimum of one click adjustment.

Overdrive Unit
Fluid and Filter Change

The fluid and filter should be changed every 30,000 miles.

1. Securely block the wheels that remain on the ground. Raise the vehicle with a jack and place it on jackstands.
2. Place a drain pan under the overdrive oil pan.
3. Remove the front and side oil pan attaching bolts.
4. Loosen the rear pan bolts about 4 turns.
5. Carefully pry oil pan free and let fluid drain.
6. When the fluid has drained to the level of the pan flange, remove pan bolts at rear of pan. Remove the pan and let the filter drain.
7. Remove the magnet from the pan. Clean all RTV sealant from pan mounting flange. Clean pan thoroughly with solvent and lint-free cloths or paper towels.
8. Remove the filter from the overdrive valve body. Discard the filter gasket.
9. Install a new filter and gasket.
10. Install magnet in pan depression and run a 1/8 in. bead of RTV sealant along the pan mounting flange. Make sure to run the bead inside the bolt holes in the pan.
11. Install pan and tighten bolts to 6-8 ft.-lb. (8-10 N•m).
12. Remove the fill plug from the driver's side of the overdrive unit.
13. Fill the overdrive unit with DEXRON II until it is level with the bottom of the fill plug hole.
14. Reinstall fill plug and tighten to 25 ft.-lb. (33 N•m).
15. Wipe any excess fluid from overdrive case.
16. Remove the jackstands and lower the vehicle to the ground.

Transmission
Removal/Installation

1. Disconnect the negative battery cable.
2. 1984—remove the air cleaner assembly. See Chapter Five.
3. Disconnect the TV cable at the throttle body. **Figure 11** shows the 1984 assembly; the 1985-on connection is similar.
4. Remove the distributor cap and place out of the way.

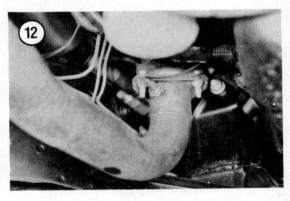

5. Securely block the wheels that remain on the ground. Raise the vehicle with a jack and place it on jackstands.
6. Disconnect the AIR pipe at the converter and AIR clamps at the exhaust manifold.
7. Disconnect the oxygen sensor lead at its connector. Disconnect the manifold pipe from the manifold. See **Figure 12**.
8. Disconnect all exhaust system hangers and brackets. Remove the exhaust system and place to one side out of the way.
9. Support the transmission with a jack and remove the bolts holding the support beam to the axle and transmission. Remove the support beam.
10. Remove the drive shaft. See Chapter Ten.
11. Disconnect the oil cooler lines at the overdrive unit. Plug the lines and fittings to prevent leakage.
12. Disconnect the TV cable at the overdrive unit. See **Figure 13**.
13. Disconnect the shift linkage at the side cover. See **Figure 6**.
14. Disconnect the electrical connectors from the side cover switches. See **Figure 14**.
15. Remove the jack supporting the transmission and position it under the engine for support.

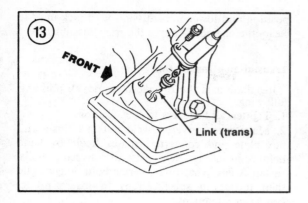

(13)

FRONT

Link (trans)

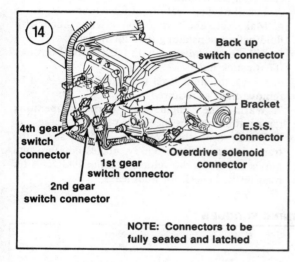

(14)

Back up
switch connector

Bracket

E.S.S.
connector

4th gear
switch
connector

Overdrive solenoid
connector

1st gear
switch connector

2nd gear
switch connector

**NOTE: Connectors to be
fully seated and latched**

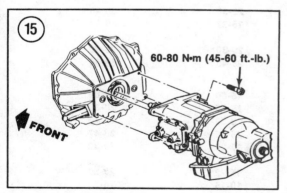

(15)

60-80 N•m (45-60 ft.-lb.)

FRONT

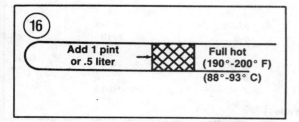

(16)

| Add 1 pint or .5 liter | → | Full hot (190°-200° F) (88°-93° C) |

16. Remove the 4 bolts holding the transmission to the bellhousing (**Figure 15**).

17. Move the transmission/overdrive assembly to the rear and disengage the input shaft from the clutch housing.

18. Installation is the reverse of removal. Tighten all fasteners to specifications and adjust TV cable as described in this chapter. Refill 4-speed transmission with SAE 80W or SAE 80W-90 GL-5 gear lubricant. Refill overdrive unit with DEXRON II automatic transmission fluid.

AUTOMATIC TRANSMISSION

The Turbo-Hydramatic 700-R4 is a 4-speed hydraulically operated unit with two planetary gear sets and a torque converter clutch controlled by the electronic control module (ECM). When engaged, the converter clutch reduces converter slippage and provides improved fuel economy with lower fluid operating temperatures.

Fluid Level Check

1. With the engine idling, shift from PARK to each of the other gear positions, then shift back to PARK.

2. Pull out the dipstick, wipe it off, reinsert it, then pull it back out.

3. Note the fluid level. If the engine is warm, it should be within the crosshatch section of the dipstick (**Figure 16**).

4. If the fluid level is low, add DEXRON II transmission fluid through the dipstick filler tube to bring the level to the top of the crosshatch section on the dipstick. Use only DEXRON II fluid.

Throttle Valve (TV) Cable Adjustment

The procedure is the same as described for the 4-speed manual transmission/overdrive unit.

Park-lock Adjustment

The procedure is the same as described for the 4-speed manual transmission/overdrive unit.

Transmission Removal

1. Disconnect the negative battery cable.

2. 1984—remove the air cleaner assembly. See Chapter Five.

3. Disconnect the TV cable at the throttle body. **Figure 11** shows the 1984 assembly; the 1985-on connection is similar.

4. Securely block the wheels that remain on the ground. Raise the vehicle with a jack and place it on jackstands.

8

5. Disconnect the AIR pipe at the converter and AIR clamps at the exhaust manifold.

6. Disconnect the oxygen sensor lead at its connector. Disconnect the manifold pipe from the manifold. See **Figure 12**.

7. Disconnect all exhaust system hangers and brackets. Remove the exhaust system and place to one side out of the way.

8. Remove the converter inspection cover and mark the relationship between the converter and flex plate for reassembly reference.

9. Remove the converter-to-flex plate bolts.

10. Disconnect the shift cable and all electrical connections at the transmission.

11. Support the engine and transmission with separate jacks.

12. Remove the torque arm. See Chapter Ten.

13. Disconnect and remove the drive shaft. See Chapter Ten.

14. Disconnect the oil cooler lines at the transmission. Plug the lines and fittings to prevent leakage.

15. Disconnect the TV cable at the transmission.

16. Remove the converter housing-to-engine bolts.

17. Carefully move the transmission to the rear until it clears the crankshaft. Hold converter in position and lower transmission with jack until it clears the engine. Remove the transmission.

Transmission Installation

Installation is the reverse of removal, plus the following:

1. Tighten all fasteners to specifications.

2. Make sure converter weld nuts are flush with flex plate and converter rotates freely by hand before installing flex plate-to-converter bolts. Install 3 flex plate-to-converter bolts finger-tight, then torque to specifications to insure proper converter alignment.

3. Install new oil seal on oil filler tube.

4. Make sure the torque converter is filled with fluid before reinstalling it in the housing.

5. Fill the transmission with DEXRON II through the dipstick hole.

6. Check the fluid level (Chapter Three). Add or remove fluid as required.

7. Warm the engine to normal operating temperature, then recheck fluid level.

8. Road test the vehicle. Make sure the transmission shifts smoothly, makes no abnormal noises and holds the vehicle when in PARK. After road testing, check for fluid leaks.

Table 1 TIGHTENING TORQUES

Fastener	ft.-lb.	N•m
Clutch		
Pedal attachment nut	22-30	30-40
Master cylinder bolts	15-22	20-30
Slave cylinder		
Attachment bolts	20-30	26-40
Hydraulic line connection	25-40	34-54
Manual transmission		
To bellhousing bolts	45-60	60-80
Drain plug	15-25	20-33
Equalizer locknuts	20-30	27-40
Fill plug	25-35	33-47
Shift rod nuts	15-23	20-32
Shifter bracket		
Front bolt	15-22	20-30
Rear bolt	10-15	14-20
Shifter mounting bolt	40-51	55-70
Overdrive unit		
Case to reverse housing bolts	34-36	46-48
Cooler block to case bolts	6-8	8-10
Cooler lines		
At radiator	15-25	20-34
At overdrive	8-11	11-16
Upper bracket clamp fastener	7-10	10-14
Lower bracket clamp fastener	3.5-5	5-7
(continued)		

Table 1 TIGHTENING TORQUES (continued)

Fastener	ft.-lb.	N·m
Automatic transmission		
Cooler lines		
At radiator	20	27
At transmission	10	13
Inspection cover	7	10
Shift lever @ transmission	24	32
Torque converter-to-flex plate bolts	35	47
Transmission-to-engine bolts	35	47

8

CHAPTER NINE

FRONT SUSPENSION AND STEERING

The independent front suspension consists of unequal upper and lower control arms, a transverse fiberglass leaf spring, tubular shock absorbers with built-in jounce/rebound bumpers, a stabilizer bar and steering knuckle. The steering knuckle contains the integral axle hub and bearing assembly.

Spindle offset is incorporated in the front suspension by moving the center of the wheel to the rear from its normal location on line through the ball-joints. This relocation of 12 mm increases directional stability.

Power assisted rack-and-pinion steering is standard. The steering gear is mounted in front of the wheels. The power steering pump uses a remote reservoir. Overall turning ratio is 15.5:1, with a faster 13.0:1 ratio used when the car is equipped with the handling package option. A tilt-telescoping steering column is standard.

Table 1 (tightening torques) and **Table 2** (ride height) are at the end of the chapter.

FRONT SUSPENSION

Figure 1 shows the major components of the front suspension.

Shock Absorber Replacement

1. Securely block the rear wheels. Raise the front of the vehicle and place it on jackstands.

2. Remove 2 lower shock absorber mounting screws (**Figure 2**) from upper control arm.
3. Remove upper mounting nut from shock absorber (**Figure 3**).
4. Remove the shock absorber and upper mounting bushings.
5. Installation is the reverse of removal. Tighten all fasteners to specifications.
6. Remove jackstands and lower vehicle to the ground.

Transverse Leaf Spring
Removal/Installation

Refer to **Figure 4** for this procedure.
1. Loosen the left wheel lug nuts.
2. Securely block the rear wheels. Raise the front of the car and place it on jackstands.
3. Remove the left wheel/tire assembly.
4. Remove the spring protectors on each side.
5. Install spring compressor part No. J-33432-4.
6. Remove the cotter pin and castellated nut from the left lower ball-joint (**Figure 5**). Separate ball-joint from knuckle with tool part No. J-33436-9 or equivalent.
7. Tighten spring compressor tool part No. J-33432-4.
8. Remove the shock absorber mount bracket from each lower control arm as described in this chapter.

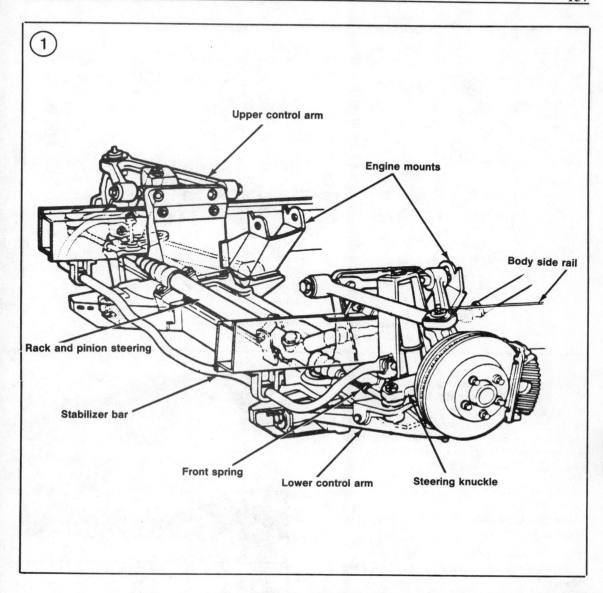

①

Upper control arm

Engine mounts

Body side rail

Rack and pinion steering

Stabilizer bar

Front spring

Lower control arm

Steering knuckle

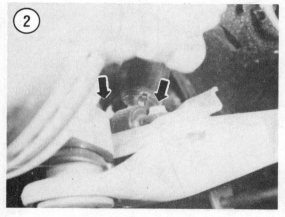

②

③

9

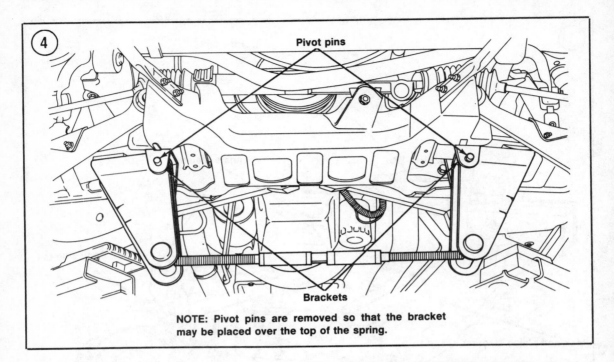

Pivot pins

Brackets

NOTE: Pivot pins are removed so that the bracket may be placed over the top of the spring.

9. Remove spring mounting bolts.
10. Release and remove the spring compressor.
11. Remove the spring from the left side.
12. Installation is the reverse of removal. Install a new cotter pin. Tighten all fasteners to specifications. Have front wheel alignment checked by a dealer or front-end shop.

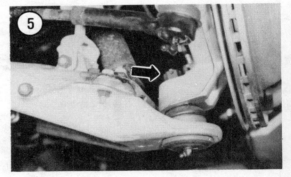

Lower Shock Absorber Bracket
Removal/Installation

Refer to **Figure 6** for this procedure.
1. Remove the shock absorber as described in this chapter.
2. Remove the bracket mounting bolts. Remove the bracket.
3. Installation is the reverse of removal. Tighten fasteners to specifications.

Lower Control Arm
Removal/Installation

1. Loosen the wheel lug nuts.
2. Securely block the rear wheels. Raise the front of the car and place it on jackstands.
3. Remove the spring protector pivot pin. Remove the spring protector and install spring compressor part No. J-33432.

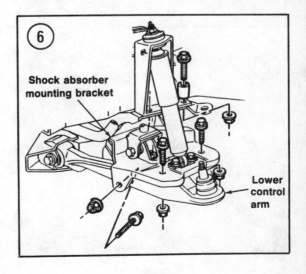

Shock absorber mounting bracket

Lower control arm

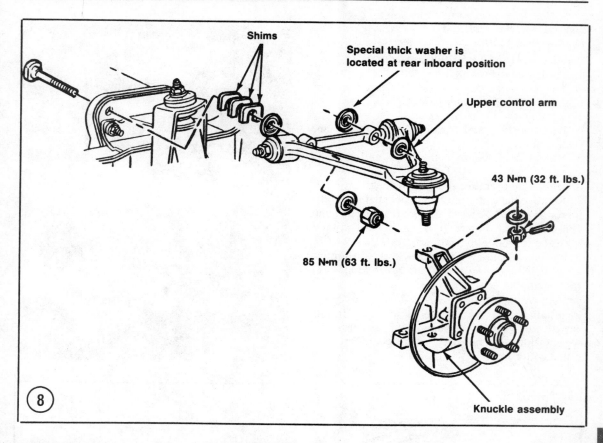

Shims

Special thick washer is
located at rear inboard position

Upper control arm

43 N•m (32 ft. lbs.)

85 N•m (63 ft. lbs.)

Knuckle assembly

⑧

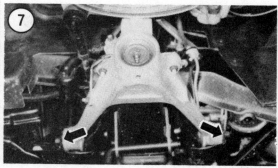

⑦

4. Remove the lower shock bracket as described in this chapter.

5. Remove the cotter pin and castellated nut from the lower ball-joint (**Figure 5**). Separate ball-joint and knuckle with tool part No. J-33436-9 or equivalent.

6. Remove the control arm mounting bolts (**Figure 7**) at the crossmember. Remove the control arm.

7. Installation is the reverse of removal. Maintain suspension at curb height after installing the control arm mounting bolts. Install new cotter pin. Tighten all fasteners to specifications with

suspension at curb height. Have front wheel alignment checked by a dealer or front-end shop.

**Upper Control Arm
Removal/Installation**

Refer to **Figure 8** for this procedure.

1. Loosen the wheel lug nuts.

2. Securely block the rear wheels. Raise the front of the car and place it on jackstands.

3. Remove the wheel/tire assembly.

4. Remove the spring protector pivot pin. Remove the spring protector and install spring compressor part No. J-33432-4. Compress and loosen spring.

5. Remove the cotter pin and castellated nut from the upper ball-joint (**Figure 9**). Separate ball-joint from control arm with tool part No. J-33436-9 or equivalent.

6. Remove upper control arm mounting bolts (**Figure 10**). Remove control arm and retrieve shims (**Figure 8**).

7. Installation is the reverse of removal. Tighten all fasteners to specifications. Install new ball-joint cotter pin from rear to front (**Figure 8**). Do not back the nut off to insert pin. Have front wheel alignment checked by a dealer or front-end shop.

Steering Knuckle Hub and Bearing Removal/Installation

Refer to **Figure 11** for this procedure.

1. Loosen the wheel lug nuts.
2. Securely block the rear wheels. Raise the front of the car and place it on jackstands.
3. Remove the wheel/tire assembly.
4. Remove the brake caliper and rotor. See Chapter Eleven.
5. Unbolt and remove the hub and bearing assembly.
6. Unbolt and remove the splash shield.
7. Remove the cotter pin and castellated nut at the tie rod (**Figure 12**), lower ball-joint (**Figure 5**) and upper ball-joint (**Figure 9**). Separate the ball-joint from the tie rod with tool part No. J-24319-01 or equivalent. Separate the upper/lower ball-joints from the knuckle with tool part No. J-33436-9 or equivalent.
8. Remove the control arm.
9. Installation is the reverse of removal. Install new cotter pins. Tighten all fasteners to specifications. Do not back off castellated nuts to install cotter pins.

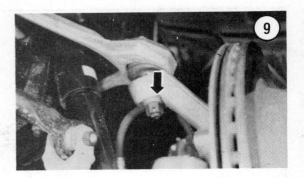

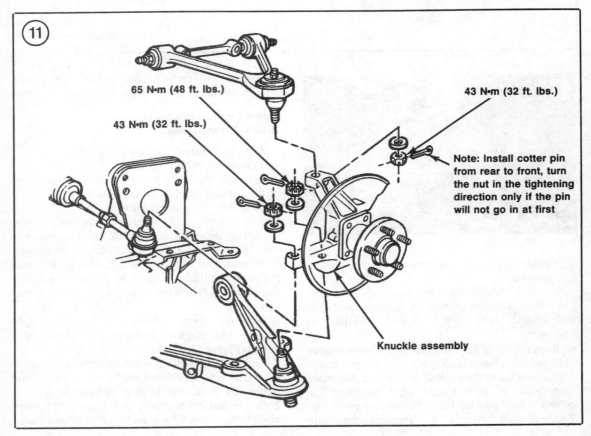

65 N•m (48 ft. lbs.)

43 N•m (32 ft. lbs.)

43 N•m (32 ft. lbs.)

Note: Install cotter pin from rear to front, turn the nut in the tightening direction only if the pin will not go in at first

Knuckle assembly

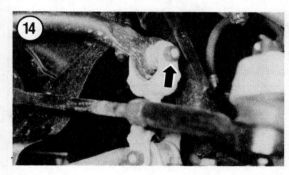

Stabilizer Bar
Removal/Installation

1. Raise the front of the car and place it on jackstands.
2. Remove bracket-to-frame attaching bolts (**Figure 13**).
3. Remove bar-to-link attaching bolt (**Figure 14**).
4. Remove the bar and bushing from the link. Remove the bar from the vehicle.
5. Installation is the reverse of removal. Remove the jackstands and lower the vehicle to the ground before tightening stabilizer bar bolts.

WHEEL ALIGNMENT

Several suspension angles affect the running and steering of the front wheels. These angles must be properly aligned to prevent excessive wear, as well as to maintain directional stability and ease of steering. The angles are:

    a. Caster.
    b. Camber.
    c. Toe-in.
    d. Steering axis inclination.
    c. Front axle height.

All except steering axis inclination are adjustable. Since these angles are critical, they must be done by a competent front-end alignment shop or your dealer.

Pre-alignment Check

Adjustment of the steering and various suspension angles is affected by several factors. Perform the following steps before any adjustments are attempted.

1. Check tire pressure and wear. See *Tire Wear Analysis*, Chapter Two.
2. Check steering gear-to-steering column alignment.
3. Check steering knuckle pivots, ball-joints and wheel bearings for looseness.
4. Check for broken or sagging front and rear springs.
5. Remove any excessive load.
6. Check brakes and shock absorbers for proper operation.
7. Check steering gear for wear or damage.
8. Check wheel balance.
9. Check rear suspension for looseness.

Front tire wear problems can indicate alignment problems. These are covered under *Tire Wear Analysis*, Chapter Two.

Caster

Caster is the inclination from vertical of the line through the ball-joints (**Figure 15**). Positive caster shifts the wheel forward; negative caster shifts the wheel rearward. The Corvette has positive caster—the bottom of the wheel is shifted forward.

Caster causes the wheels to return to a straight-ahead position after a turn. It also prevents the wheels from wandering due to wind, potholes or uneven road surfaces. By incorporating spindle offset with a slight positive caster, the resulting road feel is similar to that of higher caster, but without any sacrifice in responsiveness.

9

Caster is adjusted by adding or subtracting shims to the front or rear bolt holding the upper control arm shaft to the frame bracket. See **Figure 16**.

Camber

Camber is the inclination of the wheel from vertical (**Figure 15**). With positive camber, the top of the tire leans outward. With negative camber, the top of the tire leans inward. The Corvette uses positive camber.

Excessive camber causes tire wear. Negative camber wears the inside of the tire; positive camber wears the outside. Camber is adjusted by adding or removing shims at both front and rear bolts of the upper control arm shaft. See **Figure 16**.

Caster and Camber Adjustment

These adjustments require the use of a front end alignment rack and special tools for accurate measurement and should not be attempted by the home mechanic. Take the car to a dealer or front-end shop for caster or camber adjustment.

Toe-in

Since the front wheels tend to point outward when the car is moving in a forward direction, the

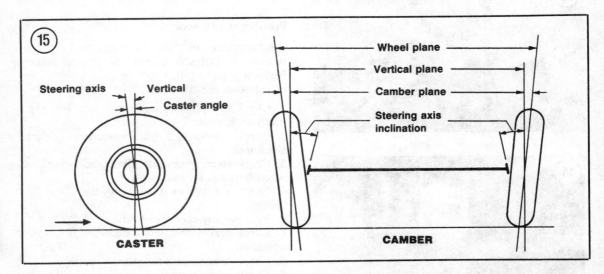

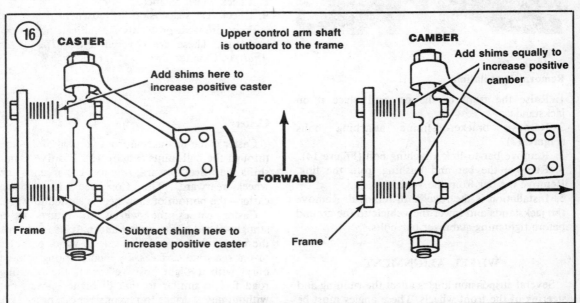

distance between the front edges of the tire (Y, **Figure 17**) is generally slightly less than the distance between the rear edges (X, **Figure 17**) when the car is at rest.

Toe Adjustment

Although toe adjustment requires only a simple homemade tool, it usually is not worth the trouble for home mechanics. Alignment shops include toe adjustment as part of the alignment procedure, so you probably will not save any money by doing it yourself. The procedure described here can be used for an initial toe setting after steering knuckle or tie rod ball-joint replacement.

1. With the steering wheel centered, roll the car forward about 15 ft. on a smooth, level surface.
2. Mark the center of the tread at the front and rear of each tire.

3. Measure the distance between the forward chalk marks (Y, **Figure 17**). Use 2 pieces of telescoping aluminum tubing. Telescope the tubing so each end contacts a chalk mark. Using a sharp center scribe, mark the small diameter tubing where it enters the large diameter tubing.
4. Measure between the rear chalk marks with the telescoping tubes. Make another mark on the small tube where it enters the large one. The distance between the 2 scribe marks is the toe-in and must be divided in half to determine the amount of toe at each wheel.
5. If toe-in is incorrect, loosen the tie rod jam nuts (**Figure 18**). Rotate inner tie rods equally in opposite directions to obtain the desired toe setting.
6. Tighten jam nuts to specifications.

Steering Axis Inclination

Steering axis inclination is the inward or outward inclination of the steering knuckle centerline from vertical. See **Figure 15**. This angle is not adjustable, but can be checked with a front-end alignment rack to determine if suspension parts are bent.

Ride Height

Before making any other suspension adjustments, check ride height as follows:

1. Park the car on a smooth, level floor. Check and adjust tire pressures. Make sure car has a full tank of gasoline.
2. Lift the front bumper up about 1 1/2 in., remove hands and let the car settle to its normal height. Repeat this step 3 times.
3. Measure and record the distance from the centerline of each lower control arm mounting bolt to the bottom of the lower ball-joint (Z, **Figure 19**).

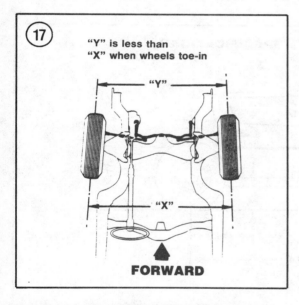

17   **"Y" is less than "X" when wheels toe-in**

"Y"

"X"

FORWARD

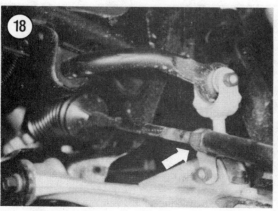

18

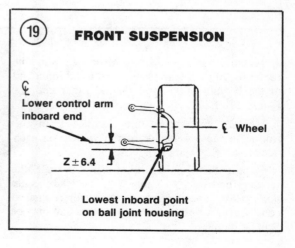

19   **FRONT SUSPENSION**

Lower control arm inboard end

₵ Wheel

Z ± 6.4

Lowest inboard point on ball joint housing

9

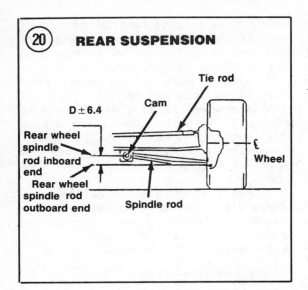

REAL SUSPENSION

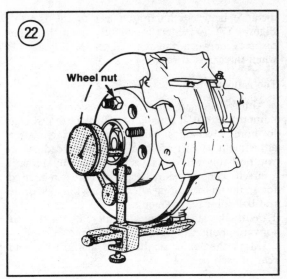

TRIM HEIGHTS SPECIFICATIONS

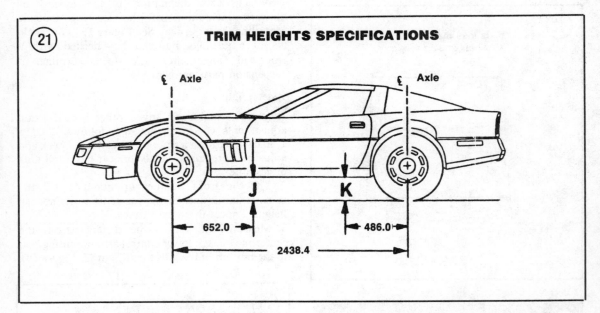

4. Measure and record the distance from the centerline of each rear wheel spindle rod inner end to the bottom of the spindle rod outer end (D, **Figure 20**).

5. Measure and record the distance from the ground to the lower edge of the vehicle on each side (J and K, **Figure 21**).

6. Repeat Steps 3-5 three times. Average the readings and refer to **Table 2**. If the readings are not within specifications, check for damaged control arms or other suspension parts that may be bent or damaged.

WHEEL BEARINGS

Front wheel bearings are a part of the hub assembly. They are permanently sealed, require no regular maintenance and cannot be adjusted.

Wheel Bearing Inspection

1. Loosen the wheel lug nuts.
2. Securely block the rear wheels. Raise the front of the car and place it on jackstands.
3. Remove the wheel/tire assembly.
4. Free the caliper shoes from the rotor or remove the caliper. See Chapter Eleven.

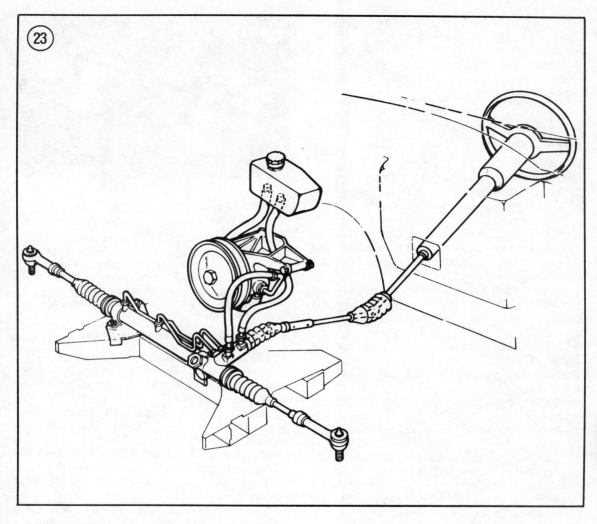

5. Install 2 lug nuts to hold the rotor to the hub/bearing assembly.

6. Attach a dial indicator as shown in **Figure 22**.

7. Grasp the rotor with a push-pull movement and read the dial indicator.

8. If the indicator reading exceeds 0.005 in. (0.127 mm), replace the hub/bearing assembly.

Removal/Installation

1. Loosen the wheel lug nuts.

2. Securely block the rear wheels. Raise the front of the vehicle and place it on jackstands.

3. Remove the wheel/tire assembly.

4. Remove the brake caliper and rotor. See Chapter Eleven.

5. Unbolt and remove the hub and bearing assembly.

6. Installation is the reverse of removal. Tighten fasteners to specifications.

STEERING LINKAGE

The power-assisted rack-and-pinion steering assembly is mounted ahead of the front wheels. See **Figure 23**.

Outer Tie Rod
Removal/Installation

1. Raise the front of the vehicle and place it on jackstands.

2. Loosen the tie rod jam nut (**Figure 18**).

3. Remove the tie rod ball-joint cotter pin and stud nut (**Figure 12**). Separate the ball-joint from the knuckle with tool part No. J-24319-01 or equivalent.

4. Unscrew outer tie rod from inner tie rod and remove from the vehicle.

9

5. Installation is the reverse of removal. Use new cotter pin. Tighten fastener and jam nut to specifications.

6. Adjust toe-in as described in this chapter.

7. Have wheel alignment checked by a dealer or front-end shop.

Power Steering Gearbox
Removal/Installation

1. Loosen the left front wheel lug nuts.

2. Securely block the rear wheels. Raise the front of the vehicle and place it on jackstands.

3. Remove the left front wheel/tire assembly.

4. Place a drain pan under the steering gearbox. Disconnect the hydraulic lines at the gearbox. Cap the lines to prevent leakage and plug the gearbox fittings to prevent contamination.

5. Remove each tie rod cotter pin and castellated nut (**Figure 12**). Separate the ball-joint from the knuckle with tool part No. J-24319-01 or equivalent.

6. Remove the mounting bolt and clamp shown in **Figure 24**.

7. Disconnect the intermediate steering shaft at the gearbox.

8. Remove the stabilizer bar as described in this chapter.

9. Remove the cooling fan assembly. See Chapter Six.

10. Remove the steering gearbox from the vehicle.

11. Installation is the reverse of removal. Install new cotter pins. Check and refill power steering reservoir as required. Have wheel alignment checked by a dealer or front-end shop.

STEERING COLUMN

Steering Wheel
Removal/Installation

1. Disconnect the negative battery cable.

2. Make sure the front wheels are in the straight-ahead position.

3. Carefully pry horn cap from steering wheel.

4. Remove telescope adjuster screws. Remove adjuster.

5. Remove the steering wheel nut and washer.

6. Note alignment marks on steering wheel and steering shaft for reassembly reference. If there are none, make your own with quick-drying paint.

7. Install a standard wheel puller and remove the wheel.

8. Installation is the reverse of removal. Tighten all fasteners to specifications.

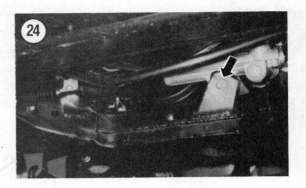

Steering Column
Removal/Installation

CAUTION
The steering column is very susceptible to damage during and after removal from the vehicle. Hammering, dropping or leaning on the column can damage internal plastic injections used to maintain rigidity.

Refer to **Figure 25** for this procedure.

1. Disconnect the negative battery cable.

2. Working in the engine compartment, remove the pinch bolt at the intermediate shaft universal joint. See **Figure 26**.

3. Working in the passenger compartment, remove the lower column bolt at the dash and toe panel support.

4. Remove the 2 column bracket bolts from the instrument panel reinforcement assembly.

5. Disconnect the steering column electrical connectors.

6. Separate the steering column from the intermediate shaft. Remove the steering column assembly from the vehicle.

7. Installation is the reverse of removal. Tighten all fasteners to specifications.

Intermediate Shaft Removal

Refer to **Figure 27** for this procedure.

1. Place the wheels in a straight-ahead position.

2. Remove the screw and U-nut from the upper and lower shields. Depress the hooked side of each shield to disengage it from the clasp. Remove the shields.

3. Remove the universal joint pinch bolts at the steering rack and steering column.

4. Remove the intermediate shaft.

Intermediate Shaft Installation

Refer to **Figure 27** for this procedure.

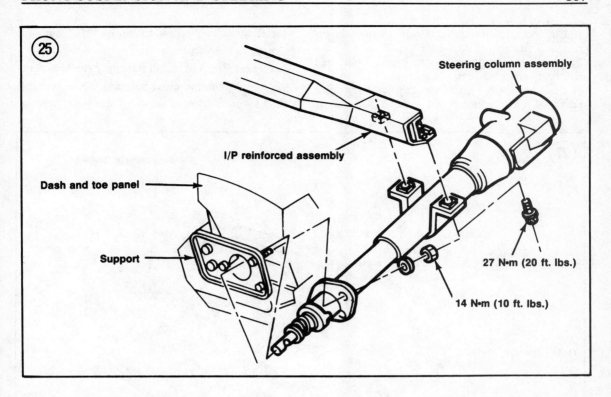

25

Steering column assembly

I/P reinforced assembly

Dash and toe panel

Support

27 N•m (20 ft. lbs.)

14 N•m (10 ft. lbs.)

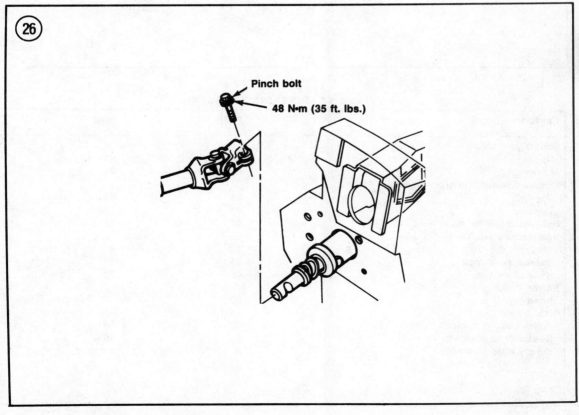

26

Pinch bolt

48 N•m (35 ft. lbs.)

9

1. Connect the intermediate shaft to the steering rack and steering column shaft.

2. Install the universal joint pinch bolts and tighten to specifications.

3. Position lower shield around steering rack universal joint. Engage shield hook in shield clasp.

Install attaching screw to engage "U" nut and tighten to specifications.

4. Repeat Step 3 to install the upper shield around the steering column universal joint. Make sure the shield groove fits over the steering column bearing.

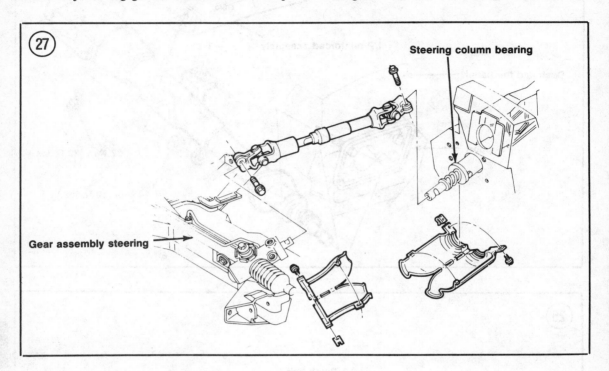

(27)

Steering column bearing

Gear assembly steering

Table 1 TIGHTENING TORQUES

Fastener	ft.-lb.	N•m
Control arm stud ball-joint nut		
Upper	32	43
Lower	48	65
Control arm shaft to crossmember		
Upper	63	85
Lower	96	130
Hub/bearing to knuckle	46	62
Intermediate shaft		
Shields	1.5	2
Column pinch bolt	35	47
Rack pinch bolt	46	62
Power steering		
Hose to pump	20	27
Pump to bracket	35	47
Pump bracket to block/head	25	34
Reservoir to alternator bracket	7	10
Supply hose clamps	2	3

(continued)

Table 1 TIGHTENING TORQUES (continued)

Fastener	ft.-lb.	N·m
Shock absorber		
Upper	22	30
Lower	22	30
Bracket to control arm	22	30
Splash shield	7.5	18
Spring protector	18	25
Spring retainer*	46	62
Stabilizer		
Clamp to frame*	40	54
Link*	35	48
Bracket to control arm	22	30
Steering column		
Bracket to frame bolts	20	27
Telescope adjustment screws	2	2.8
To dash/toe panel support	10	14
Steering gear		
Clamp	18	25
To crossmember	25	34
Steering wheel nut	30	40
Tie rod stud to knuckle	32	43

* Car must be on ground when torque is applied.

Table 2 RIDE HEIGHT SPECIFICATIONS

Suspension type	Dimension (mm)			
	Z*	D*	J	K
1984				
Standard	51.8	77.4	191.8	193.5
FE 7	50.9	76.1	190.9	192.5
1985				
Standard	46.5	80.9	188.1	194.5
FE 7	51.8	78.7	191.4	193.8

* ±6.4 mm

9

CHAPTER TEN

REAR SUSPENSION, DRIVE SHAFT AND DIFFERENTIAL

The 5-link independent rear suspension uses tubular shock absorbers and a transverse-mounted fiberglass leaf spring. The axle drive shafts and camber control support rods maintain a near-constant camber change throughout wheel travel. Aluminum upper and lower control arms control the front/rear action of the wheels. The lateral position of the wheels is maintained by the links, which transmit side forces to the fixed differential.

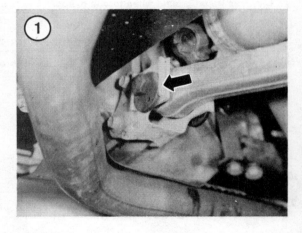

The fiberglass leaf spring is clamp-bolted to the lower mounting surface on the differential carrier cover beam. The outer spring ends are link-bolted to the rear of the wheel knuckles. A stabilizer bar connecting the 2 knuckles extends to the rear and is bracket-mounted to the frame.

A hub and bearing unit bolted to the knuckle support the axle drive shaft and spindle. The hub and bearing unit is a sealed assembly, requires no maintenance or adjustment and is serviced by replacement only.

This chapter contains repair and replacement procedures for the rear suspension, drive shaft, rear axles and differential carrier. **Table 1** (tightening torques) is at the end of the chapter.

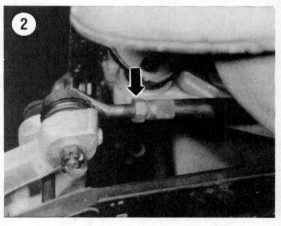

WHEEL ALIGNMENT

Wheel alignment on an independent rear suspension is as important to handling and tire wear as front suspension wheel alignment. Wheel camber and toe-in are adjustable and should be checked periodically on an alignment rack.

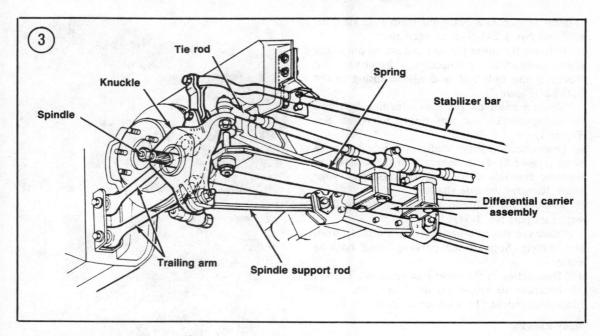

③ Tie rod
Knuckle
Spindle
Spring
Stabilizer bar
Differential carrier assembly
Trailing arm
Spindle support rod

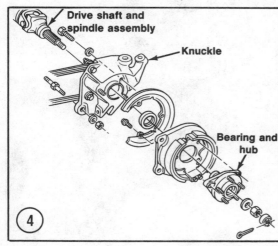

④ Drive shaft and spindle assembly
Knuckle
Bearing and hub

It is not possible to adjust camber or toe-in without an alignment rack. If you have disassembled any part of the rear suspension, take the car to your dealer or other front-end specialist immediately after reassembling.

> *CAUTION*
> *Drive slowly and carefully as handling is affected. Do not drive too far as tires can wear rapidly when scrubbed sideways by a misaligned suspension.*

Camber

Camber is the inclination of the wheel from vertical. Rear wheel camber is adjusted by rotating an eccentric cam at the inner mounting of the support rods (**Figure 1**). This moves the support rod in or out to achieve the correct amount of camber (0.7° ±0.5°).

Toe-in

Camber and rolling resistance tend to force the front wheels outward at their forward edge. To compensate for this tendency, the front edges are turned slightly inward when the car is at rest; this is toe-in.

To adjust toe-in, loosen the locknuts on the tie rod ends and rotate the tie rod shaft (**Figure 2**) to obtain the correct setting (0° ±0.06° per wheel).

REAR SUSPENSION

Figure 3 shows the major components of the rear suspension.

Hub and Bearing
Removal/Installation

Refer to **Figure 4** for this procedure.
1. Remove the center cap from the wheel. Loosen the wheel lug nuts.
2. Securely block the front wheels. Raise the rear of the vehicle and place it on jackstands. Remove the wheel/tire assembly.
3. Remove the cotter pin, spindle nut and washer (**Figure 5**).
4. Remove the brake caliper, support and brake rotor. See Chapter Eleven.
5. Remove the cotter pin and castellated nut holding the tie rod end ball-joint to the knuckle

10

(**Figure 6**). Separate ball-joint from knuckle with tool part No. J-24319-01 or equivalent.

6. Remove the cotter pin and castellated nut at the spring-to-knuckle connection. Remove the bushings and link bolt holding the spring to the knuckle (**Figure 7**).

7. Scribe a mark on the cam adjusting bolt and mounting bracket for reassembly reference. See **Figure 1**.

8. Disconnect the drive shaft at the side gear yoke shaft (**Figure 8**). Push outward on the knuckle to separate the axle shaft from the side gear yoke shaft. Remove the axle shaft.

9. Remove the hub and bearing mounting bolts with tool part No. J-34161.

10. Remove the hub and bearing assembly from the vehicle. Support the parking brake backing plate.

11. Installation is the reverse of removal. Tighten all fasteners to specifications. Have rear wheel alignment checked by a dealer or front-end shop.

Rear Knuckle
Removal/Installation

1. Perform Steps 1-6 of *Hub and Bearing Removal/Installation* in this chapter.

2. Disconnect the stabilizer bar at the knuckle (**Figure 9**).

3. Disconnect the parking brake cable at the backing plate (**Figure 10**).

4. Disconnect the shock absorber at the knuckle (A, **Figure 11**).

5. Disconnect the spindle support rod at the knuckle (B, **Figure 11**).

6. Disconnect the upper and lower control arms at the knuckle (**Figure 12**).

7. Lower the knuckle and slide the spindle from the hub and bearing assembly.

8. Remove the hub and bearing assembly from the knuckle with tool part No. J-24161.

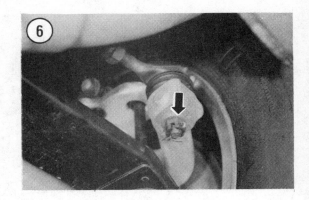

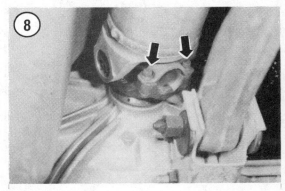

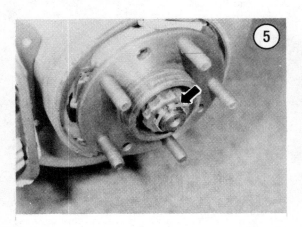

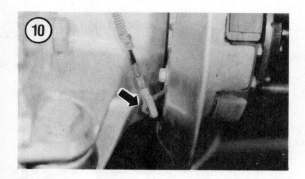

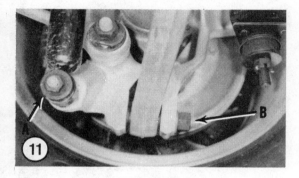

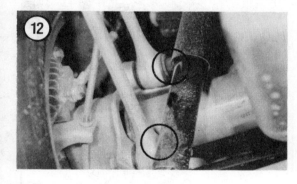

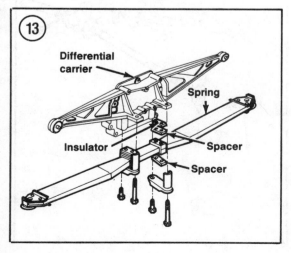

Figure 13: Differential carrier, Spring, Insulator, Spacer, Spacer

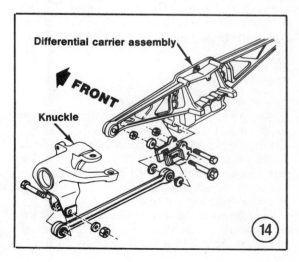

Figure 14: Differential carrier assembly, Knuckle, FRONT

9. Remove splash shield from knuckle.
10. Installation is the reverse of removal. Tighten all fasteners to specifications. Have rear wheel alignment checked by a dealer or front-end shop.

**Transverse Leaf Spring
Removal/Installation**

Refer to **Figure 13** for this procedure.
1. Remove the center cap from the wheels. Loosen the wheel lug nuts.
2. Securely block the front wheels. Raise the rear of the vehicle and place it on jackstands.
3. Remove the wheel/tire assemblies.
4. Remove the cotter pin, castellated nut, bushings and link bolt holding the spring ends to the knuckles. See **Figure 7**.
5. Remove the bolts, spacers and insulators holding the spring at the cover beam (**Figure 13**).
6. Remove the spring from the vehicle.
7. Installation is the reverse of removal. Tighten all fasteners to specifications.

**Spindle Support Rod
Removal/Installation**

Refer to **Figure 14** for this procedure.
1. Securely block the front wheels. Raise the rear of the car and place it on jackstands.
2. Scribe marks on the cam adjusting bolt and mounting bracket for reassembly reference. See **Figure 1**.
3. Remove cam adjusting bolt. Separate spindle rod from mounting bracket.
4. Remove spindle rod bolt at the knuckle. Remove spindle rod.
5. Installation is the reverse of removal. Tighten all fasteners to specifications. Have rear wheel alignment checked by a dealer or front-end shop.

10

Upper/Lower Control Arm
Removal/Installation

1. Securely block the front wheels. Raise the rear of the car and place it on jackstands.
2. Remove the shock absorber as described in this chapter.
3. Remove the bolt holding the control arm to the knuckle (**Figure 12**).
4. Remove the bolt holding the control arm to the body bracket (**Figure 15**). Remove the control arm.
5. Installation is the reverse of removal. Tighten all fasteners to specifications.

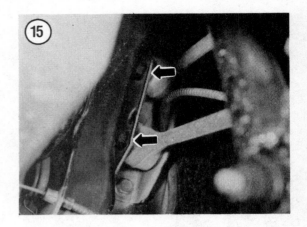

Shock Absorber
Removal/Installation

1. Securely block the front wheels. Raise the rear of the car and place it on jackstands.
2. Remove the shock absorber lower mounting nut/washer (A, **Figure 11**).
3. Remove the upper shock absorber mounting bolt (**Figure 16**). Remove the shock absorber.
4. Installation is the reverse of removal. Install upper bolt with the nut facing toward the rear of the vehicle. Tighten all fasteners to specifications.

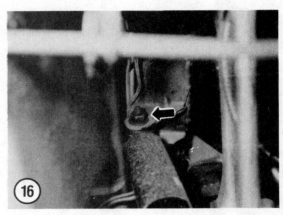

Rear Axle Tie Rod
Removal/Installation

Refer to **Figure 17** for this procedure.
1. Securely block the front wheels. Raise the rear of the car and place it on jackstands.
2. Remove the cotter pin and castellated nut from the tie rod ball-joint. Separate tie rod from knuckle with tool part No. J-24319-01 or equivalent.
3. Remove the bolts holding the tie rod to the differential carrier assembly. Remove the tie rod.
4. Installation is the reverse of removal. Tighten all fasteners to specifications. Have rear wheel alignment checked by a dealer or front-end shop.

Tie Rod End
Removal/Installation

Refer to **Figure 17** for this procedure.
1. Securely block the front wheels. Raise the rear of the car and place it on jackstands.
2. Remove the cotter pin and castellated nut from the tie rod ball-joint. Separate tie rod from knuckle with tool part No. J-24319-01 or equivalent.
3. Loosen tie rod jam nut.
4. Unscrew tie rod end from shaft.
5. Installation is the reverse of removal. Tighten all fasteners to specifications. Have rear wheel alignment checked by a dealer or front-end shop.

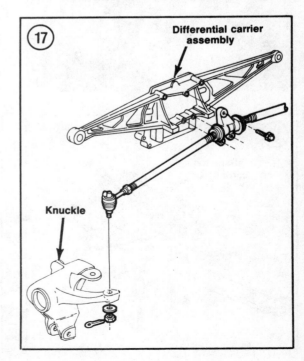

Differential carrier assembly

Knuckle

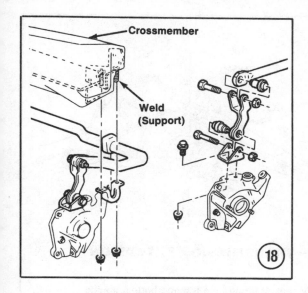

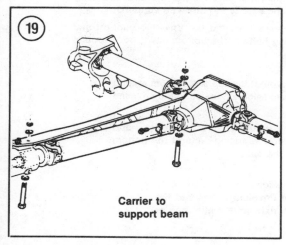

Stabilizer Bar
Removal/Installation

Refer to **Figure 18** for this procedure.
1. Securely block the front wheels. Raise the rear of the car and place it on jackstands.
2. Remove the spare tire and tire carrier.
3. Disconnect the stabilizer bar at the knuckles.
4. Remove stabilizer bar bushing retainers, bushings and bar from the vehicle.
5. Installation is the reverse of removal. Tighten all fasteners to specifications.

Support Beam
Removal/Installation

Refer to **Figure 19** for this procedure.
1. Securely block the front wheels. Raise the rear of the car and place it on jackstands.

2. Remove the complete exhaust system as an assembly. See Chapter Five.
3. Support the transmission with a jack.
4. Remove the support beam bolts at the differential carrier and transmission extension housing.
5. Remove the drive shaft as described in this chapter.
6. Pry the transmission to the driver's side of the car and remove the support beam.
7. Installation is the reverse of removal. Tighten all fasteners to specifications. Seal the drive line support as described in this chapter.

Drive Line Support Sealing

Whenever the support beam is removed and reinstalled, it must be sealed at the mating surfaces of the transmission extension housing and differential carrier. Refer to **Figure 20** for this procedure.
1. Apply sealant at the top and bottom surfaces where the axle (1, **Figure 20**) and transmission extension housing (3, **Figure 20**) meet the drive line support.
2. Apply sealant at the bottom cavity where the axle bolts (2, **Figure 20**) and transmission extension housing bolts (4, **Figure 20**) meet the drive line support. Sealant must be applied completely around the bolts.

DRIVE SHAFT

Corvettes equipped with the automatic transmission (without the power seat option) use a one-piece steel drive shaft; all others use an aluminum drive shaft. A universal joint and splined slip yoke is used at the transmission end of the shaft. A second universal joint connects the drive shaft with the pinion flange at the rear axle.

The universal joints are factory-lubricated and cannot be lubricated while on the car. Cars from the factory may have universal joint bearings installed with a snap ring or a nylon injection ring. A repair kit is available containing a new spider with bearing assemblies and snap rings to overhaul worn universal joints.

Figure 21 shows the drive shaft design.

Removal

> *CAUTION*
> *Do not pound on the yoke ears while removing or installing the drive shaft. This can fracture the nylon injection rings if so equipped.*

1. Securely block the wheels that remain on the ground. Raise the car and place it on jackstands.

10

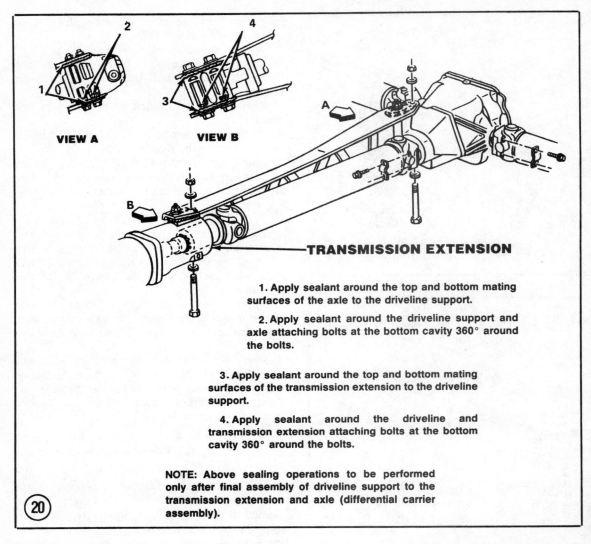

VIEW A

VIEW B

TRANSMISSION EXTENSION

1. Apply sealant around the top and bottom mating surfaces of the axle to the driveline support.

2. Apply sealant around the driveline support and axle attaching bolts at the bottom cavity 360° around the bolts.

3. Apply sealant around the top and bottom mating surfaces of the transmission extension to the driveline support.

4. Apply sealant around the driveline and transmission extension attaching bolts at the bottom cavity 360° around the bolts.

NOTE: Above sealing operations to be performed only after final assembly of driveline support to the transmission extension and axle (differential carrier assembly).

⑳

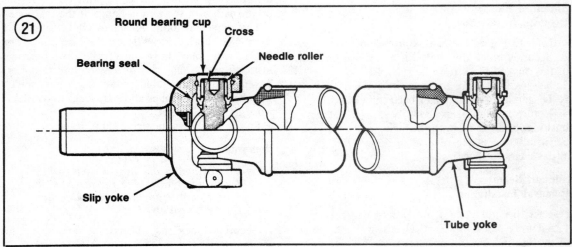

㉑

Round bearing cup

Cross

Bearing seal

Needle roller

Slip yoke

Tube yoke

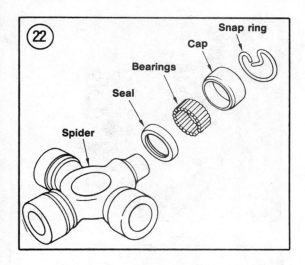

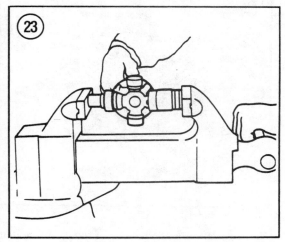

2. Align the rear universal joint to the companion flange. Make sure the bearings are properly seated in the companion flange yoke and that the alignment marks scribed during removal are aligned.

3. Install the retaining bolts and tighten to specifications.

4. Install the support beam as described in this chapter. Apply sealant as described under *Drive Line Support Sealing* in this chapter.

5. Install the exhaust system. See Chapter Five.

6. Remove the jackstands and lower the vehicle to the ground.

UNIVERSAL JOINT SERVICE

The single cardan joint consists of a single spider and 4 sets of needle bearings, bearing seals, caps and snap rings (**Figure 22**). Clamp straps attach the joints to the rear axle and transmission case yokes.

Disassembly (Nylon Injection Rings)

Some production universal joints may be retained by nylon injected rings. Removal of the universal joint destroys the nylon ring and the universal joint must be discarded.

1. Support the lower ear of the drive shaft yoke with a 1 1/8 in. socket on the base plate of a hydraulic press.

2. Install a cross press such as tool part No. J-9522-3 over the open horizontal bearing cup and press the cup from the yoke ear.

3. Rotate the drive shaft 180° and repeat Step 1 and Step 2 to press the opposite bearing cup from the yoke.

4. Remove the spider from the yoke.

Disassembly (Snap Rings)

1. Remove the bearing snap rings from the yoke.

2. Use appropriate size sockets to press bearing cup from yoke with a vise as shown in **Figure 23**.

3. Rotate the drive shaft 180° and repeat Step 2 to remove the opposite bearing cup from the yoke.

4. Remove the spider from the yoke.

Cleaning and Inspection

1. Clean the yoke bearing cap bores with solvent and a wire brush.

2. Wash the bearing caps, bearings and spider in solvent. Wipe dry with a clean shop cloth.

3. Check the caps, bearings and spider for brinelling, flat spots, scoring, cracks or excessive wear. Replace the entire assembly if any part(s) shows such conditions.

2. Disconnect and remove the exhaust system as an assembly. See Chapter Five.

3. Remove the support beam as described in this chapter.

4. Scribe or chalk alignment marks on the shaft and pinion flange for reassembly reference.

5. Disconnect the rear universal joint from the companion flange.

6. Support the drive shaft and tape the bearing cups to the yoke to prevent a loss of the bearing rollers.

7. Move the drive shaft to the rear to disengage it from the transmission, then remove from the vehicle.

Installation

1. Slide the drive shaft into the transmission extension housing carefully to prevent damage to the housing seal.

10

Assembly

1. If replacing original universal joints that had nylon injected retaining rings, remove any remaining sheared plastic from the yoke grooves.
2. Lubricate all components with chassis grease. Wipe the outside of the bearing caps with a thin film of chassis grease.
3. Install the bearing cap seals on the spider.
4. Partially install a bearing cap and needle bearing assembly in the shaft yoke.
5. Place the spider in the shaft yoke. Install the opposite bearing cap and needle bearing assembly in the yoke.
6. Place shaft yoke in vise. Press bearing caps into yoke with an appropriate size socket.
7. Install the bearing cap snap rings.
8. Install the remaining 2 bearing cap and needle bearing assemblies in the spider.
9. Tape the caps on the spider to hold them in place until the drive shaft is reinstalled.

REAR AXLE AND AXLE SHAFTS

This section includes removal, installation and inspection procedures for the rear axle and axle shafts. Rear axle repair requires special skills and many expensive special tools. The inspection procedures will tell you if repairs are necessary.

Axle Shaft
Removal/Installation

1. Remove the center cap from the wheel. Loosen the wheel lug nuts.
2. Securely block the front wheels. Raise the rear of the car and place it on jackstands.
3. Remove the wheel/tire assembly. Remove the cotter pin, spindle nut and washer (**Figure 4**).
4. Remove the cotter pin and castellated nut from the leaf spring link bolt at the knuckle (**Figure 7**). Remove the bushings and link bolt.
5. Remove the cotter pin and castellated nut from the tie rod ball-joint at the knuckle (**Figure 6**). Separate the tie rod from the knuckle with tool part No. J-24319-01 or equivalent.
6. Scribe marks on the cam adjusting bolt and mounting bracket (**Figure 1**) for reassembly reference.
7. Remove the bolt and separate the spindle support rod from the mounting bracket.
8. Disconnect the axle shaft at the spindle and side gear yoke (**Figure 8** shows the side gear yoke).
9. Push outward on the spindle and remove the axle shaft.

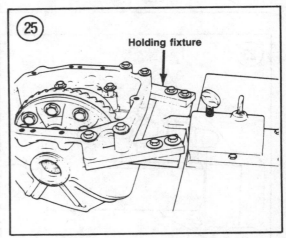

Holding fixture

10. Installation is the reverse of removal. Tighten all fasteners to specifications. Have rear wheel alignment checked by a dealer or front-end shop.

Axle Shaft Universal
Joint Replacement

See *Universal Joint Service* in this chapter.

Differential Carrier and
Cover Removal/Installation

1. Remove the air cleaner. See Chapter Five.
2. Remove the distributor cap. See Chapter Five.
3. Securely block the front wheels. Raise the rear of the car and place it on jackstands.
4. Remove the spare tire. Remove the support hook holding the spare tire cover (**Figure 24**). Remove the cover.
5. Disconnect and remove the exhaust system as an assembly. See Chapter Five.
6. Remove the leaf spring as described in this chapter.

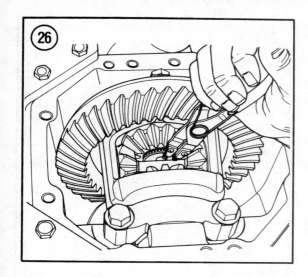

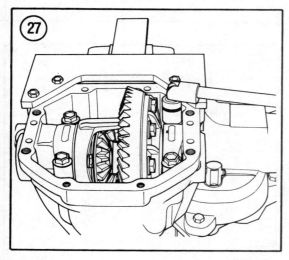

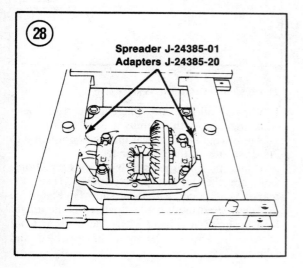

Spreader J-24385-01
Adapters J-24385-20

7. Scribe marks on the cam adjusting bolts and mounting bracket (**Figure 1**) for reassembly reference. Remove the bolts.

8. Remove the cotter pin and castellated nut at each tie rod ball-joint (**Figure 6**). Separate ball-joints from knuckles with tool part No. J-24319-01 or equivalent.

9. Disconnect the axle shafts at the side gear yokes.

10. Push wheel/tire assemblies outward and disengage the axle shafts from the differential.

11. Disconnect the drive shaft at the pinion flange. Push the drive shaft toward the transmission and wire it to the support beam.

12. Support the transmission with a jack.

13. Remove the bolts holding the differential cover/beam to the frame brackets.

14. Remove the bolts holding the support beam at the front of the differential carrier. Remove the carrier from the vehicle.

15. Installation is the reverse of removal. Tighten all fasteners to specifications. Apply sealant to the differential carrier and support beam as described in *Drive Line Support Sealing* in this chapter. Have rear wheel alignment checked by a dealer or front end shop.

Differential
Removal/Installation

1. Remove the differential carrier as described in this chapter.

2. Remove the cover and drain the lubricant.

3. Bolt the carrier to holding fixture part No. J-34162 and mount in base plate part No. J-3389-20. See **Figure 25**.

4. Remove the snap rings holding the yoke shafts in the carrier (**Figure 26**). Remove the yoke shafts.

5. Remove the bearing caps (**Figure 27**), noting the stamped letters on the caps and carrier. Cap letters must be correctly positioned to carrier letters when reinstalled.

6. Mount spreader part No. J-24385-01 and adapter part No. J-24385-20 to carrier. See **Figure 28**.

7. Install a dial indicator as shown in **Figure 29** to measure carrier spread. Spread must not exceed 0.010 in. (0.25 mm).

8. Use a pair of pry bars as shown in **Figure 30** to pry the differential from the carrier. Work carefully to prevent damage to any machined surface.

9. Remove the spreader from the carrier to prevent distortion.

10. Identify and tag the bearing cups for proper reinstallation.

10

11. Installation is the reverse of removal. Use a rawhide or plastic hammer to seat differential in carrier cross bore. Perform *Differential Inspection (In Carrier)* as described in this chapter. Apply a continuous 1/8 in. (3 mm) bead of Loctite 515 or equivalent to carrier and cover sealing surfaces. Tighten all fasteners to specifications.

Differential Inspection (Out of Carrier)

1. Rotate the ring gear and check for broken, chipped or worn teeth. Check the differential for rough movement. Have the differential repaired if these conditions are found.
2. Inspect all bearings and cups for pitting, galling, flat spots or cracks. Replace as necessary.
3. Check the differential case for an elongated or enlarged pinion mate shaft bore.
4. Inspect the mechined surface areas for nicks, gouges, cracks or burrs.
5. Check the carrier for cracks or other damage. Replace the carrier if any of these conditions are found.

Differential Inspection (In Carrier)

1. Mount a dial indicator on the carrier to measure ring gear backlash. The indicator plunger should touch the drive side of a ring gear tooth at right angles to the tooth. Hold the pinion from turning with one hand and rotate the ring gear against the dial indicator with the other.
2. Check at 3 points around the ring gear. Backlash should be 0.005-0.008 in. (0.13-0.20 mm), with less than 0.003 in. (0.08 mm) variation between points checked.
3. If backlash is excessive, remove the differential from the carrier and move some of the shims from the opposite side of the differential case to the ring gear side. This will position the ring gear closer to the pinion.
4. If backlash is low, remove the differential from the carrier and move some of the shims from the ring gear side of the differential case to the opposite side. This will position the ring gear away from the pinion.
5. Install the dial indicator to measure yoke shaft end play. Move yoke shaft in and out and read the indicator. If end play is not 0.0005 in. (0.013 mm), replace the yoke shaft snap rings with thicker or thinner rings as required.

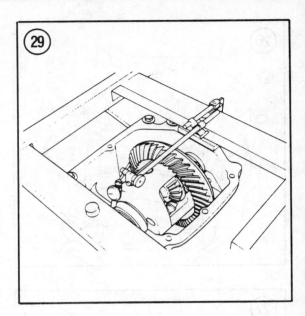

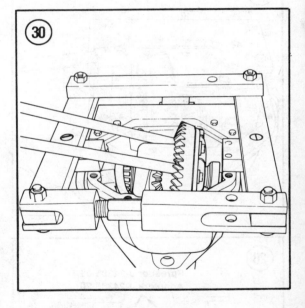

Tooth Contact Pattern Test

1. Wipe all oil from the differential carrier. Clean each ring gear tooth carefully.
2. Apply a light coat of gear marking compound to the drive side of the ring gear teeth.
3. Rotate the ring gear slowly in both directions. Compare the contact pattern pressed into the marking compound with those shown in **Figure 31**.
4. The desired tooth contact pattern under a light load is shown in **Figure 32**. If the pattern is not correct, have the differential disassembled and adjusted.

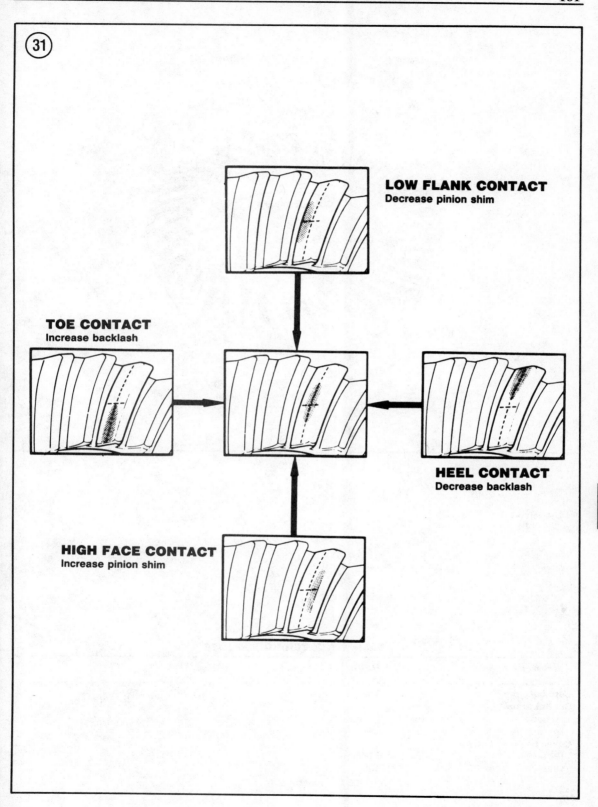

LOW FLANK CONTACT
Decrease pinion shim

TOE CONTACT
Increase backlash

HEEL CONTACT
Decrease backlash

HIGH FACE CONTACT
Increase pinion shim

10

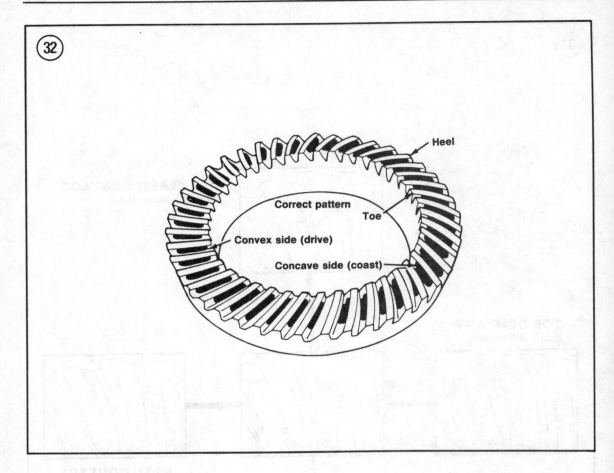

(32)

Heel

Correct pattern   Toe

Convex side (drive)

Concave side (coast)

Table 1 TIGHTENING TORQUES

Fastener	ft.-lb	N•m
Cam bolt	186	252
Control arms		
To body	63	85
To knuckle	140	190
Cover beam to body		
1984-1985	81-95	110-130
1986-on	100	135
	(continued)	

Table 1 TIGHTENING TORQUES (continued)

Fastener	ft.-lb.	N·m
Differential		
Carrier to cover beam		
1984-1985	20-25	27-34
1986-on		
Model 36	21-24	28-33
Model 44	32-38	43-52
Side bearing caps		
1984-1985	40-50	54-68
1986-on		
Model 36	42-48	57-65
Model 44	58-68	79-92
Fill plug	8-11	10-15
Dust shield to backing plate	7	10
Hub and bearing to knuckle	66	90
Jounce bumper to body	35	45
Shock absorber		
Stud to knuckle nut		
1984	51-66	70-90
1985	59-74	80-100
1986-on	80	120
To body		
1984-1985	40-51	55-70
1986-on	66	90
To knuckle		
1984-1985	55-73	75-100
1986-on	65	88
Spindle to hub and bearing	164	222
Stablizer bar to body	18	25
Stabilizer link		
To bracket and bar		
1984-1985	25-35	35-48
1986-on	38	52
Bracket to knuckle	18	25
Support beam		
To differential carrier	60	80
To transmission	52	70
Support rod		
To knuckle	107	145
Bracket to differential	55	75
Tie rod end		
To knuckle	33	45
Locking nut	46	63
Tie rod housing to cover beam		
1984-1985	35-44	48-60
1986-on	54	74

10

(continued)

Table 1 TIGHTENING TORQUES (continued)

Fastener	ft.-lb.	N·m
Transverse spring		
Link bolt	*	*
To cover beam	37	50
Trunnion straps	26	35
Underbody brace		
Nuts	18	25
Bolts	48	65
Wheel lug nuts		
Except spare	100	140
Spare	80	110

* Install nut to expose hole and insert cotter pin.

BRAKES

The Corvette uses 4-wheel disc brakes and a dual hydraulic brake system with 2 independent circuits. A failure in one circuit leaves the other circuit intact and functional. One circuit operates the front disc brakes and the other circuit operates the rear disc brakes. A dual reservoir master cylinder is used, with the front reservoir connected to the front wheels and the rear reservoir connected to the rear wheels.

An anti lock braking system (ABS) is used on 1986 and later Corvettes to maintain vehicle control and stability under severe braking conditions in conjuction with the conventional brake system.

The master cylinder contains an integral proportioning valve/warning switch to regulate outlet pressure to the rear brakes once a predetermined rear input pressure is obtained. The warning switch indicates when pressure in one circuit is low. Increased pedal travel and decreased braking also indicate trouble.

Power brakes are standard. A single diaphragm vacuum booster is mounted on the firewall.

A hand-operated ratchet-type parking brake lever is located between the driver's seat and the door. The handle returns to a horizontal position after application to ease vehicle entry and exit. This lever operates the rear wheels through a series of cables underneath the floor pan.

Tightening torques are provided in **Table 1** at the end of the chapter.

DISC BRAKES

The Corvette front and rear disc brake assemblies use a single piston, sliding caliper. The finned aluminum caliper is suspended in an iron reaction bracket and slides on 2 mounting pins which maintain its position in relation to the rotor and bracket. The vented rotor is separate from the hub.

Pad Removal

NOTE
Work only on one wheel at a time.

Refer to **Figure 1** for this procedure.
1. Set the parking brake. Place the transmission in 1st gear (manual) or PARK (automatic).

① DISC BRAKE

1. Caliper housing
2. Mounting bracket
3. Guide pin boots
4. Guide pins
5. Mounting bolt (self-locking)
6. Outer shoe
7. Inner shoe

11

2. Remove the master cylinder covers. Use a large syringe to remove about two-thirds of the brake fluid from the reservoir.

> *WARNING*
> *Discard this brake fluid. Do not reuse.*

3. Loosen the wheel lug nuts.

4. Securely block the wheels that remain on the ground. Raise the front or rear of the vehicle as required and place it on jackstands.

5. Remove the wheel/tire assembly. Reinstall 2 lug nuts to hold rotor in place.

6. Install a C-clamp as shown in **Figure 2**. One leg of the clamp should rest on the inlet fitting bolt and the other leg against the outer shoe. Tighten clamp until caliper piston bottoms in its bore.

7. Remove and discard the upper caliper self-locking bolt. Pull caliper housing down, rotating it on lower bolt to position shown in **Figure 3**.

8. Remove inner and outer shoes from mounting bracket (**Figure 3**).

Cleaning and Inspection

1. Inspect the disc shoes. Light surface dirt, oil or grease stains may be sanded off. If oil or grease has penetrated the surface, replace the shoes. Since brake fluid will ruin the friction material, the shoes must be replaced if any brake fluid has touched them.

2. Wipe the inside of the caliper housing with a clean dry cloth. Check the piston seal and boot area for brake fluid leaks. If brake fluid has leaked from the caliper housing, replace the caliper. If the leak appears to come from the seal area, rebuild the caliper as described in this chapter.

3. Inspect the brake rotor as described in this chapter.

4. Check guide pin dust boots. If cracked or deteriorated, remove and rebuild caliper as described in this chapter.

5. Clean the mounting bracket abutment surfaces and the inside of the caliper housing legs with a wire brush and crocus cloth to remove any residue, then lubricate lightly with molybdenum-disulfide grease.

Pad Installation

1. Install new inner and outer shoes in the mounting bracket. The shoe with the lining wear sensor is the outer shoe.

2. Rotate caliper housing back into position on the mounting bracket. When properly seated, the shoe springs will not protrude through the caliper inspection hole. If they do, rotate caliper down and reseat.

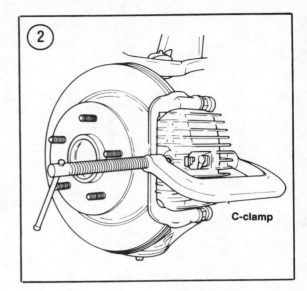

C-clamp

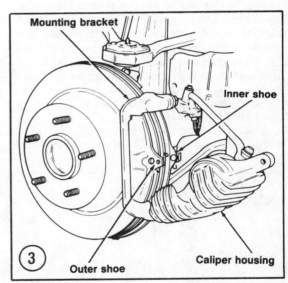

Mounting bracket

Inner shoe

Outer shoe

Caliper housing

3. Install a new self-locking upper mounting bolt and tighten to specifications.

4. Remove lug nuts holding rotor in place. Install wheel/tire assembly.

5. Remove jackstands and lower vehicle to the ground. Tighten lug nuts to specifications.

6. Fill master cylinder reservoir to the proper level with DOT 3 brake fluid. See Chapter Three.

> *WARNING*
> *Do not use brake fluid from a previously opened container. Brake fluid absorbs moisture from the air, which can cause erratic or slow braking.*

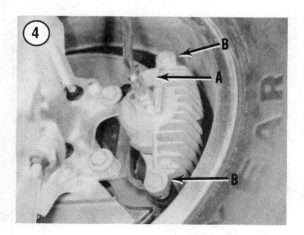

7. Pump brake pedal slowly but firmly 3 times to seat shoes against rotor.

8. Recheck master cylinder fluid level and top up reservoir, if necessary.

9. Road test the car to make sure the brakes operate properly.

Caliper Removal

> *CAUTION*
> *Chevrolet has indicated that incorrectly coated bolts were used on cars manufactured before June 16, 1983 to attach the front brake caliper to the steering knuckle. Return your vehicle to a dealer for inspection and correction, if not already done.*

Omit Step 1 if caliper is being removed only for rotor replacement.

1. Disconnect the inlet fitting at the caliper (A, **Figure 4**). Cap the line to prevent leakage. Discard fitting washers.

> *NOTE*
> *It is not necessary to remove the shoes for caliper removal unless they are being replaced or if the rotor is being removed for service.*

2. Remove and discard the 2 mounting bolts (B, **Figure 4**).

3. Reinstall 2 lug nuts to retain rotor in place (unless rotor is also being removed).

4. Mark the left and right calipers for identification if both are removed.

5. If hydraulic line was not disconnected in Step 1, suspend caliper with a length of wire to prevent stressing the line.

Caliper Overhaul

Refer to **Figure 5** for this procedure.

1. Place the caliper on a clean workbench and drain any remaining fluid.

> *WARNING*
> *Do not attempt to remove the piston from the caliper bore in Step 2 by catching it with your fingers. This can cause serious personal injury.*

2. Fill the caliper interior with shop cloths. Apply compressed air to the brake hose port (**Figure 6**) to remove the piston from the caliper bore.

3. Remove and discard the piston dust boot.

> *CAUTION*
> *Use a plastic or wooden dowel for seal removal in Step 4. Do not pry the seal out with a screwdriver or other metal tool. This can damage the piston bore or burr the seal groove edge.*

4. Remove the piston seal from the caliper bore. Discard the seal.

5. Remove the bleeder screw. Remove the cap from the screw.

6. Remove caliper guide pins and pin boots.

7. Clean the caliper, piston and all other parts not included in the overhaul kit with rubbing alcohol. Make sure all grooves and passages are clean, then blow dry with filtered compressed air.

8. Inspect the caliper piston for wear or damage. The piston has a chrome plating and cannot be refinished. Replace if scored, pitted, nicked, scratched or otherwise damaged.

9. Inspect the caliper bore. If bore is corroded or scored around the seal area, replace caliper housing.

> *CAUTION*
> *Do not use emery cloth, sandpaper or similar abrasives on caliper bore.*

10. Check guide pins. If corroded, install new pins during reassembly.

11. Install bleeder screw and cap. Tighten screw to specifications.

12. Lubricate a new piston seal with clean brake fluid and install it in the bore. The seal should be seated firmly in the groove without twisting it.

13. Lubricate piston and caliper bore with clean brake fluid. Install boot over piston end so that fold in boot faces outward. See **Figure 7**.

14. Hold piston over caliper and seat boot into caliper bore groove by hand. Push piston into caliper until it bottoms in the bore. Check that the boot seats into the piston and caliper bore grooves.

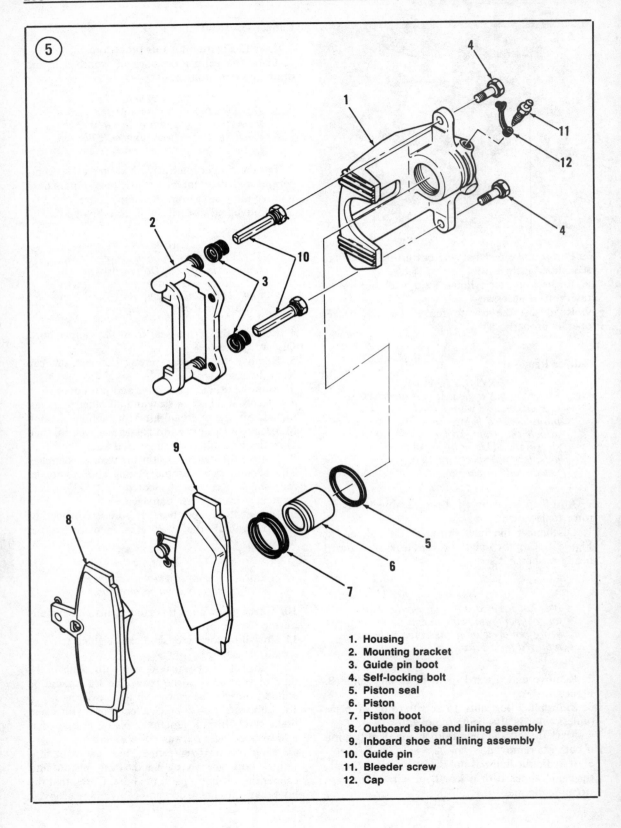

1. Housing
2. Mounting bracket
3. Guide pin boot
4. Self-locking bolt
5. Piston seal
6. Piston
7. Piston boot
8. Outboard shoe and lining assembly
9. Inboard shoe and lining assembly
10. Guide pin
11. Bleeder screw
12. Cap

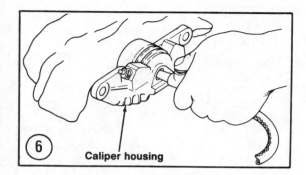

6 Caliper housing

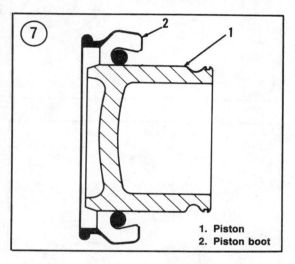

7
1. Piston
2. Piston boot

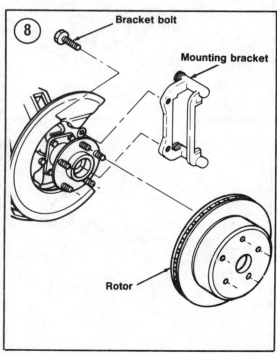

8 Bracket bolt

Mounting bracket

Rotor

15. Coat guide pins with silicone grease and install new pin boots over pins.

16. Fit guide pins into mounting bracket. Boots should fit into the pin grooves and mounting bracket.

Caliper Installation

1. Position caliper housing over rotor and into mounting bracket. Make sure shoe springs do not protrude through the caliper inspection hole.

2. Install new self-locking mounting bolts (B, **Figure 4**) and tighten to specifications.

3. Install inlet fitting to caliper with 2 new washers (if removed) and tighten to specifications.

4. Remove the 2 lug nuts holding the rotor in place. Install the wheel/tire assembly and lower the vehicle to the ground. Tighten the lug nuts to specifications.

5. Refill the master cylinder reservoir to the proper level. See Chapter Three. Use only fresh DOT 3 brake fluid from an unopened container.

> *CAUTION*
> *Do not use brake fluid from a previously opened container. Brake fluid absorbs moisture from the air which can cause erratic or slow braking.*

6. Bleed the brake system as described in this chapter.

7. Pump the brake pedal 3 times to seat the shoes and road test the vehicle to make sure the brakes operate properly.

Front Caliper Mounting Bracket Removal/Installation

Refer to **Figure 8** for this procedure.

1. Remove the caliper housing as described in this chapter.

2. Remove and discard the 2 mounting bracket bolts. Remove mounting bracket.

3. Clean any residual bolt adhesive from mounting bracket mating surface, knuckle mating surface and bracket threads.

4. Installation is the reverse of removal. Use new bracket bolts and tighten to specifications (new bolts are pre-coated with adhesive). Recheck torque immediately, then allow bolt adhesive to dry for 2 hours before driving the car.

Rear Caliper Mounting Bracket Removal/Installation

Refer to **Figure 9** for this procedure.

1. Remove the caliper housing as described in this chapter.

11

2. Remove and discard the upper bracket bolt.

3. Note position of cable bracket, then remove and discard the lower bolt.

4. Remove the mounting bracket.

5. Clean any residual bolt adhesive from mounting bracket mating surface and bracket threads.

6. Install mounting bracket. Position cable bracket tang into mounting plate recess with a new lower bracket bolt.

7. Install new upper mounting bolt (bolt is pre-coated with adhesive). Tighten both bolts to specifications. Recheck torque immediately, then allow bolt adhesive to cure for 2 hours before driving car.

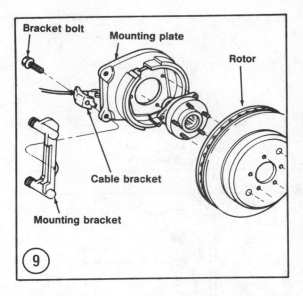

Rotor Runout Measurement

1. Loosen the wheel lug nuts.

2. Securely block the rear wheels. Raise the front of the vehicle and place it on jackstands.

3. Remove the wheel/tire assembly.

4. Reinstall 2 lug nuts to retain rotor on hub.

5. Mount a dial indicator as shown in **Figure 10**. Turn the rotor 360° and note the runout reading on the indicator gauge.

6. If the lateral runout reading obtained in Step 5 is greater than 0.006 in. (0.15 mm), resurface or replace the rotor.

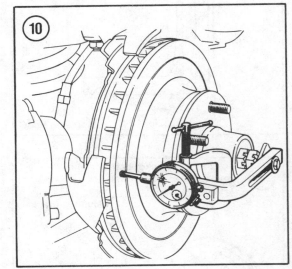

Rotor Removal/Installation

1. Loosen the wheel lug nuts.

2. Securely block the rear wheels. Raise the front of the vehicle and place it on jackstands.

3. Remove the wheel/tire assembly.

4. Remove brake caliper housing as described in this chapter. Do not disconnect the hydraulic line at the caliper inlet fitting. Suspend caliper from knuckle with a length of wire.

5. Remove the caliper mounting bracket as described in this chapter.

6. Remove the rotor from the hub.

7. Installation is the reverse of removal. Tighten all fasteners to specifications.

Rotor Inspection

1. Inspect the rotor for cracks, rust or scratches. Replace the rotor if cracked. Light scoring of the rotor surface that does not exceed 0.015 in. (0.38 mm) in depth is considered normal and does not affect braking action. Light rust can be removed with crocus cloth or medium emery paper. Heavy rust or scratches deeper than 0.015 in. (0.38 mm)

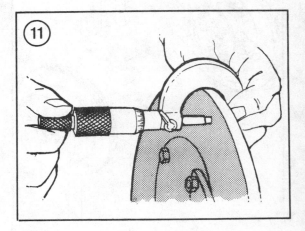

1. Brake line   3. Master cylinder
2. Tubing nut   4. Attaching nut

should be removed by resurfacing the rotor. This can be done by a dealer or a machine shop.

NOTE
If the rotor is resurfaced, equal amounts should be removed from both rotor faces and the finished thickness should not be less than 0.724 in. (18.4 mm). If it is, replace the rotor.

2. Check the rotor thickness with a micrometer at 4 equal points. Take each reading with the micrometer positioned one inch from the edge of the rotor, as shown in **Figure 11**. Resurface or replace the rotor if the measurements vary by more than 0.0005 in. (0.013 mm).

MASTER CYLINDER

The Corvette uses an aluminum and plastic composite master cylinder attached to the power brake booster (**Figure 12**).

Removal/Installation

Refer to **Figure 13** for this procedure.
1. Loosen the tube nuts and disconnect the 3 brake lines at the master cylinder. Cap the lines to prevent leakage.
2. Tape the master cylinder outlet ports closed.

CAUTION
Brake fluid will damage paint. Wipe up any spilled fluid immediately, then wash the area with soap and water.

3. Remove the nuts holding the master cylinder to the power brake booster. Remove the master cylinder.
4. Installation is the reverse of removal. Tighten the attaching nuts to specifications. Fill the master cylinder reservoir with clean DOT 3 brake fluid. See Chapter Three. Bleed the brakes as described in this chapter. Start the engine and depress the brake pedal. Check for external leaks.

Overhaul

Refer to **Figure 14** for this procedure.
1. Clean the outside of the master cylinder with fresh brake fluid or rubbing alcohol.
2. Remove the reservoir caps and diaphragms. Drain the reservoir and discard the fluid.
3. Clamp the master cylinder by one mounting flange in a vise equipped with protective jaws. If protective jaws are not available, wrap the cylinder in shop cloths.
4. Use a wooden dowel to push the primary piston inward and remove the stop bolt from the master cylinder.
5. Holding primary piston assembly depressed, remove snap ring from cylinder bore groove.
6. Remove the primary piston assembly from the bore.
7. Gently tap end of master cylinder housing on workbench to dislodge and remove secondary piston.
8. Remove the primary piston spring.
9. Remove the seal retainer with a small screwdriver. Discard retainer.
10. Remove the primary seal, secondary seal and primary seal washer from the primary piston (**Figure 15**). Discard these parts.
11. Remove the spring locator and spring from the secondary piston.
12. Remove the seal retainer with a small screwdriver. Discard retainer.
13. Remove the primary seal, secondary seals and primary seal washer from the secondary piston (**Figure 16**). Discard these parts.

11

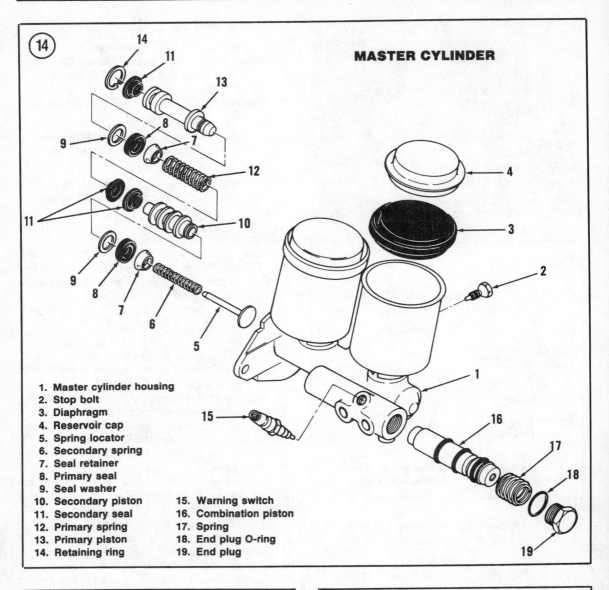

MASTER CYLINDER

1. Master cylinder housing
2. Stop bolt
3. Diaphragm
4. Reservoir cap
5. Spring locator
6. Secondary spring
7. Seal retainer
8. Primary seal
9. Seal washer
10. Secondary piston
11. Secondary seal
12. Primary spring
13. Primary piston
14. Retaining ring
15. Warning switch
16. Combination piston
17. Spring
18. End plug O-ring
19. End plug

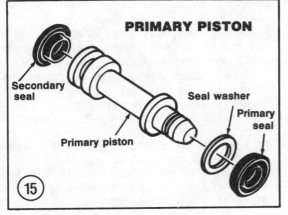

PRIMARY PISTON

Secondary seal

Seal washer

Primary seal

Primary piston

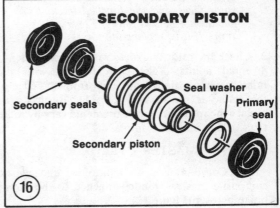

SECONDARY PISTON

Secondary seals

Secondary piston

Seal washer

Primary seal

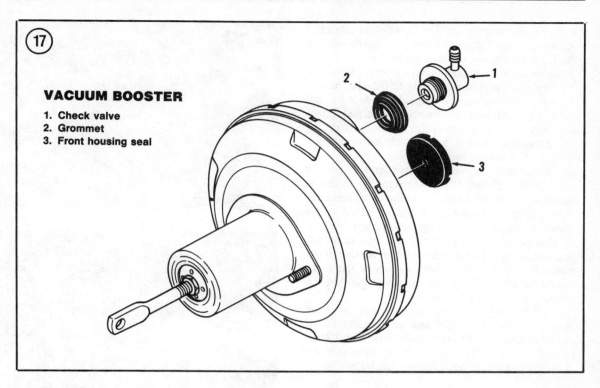

(17)

VACUUM BOOSTER

1. **Check valve**
2. **Grommet**
3. **Front housing seal**

14. Remove the switch assembly from the master cylinder housing. The plastic body, spring and probe should be retained as an assembly.

15. Remove the end plug. Remove the O-ring from the end plug and discard it.

16. Gently tap end of master cylinder housing on workbench to dislodge the combination piston and ground spring. Discard the entire assembly.

17. Clean all parts not included in overhaul kit in rubbing alcohol. Do not clean with gasoline, kerosene or solvents. These leave a residue which can cause rubber parts to soften or swell. Blow dry with filtered compressed air.

18. Check the cylinder bore. Replace if any signs of wear, scoring, pitting or corrosion are found. Do not attempt to refinish the bore by honing.

19. Lubricate secondary piston and new seals with clean brake fluid. Install seals and seal washer. Install seal retainer so that it snaps into the piston groove. See **Figure 16**.

20. Install the secondary spring and spring locator to the secondary piston.

21. Lubricate the master cylinder bore with clean brake fluid. Install the secondary piston and spring assembly.

22. Repeat Steps 19-21 with the primary piston. See **Figure 15**.

23. Depress piston assemblies in master cylinder bore with a wooden or plastic dowel. When both

pistons have bottomed in the bore, install the stop bolt and tighten to specifications.

24. Holding the piston assemblies depressed, install a new snap ring in the bore groove.

25. Install the combination piston spring over the capped end of the new piston included in the overhaul kit.

26. Lubricate the combination piston bore with clean brake fluid. Insert open end of piston in bore and push in place until fully seated.

27. Coat a new O-ring with clean brake fluid and fit it over the threaded end of the end plug.

28. Install and tighten end plug to specifications.

29. Install new diaphragms to the reservoir caps.

POWER BRAKE VACUUM BOOSTER

The power brake vacuum booster (**Figure 17**) is serviced by replacement only. All units have a preset, nonadjustable pushrod. When installing a new booster unit, use the pushrod supplied with the replacement unit, as it has been correctly adjusted to the replacement booster.

Testing

1. Check the brake system for hydraulic leaks. Make sure the master cylinder reservoirs are filled to within 1/4 in. of the rim.

2. Start the engine and let it idle for about 2 minutes, then shut it off. Place the transmission in NEUTRAL and set the parking brake.

3. Depress the brake pedal several times to exhaust any vacuum remaining in the system.

4. When the vacuum is exhausted, depress and hold the pedal. Start the engine. If the pedal does not start to fall away under foot pressure (requiring less pressure to hold it in place), the power booster unit is not working properly.

5. Disconnect the vacuum hose at the booster check valve (**Figure 18**). If vacuum can be felt at the hose with the engine running, reconnect the hose and repeat Step 4. If the brake pedal does not move downward, replace the booster unit.

6. If vacuum cannot be felt at the hose in Step 5, disconnect the vacuum hose filter at the intake manifold (**Figure 19**). If vacuum can be felt at the manifold with the engine running, the filter is plugged and must be replaced.

7. Run the engine for at least 10 minutes at fast idle. Shut the engine off and let it stand for 10 minutes. Depress the brake pedal with about 20 lb. of force. If the pedal feel is not the same as it was with the engine running, replace the booster unit.

**Vacuum Hose and
Filter Inspection**

1. Check the intake manifold-to-vacuum filter and vacuum filter-to-booster check valve for leaks or loose connections.

2. Remove the vacuum filter (**Figure 19**). It should be possible to blow air into one end of the filter but not the other. If air flows both ways or neither way, replace the filter.

Booster Replacement

1. From inside the passenger compartment, remove the pushrod-to-brake pedal retainer clip and washer. Disconnect the booster unit pushrod from the brake pedal.

2. Disconnect vacuum hose at the booster check valve (A, **Figure 20**).

3. Remove the nuts and washers holding the master cylinder to the booster unit (B, **Figure 20**). Do not remove the brake lines from the master cylinder. Set the master cylinder to one side out of the way.

4. From inside the passenger compartment, remove the nuts and washers holding the booster unit to the dash panel. Remove the booster unit.

5. Installation is the reverse of removal. Tighten all fasteners to specifications.

STOPLIGHT SWITCH

The stoplight switch is mounted on the brake pedal arm with a tubular clip (**Figure 21**). Switch design and mounting provides automatic adjustment when the brake pedal is manually returned to its stop position.

Adjustment

1. Hold brake pedal depressed and make sure that switch body is properly seated in tubular clip. As

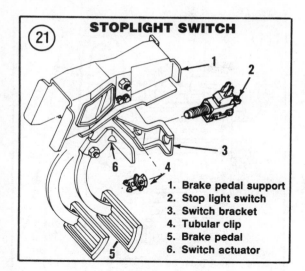

STOPLIGHT SWITCH

1. Brake pedal support
2. Stop light switch
3. Switch bracket
4. Tubular clip
5. Brake pedal
6. Switch actuator

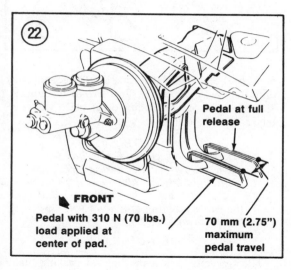

Pedal at full release

FRONT

Pedal with 310 N (70 lbs.) load applied at center of pad.

70 mm (2.75") maximum pedal travel

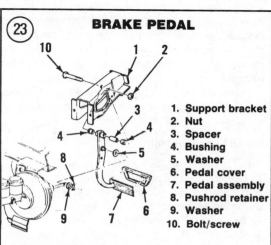

BRAKE PEDAL

1. Support bracket
2. Nut
3. Spacer
4. Bushing
5. Washer
6. Pedal cover
7. Pedal assembly
8. Pushrod retainer
9. Washer
10. Bolt/screw

the threaded portion of the switch is pushed through the clip, you will hear audible clicks.

2. Pull the brake pedal to the rear against its mechanical stop until no clicks can be heard.

3. Release brake pedal and repeat Step 2 to make sure no clicks can be heard. The switch is now properly adjusted.

Removal/Installation

1. Disconnect the switch connector.
2. Rotate the switch and tubular clip to align the clip tang with the bracket slot.
3. Remove the switch.
4. Installation is the reverse of removal. Adjust switch as described in this chapter.

BRAKE PEDAL

Corvettes use a one-piece suspended brake pedal.

Pedal Travel

Refer to **Figure 22** for this procedure.
1. Depress and release the brake pedal several times to exhaust any remaining vacuum in the power assist system.
2. With the brake pedal fully released, measure the distance between the pedal and floorboard.
3. Have an assistant depress and hold the pedal with approximately 70 lb. pressure applied at the center of the pedal pad.
4. Remeasure the distance between the pedal and floorboard. Subtract this from the distance measured in Step 2. If the difference between the 2 measurements exceeds 2.75 in. (68 mm), check the brake shoes for excessive wear. Check brake fluid level.

Pedal Removal/Installation

Refer to **Figure 23** for this procedure.
1. Disconnect the negative battery cable.
2. Remove the close-out panel and disconnect the courtesy light.
3. Remove the pushrod-to-pedal retainer and washer. Disconnect the pushrod from the pedal.
4. Remove the pedal pivot bolt, spacer and bushings. Remove the pedal.
5. Installation is the reverse of removal. Lubricate bushings and all pivot parts with Delco Brake Lube or equivalent. Tighten pedal bolt to specifications. Adjust stoplight switch as described in this chapter.

BRAKE BLEEDING

The hydraulic system should be bled whenever air enters it. Air in the brake lines will compress,

11

rather than transmit pedal pressure to the brake operating parts. If the pedal feels spongy or if pedal travel increases considerably and the pushrod shows no signs of excessive wear, the brakes need to be bled. Bleeding is also necessary whenever a brake line has been disconnected. In general, it is only necessary to bleed that part of the brake system (front or rear) which has been serviced. The following procedure, however, covers bleeding of the entire brake system.

This procedure requires handling brake fluid. Be careful not to get any fluid on brake rotors or pads. Clean all dirt from the bleed valves before beginning. Two people are needed: one to operate the brake pedal and the other to open and close the bleed valves.

Since the brake system consists of 2 individual circuits, each is bled separately. When the rear brake system is bled, raise the front of the car. This is required to properly position the bleed valve and prevent air from being trapped in the caliper. Bleeding should be done in the following order: left rear, right rear, left front, right front.

1. Clean away any dirt around the master cylinder reservoir caps. Remove the caps and top up the master cylinder with Delco Supreme 11 or another brake fluid marked DOT 3.

> *CAUTION*
> *DOT 3 means that the brake fluid meets current Department of Transportation quality standards. If the fluid does not say DOT 3 somewhere on the label, buy a brand that does. Do not use any brake fluid containing silicone. Chevrolet states that this can damage the rubber components in the system.*

2. Attach a plastic tube to the bleed valve. Immerse the other end of the tube in a jar containing several inches of clean brake fluid. See **Figure 24**.

> *NOTE*
> *Do not allow the end of the tube to come out of the brake fluid during bleeding. This could allow air into the system and the bleeding procedure would have to be done over.*

3. Slowly depress the brake pedal 2 or 3 times, then hold it down.
4. With the brake pedal depressed, open the bleed valve 3/4 turn. Let the brake pedal sink to the floor, then close the bleed valve. Do not let the pedal up until the bleed valve is closed.
5. Let the pedal back up slowly. Wait 15 seconds.

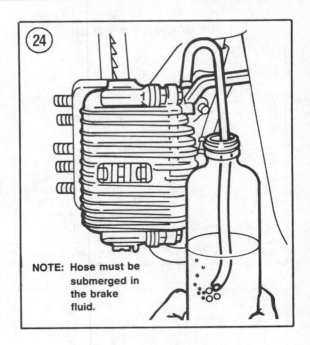

NOTE: Hose must be submerged in the brake fluid.

6. Repeat Steps 3-5 (including the 15 second wait) until the fluid entering the jar is free of air bubbles.
7. Repeat the process for the other bleed valves in the sequence specified.

> *NOTE*
> *Periodically check the brake fluid level in the master cylinder during bleeding. If the fluid level is allowed to drop too low, air will enter the brake lines and the entire bleeding procedure will have to be repeated.*

PARKING BRAKE

The Corvette uses a mechanical parking brake which operates on the duo-servo principle. Applying the parking brake forces the primary shoe against the rotor drum. Force from the primary shoe is transferred to the secondary shoe and multiplied by the wrapping action of drum rotation. Stainless steel strips attached to the aluminum housing prevent excessive or premature wear. All springs and other attaching components are either stainless steel or plated.

Brake Shoe Removal

Refer to **Figure 25** for this procedure.
1. Loosen the rear wheel lug nuts.
2. Securely block the front wheels. Raise the rear of the car and place it on jackstands.
3. Remove the wheel/tire assemblies.
4. Remove the brake caliper housing and mounting bracket as described in this chapter.

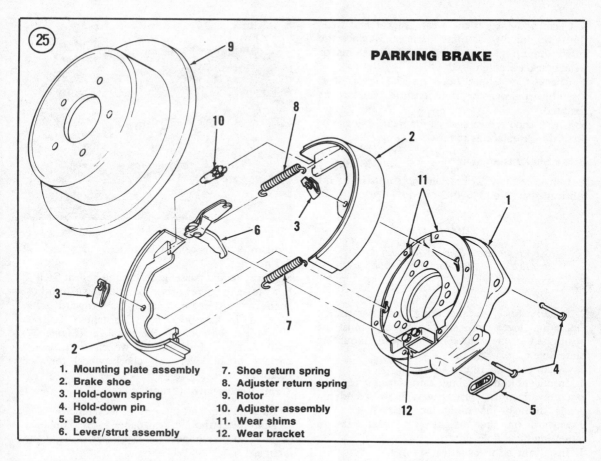

㉕

PARKING BRAKE

1. Mounting plate assembly
2. Brake shoe
3. Hold-down spring
4. Hold-down pin
5. Boot
6. Lever/strut assembly
7. Shoe return spring
8. Adjuster return spring
9. Rotor
10. Adjuster assembly
11. Wear shims
12. Wear bracket

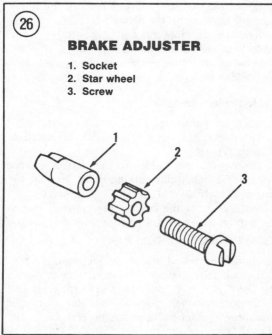

㉖

BRAKE ADJUSTER

1. Socket
2. Star wheel
3. Screw

5. Remove the rotor.

CAUTION
Use care when working near the wear shims on the mounting plate assembly. If shims are damaged, entire mounting plate assembly must be replaced.

6. Spread the primary/secondary shoes and remove the adjuster screw assembly and adjuster spring.
7. Depress hold-down spring and rotate pin until it can be removed from the spring slot. Repeat procedure with remaining spring/pin.
8. Remove the shoe return spring. Remove the primary/secondary shoe assembly. Mark the shoes for reinstallation in the same position as removed.

Cleaning and Inspection

1. Unscrew adjuster assembly and separate into 3 parts as shown in **Figure 26**. Check threads for wear, damage or burring. Replace as required.
2. Clean adjuster assembly components in rubbing alcohol and blow dry with filtered compressed air. Reassemble adjuster.

11

3. Clean and inspect the wear bracket and wear shims for burring or other damage. Replace the entire mounting plate assembly if the shims or wear bracket are damaged.

4. Check the rubber boot on the lever strut assembly for wear or deterioration. Replace as required.

5. Check shoe return springs for wear, damage or distortion. Replace as required.

Brake Shoe Installation

1. Lubricate the wear bracket and shims with GM lubricant part No. 5450032 or equivalent.

> *NOTE*
> *Primary and secondary shoe assemblies are identical but should be installed in the same position as removed.*

2. Install shoes to mounting plate assembly. Operating lever and strut assembly must be positioned on the wear shim, not in the mounting plate hole.

3. Install the shoe return spring.

4. Install hold-down pins and springs to shoe assembly. Depress springs enough to extend pin heads through the mounting plate holes. Pull downward on shoe assembly to seat pins in mounting plate hole slots.

5. Install the adjuster return spring.

6. Install adjuster assembly with star wheel facing toward front of vehicle.

7. Install the rotor, mounting bracket and caliper as described in this chapter. Adjust parking brake as described in this chapter.

Adjustment

1. Loosen the rear wheel lug nuts.

2. Securely block the front wheels. Raise the rear of the car and place it on jackstands.

3. Remove the wheel/tire assemblies. Reinstall 2 lug nuts to hold the rotor in place.

4. Install a C-clamp as described in Step 6, *Pad Removal* and seat caliper piston in bore. Repeat on other wheel.

5. Loosen the parking brake cable to relieve any tension at the parking brake shoes.

6. Turn the rotor to align the hole in the rotor/drum face with the adjuster star wheel.

7. Insert a flat blade screwdriver through the hole in the rotor/drum face on the driver's side and engage the adjuster star wheel. Move the screwdriver handle up to adjust shoes outward or down to adjust the shoes inward. Turn star wheel

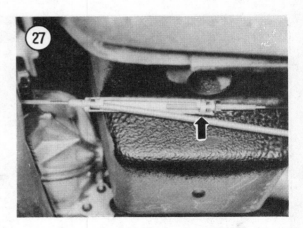

until rotor/drum cannot be turned, then back off 5-7 notches.

8. Move to the passenger side and repeat Step 7, but move the screwdriver handle down to adjust shoes outward or up to adjust them inward.

9. Apply parking brake lever 2 notches.

10. Adjust the cable at the equalizer (**Figure 27**) until there is drag on the wheel. Release the parking brake lever and check wheel for free rotation.

Cable Replacement (Front)

1. Raise the car and place it on jackstands.

2. Disconnect the left rear cable at the equalizer (**Figure 27**). Disconnect the right rear cable at the retainer.

3. Lower the car part-way and remove the lower door sill molding on the driver's side.

4. Remove the cable nut and guide. Remove the cable from the vehicle.

5. Installation is the reverse of removal. Adjust the parking brake as described in this chapter.

Cable Replacement (Left Rear)

1. Raise the car and place it on jackstands.

2. Disconnect the left rear cable at the equalizer (**Figure 27**).

3. Disconnect the cable at the frame, caliper mounting bracket and parking brake lever at the rear of the wheel.

4. Installation is the reverse of removal. Adjust the parking brake as described in this chapter.

Cable Replacement (Right Rear)

1. Raise the car and place it on jackstands.

2. Loosen the equalizer tension enough to permit the right cable to be disconnected at the retainer.

3. Disconnect the cable at the frame, caliper mounting bracket and parking brake lever at the rear of the wheel.

4. Installation is the reverse of removal. Adjust the parking brake as described in this chapter.

Parking Brake Lever
Removal/Installation

Refer to **Figure 28** for this procedure.
1. Securely block the wheels that remain on the ground. Raise the car and place it on jackstands.
2. Loosen the equalizer tension enough to permit cable removal at the parking brake lever clevis. Disconnect the cable at the clevis.
3. Remove the jackstands and lower the car to the ground.
4. Remove the lower door sill molding on the driver's side.
5. Disconnect the parking brake electrical connector.
6. Remove the 2 parking brake lever attaching bolts. Remove the lever assembly.
7. Installation is the reverse of removal. Tighten fasteners to specifications. Adjust the parking brake as described in this chapter.

ANTI-LOCK BRAKING SYSTEM (ABS)

An electronically-controlled system on 1986 and later Corvettes monitors the rotational speed of all four wheels, modulating hydraulic pressure to each wheel during braking. This prevents wheel lock-up, giving the driver maximum control during severe braking conditions. **Figure 29** shows the anti-lock braking system components.

When the ignition is turned ON, an amber Anti-Lock warning lamp on the instrument panel lights. Once the engine starts, the light goes out. If it does not go out, or if it comes on and stays on during driving, there is a malfunction in the system.

The electronic control unit (ECU) monitors battery voltage. If battery voltage drops below a specified value, the ECU turns off the ABS system and the amber warning light will come on until battery voltage rises above the specified level. If the ABS malfunctions, the ECU will shut the system off. The conventional braking system is

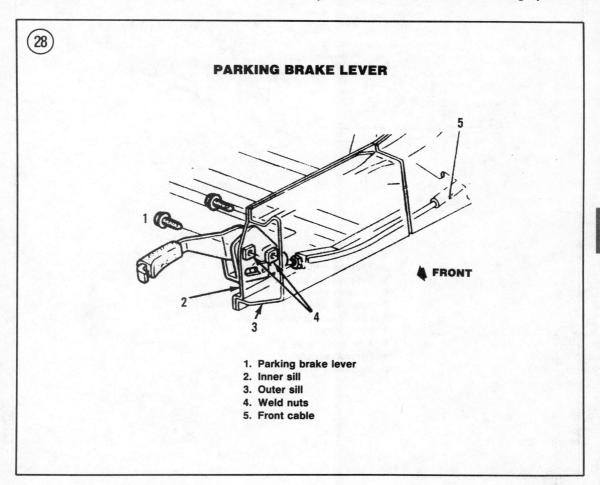

(28)

PARKING BRAKE LEVER

FRONT

1. Parking brake lever
2. Inner sill
3. Outer sill
4. Weld nuts
5. Front cable

11

fully operational at all times, whether or not the ABS is working.

Since the ABS components are not adjustable or repairable, any malfunction of the system should be referred to a dealer for testing and service. The only recommended owner service is to check the fuses in the main fuse panel. The GAUGE and BRAKE fuses protect the ABS main power feed circuit.

The function of this system is directly related to your safety and only a qualified technican should troubleshoot and service a malfunction.

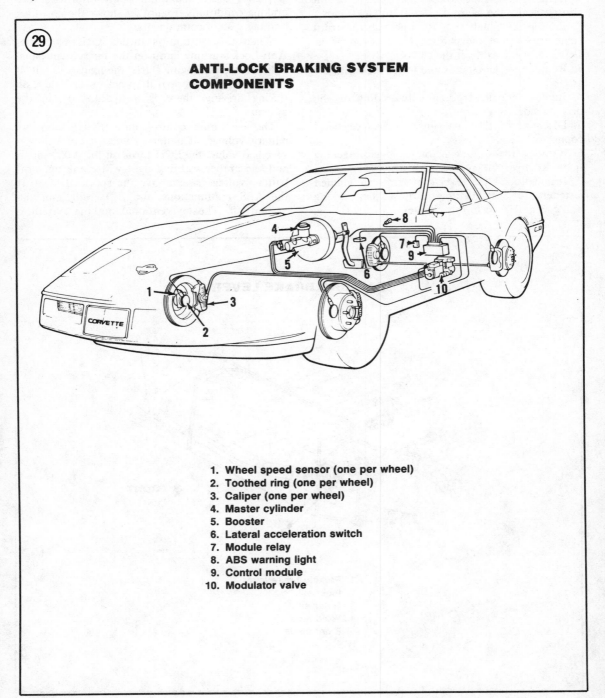

(29)

ANTI-LOCK BRAKING SYSTEM COMPONENTS

1. Wheel speed sensor (one per wheel)
2. Toothed ring (one per wheel)
3. Caliper (one per wheel)
4. Master cylinder
5. Booster
6. Lateral acceleration switch
7. Module relay
8. ABS warning light
9. Control module
10. Modulator valve

Table 1 TIGHTENING TORQUES

Fastener	ft.-lb.	N·m
Brake line		
Clip-to-frame	4	6
Clip-to-sill	7	9.5
Nut-to-master cylinder	13	18
Nut-to-front brake hose	13	18
Nut-to-rear brake hose	13	18
Caliper		
Bleeder screw	6-8	8-11
Hose fitting	32	44
Mounting bolts		
Front	70	95
Rear	44	60
Mounting bracket bolts		
Front	63-70	85-95
Rear	30-44	40-60
Front brake shield	7	10
Master cylinder attaching nuts	15	21
Parking brake lever bolts		
Front	26	35
Rear	19	25
Pedal pivot nut	22	30
Power booster attaching nuts	15	21
Rear cable bracket	35	47
Stoplight switch		
Bracket-to-pedal support	3	4.5
Actuator-to-pedal arm	18	24
Wheel hub-to-knuckle	46	62
Wheel lug nut	100	140

11

CHAPTER TWELVE

BODY

The Corvette uses a new type of unitized construction consisting of an integral perimeter birdcage frame (**Figure 1**). The all-welded birdcage is galvanized steel, with bolted-on aluminum front and rear extensions. Exterior panels manufactured of various molding compounds are attached to the birdcage to form the finished body. The dash, plenum, front/rear underbody panels, door sealing panel, roof and quarter panels are adhesively bonded to the uniframe.

This chapter provides service procedures for the front/rear fascia/bumpers, front fenders, hood, doors, door windows, seats, instrument panel trim pads and console. Where appropriate, electrical wiring connectors and switch/relay locations are shown.

No special tools are required for any of these procedures. Other body repairs require special skills and tools and should be left to a dealer or body shop.

FRONT FASCIA

Refer to **Figure 2** for this procedure.
1. Remove the fascia-to-chassis attaching screws.
2. Remove the side marker lamp assemblies. See Chapter Seven.
3. Remove the fascia-to-fender bolts at the side marker lamp openings.
4. Remove the inner wheelwell-to-fascia bolts.
5. Remove the fascia-to-support bolts.
6. Remove the fascia.
7. Installation is the reverse of removal. Make sure the clearance between the fascia and hood does not exceed 5/32 in. (4 mm).

REAR FASCIA

Refer to **Figure 2** for this procedure.
1. Remove the tail lamp assemblies. See Chapter Seven.
2. Remove the push retainers from along the upper and under edges of the fascia.
3. Remove the side marker lamp assemblies. See Chapter Seven.
4. Remove the bolts on each side of the fascia.
5. Remove the wheelwell bolts on each side of the fascia.
6. Remove the fascia.
7. Installation is the reverse of removal.

FRONT/REAR BUMPERS

The fascias form the bumper face bars. A honeycomb energy absorbing unit attached to a metal bar under the fascia constitutes the bumper.

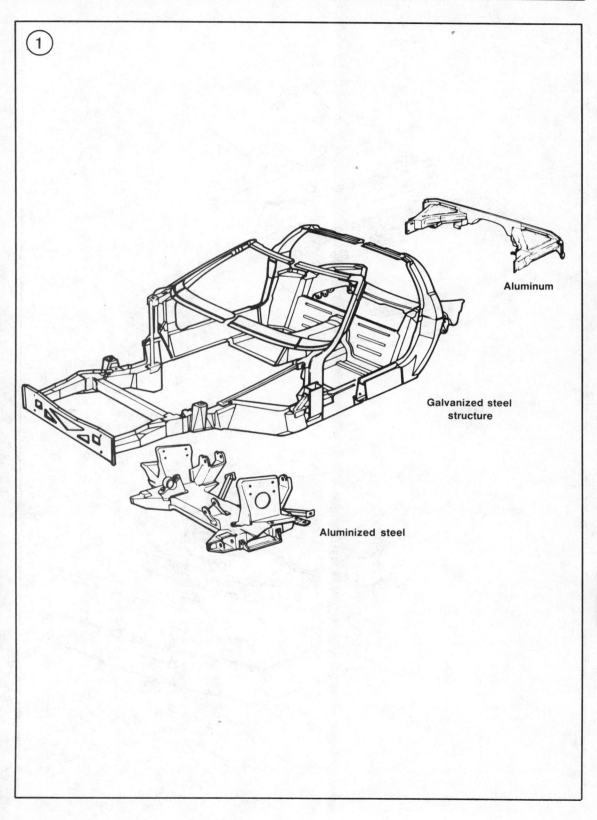

Aluminum

Galvanized steel
structure

Aluminized steel

12

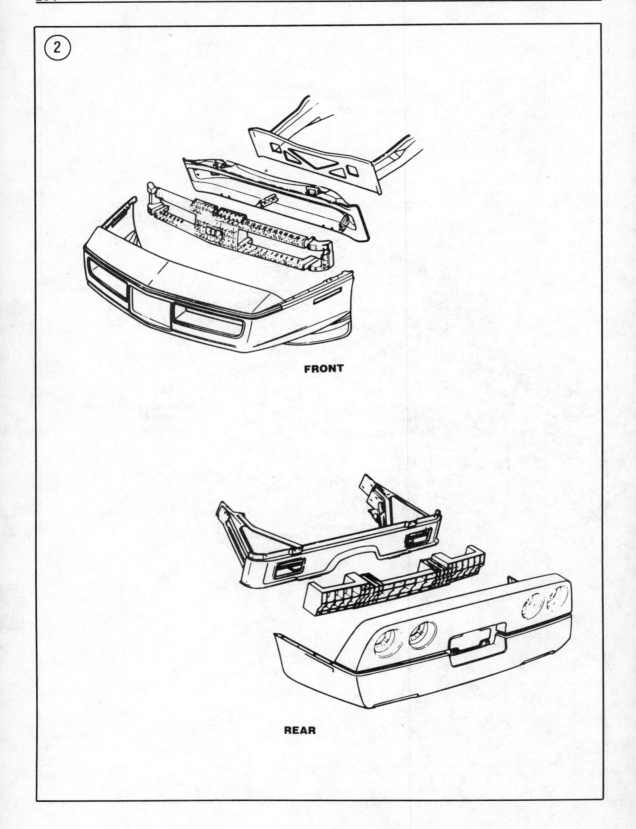

②

FRONT

REAR

This energy absorbing unit is designed to withstand a 2.5 mph impact. If the bumper does not return to its original position, the energy absorbing unit must be replaced.

1. Remove the front or rear fascia, as required.

2. Front bumper—Remove the reinforcement assembly along the upper edge of the bumper.

3. Remove the absorber and bumper bar assembly.

4. Drill out the push retainers holding the energy absorbing unit to the bumper bar. Remove and discard the energy absorbing unit.

5. Install a new energy absorbing unit to the bumper bar with new push retainers.

6. Reverse Steps 1-3 to complete installation.

FRONT FENDER

Refer to **Figure 3** for this procedure.
1. Raise and support the hood.
2. Disconnect the negative battery cable.
3. Remove the 3 fender-to-splash shield screws.
4. Remove the 2 fender-to-brace retaining screws at the rear of the fender. Remove the fender seal.
5. Carefully separate fender tabs from rocker and inner wheelwell panels, then remove the fender from the vehicle.
6. Installation is the reverse of removal.

HOOD

Adjustment

Make hood adjustments in the order specified. Refer to **Figure 4** for this procedure.

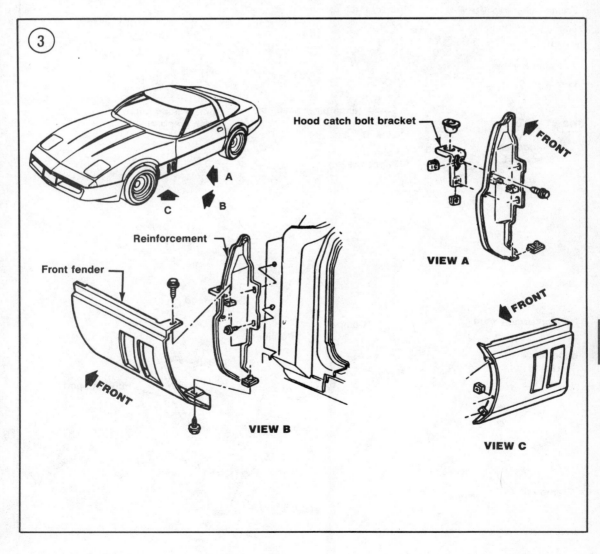

③

Hood catch bolt bracket

A
B
C

VIEW A

Reinforcement

Front fender

FRONT

VIEW B

FRONT

VIEW C

12

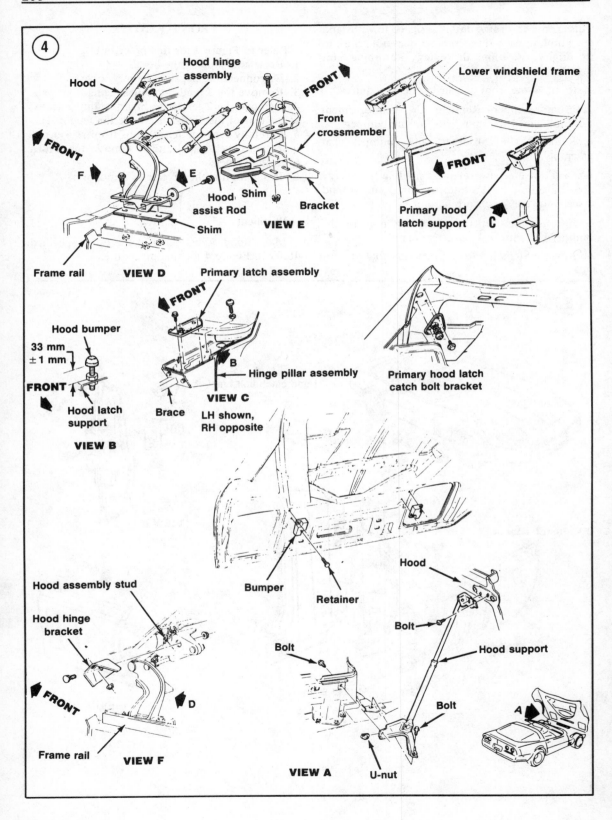

④

Hood

Hood hinge
assembly

FRONT

Front
crossmember

Lower windshield frame

FRONT

FRONT

F

E

Hood
assist Rod

Shim

Bracket

Primary hood
latch support

C

Shim

VIEW E

Frame rail

VIEW D

Primary latch assembly

FRONT

Hood bumper

33 mm
± 1 mm

B

Hinge pillar assembly

Primary hood latch
catch bolt bracket

FRONT

Hood latch
support

Brace

VIEW C

LH shown,
RH opposite

VIEW B

Hood assembly stud

Hood hinge
bracket

Hood

Bolt

FRONT

D

Bumper

Retainer

Bolt

Hood support

Bolt

Frame rail

VIEW F

Bolt

VIEW A

U-nut

A

1. To align hood laterally:
   a. Loosen the hinge nuts at each side.
   b. Reposition hood and tighten nuts.
2. To move the hood forward or to the rear:
   a. Loosen the hood hinge frame bolts at each side.
   b. Align the hood as necessary, then tighten the bolts.
3. If the hood is too high or low at the rear corners:
   a. Determine how much adjustment is required and in what direction.
   b. Loosen either the lock and bolt assemblies or the latch assembly.
   c. Reposition the hood as required, then tighten the lock/bolt assemblies or latch assembly.

Removal/Installation

This procedure requires the help of an assistant. Refer to **Figure 4**.
1. Raise and support the hood.
2. Disconnect the underhood lamp wire, if so equipped.
3. Disconnect the negative battery cable.
4. Remove the 8 upper wheelhouse screws at the hood panel on each side of the vehicle.
5. Remove the 2 underhood lamps.
6. Remove the 3 bolts holding the bolt/spring assemblies on each side of the vehicle.
7. Disconnect the headlamp wire connectors, then remove the lamps from the hood. See Chapter Seven.
8. Remove all remaining fasteners and clips.
9. Remove the hood support rod.
10. Use a soft lead pencil to make alignment marks around the hinges and hood supports directly on the hood. The marks will make installation easier.
11. While an assistant supports one side of the hood, remove the 2 hinge-to-hood nuts.
12. Support your side of the hood while the assistant removes the other 2 hinge-to-hood nuts. Lift the hood off and place it out of the way. If hinges are removed, note the location and number of shims used on each side for reinstallation reference.

> *CAUTION*
> *Do not place the hood flat on the floor or ground. Lean it up against a wall or other solid object to prevent damage.*

13. Installation is the reverse of removal. Align the marks made before removal. If necessary, adjust the hood as described in this chapter.

DOORS

Removal/Installation

Refer to **Figure 5** for this procedure.
1. Raise and support the hood.
2. Disconnect the negative battery cable.
3. Tape the door and body pillars with cloth-backed body tape.
4. Remove the trim panel as described in this chapter.
5. Carefully remove the water deflector with a putty knife.
6. Disconnect all electrical connectors inside the door and pull the wiring harness conduit out of the door.
7. Mark the location of the hinges on the door with a soft lead pencil.
8. Remove the door-to-upper hinge attaching bolts.
9. Support the door. Remove the door-to-lower hinge attaching bolts.
10. Slide the door off its hinges and remove from the vehicle.
11. Installation is the reverse of removal. Tighten hinge attaching bolts to 15-25 ft.-lb. Check for proper engagement with striker and adjust as described in this chapter, if necessary.

Striker Adjustment

The striker bolt can be shimmed with washers to obtain the desired clearance between the door lock fork and striker. Four thicknesses of washers are available from your dealer.
1. Clean the lock fork and striker area, then apply modeling clay or body caulking to the lock bolt opening. See **Figure 6**.
2. Close the door just enough to make a visible impression in the clay or caulking. Dimension X in **Figure 6** should be a minimum of 3/32 in. (2 mm).
3. If adjustment is required, remove the striker bolt with tool part No. J-23457.
4. Install the appropriate spacers under the striker bolt to obtain the desired clearance.
5. Install the striker bolt with the spacers and tighten to 40 ft.-lb.
6. Repeat Step 1 and Step 2 to recheck clearance.

Trim Panel
Removal/Installation

The trim panel is attached to the door inner panel by screws. The armrest and accessory trim plate are fastened in place with screws after the trim panel is installed. Refer to **Figure 7** for this procedure.

12

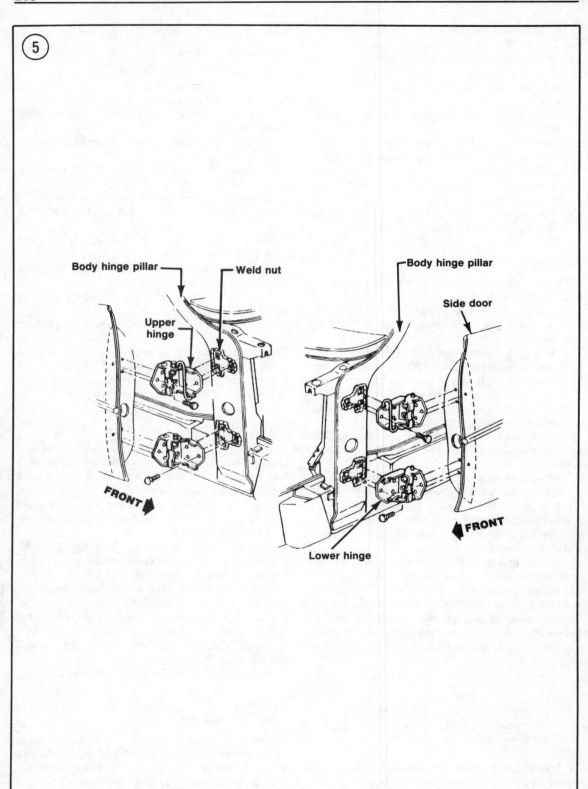

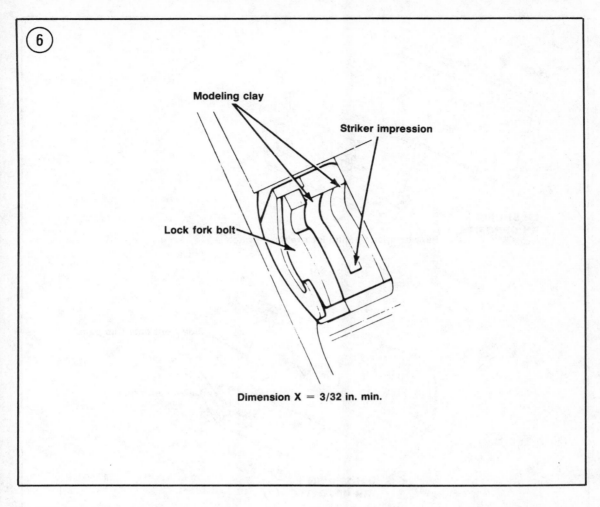

Dimension X = 3/32 in. min.

1. Disconnect the negative battery cable.

2. Remove the 2 armrest attaching screws. Push inward on the armrest to disengage its plastic hooks from the trim panel slot, then remove the armrest.

3. Remove the speaker grille.

4. Remove the 5 accessory trim plate screws. One screw is located behind the door release handle.

5. Left door—Disconnect the hatch lid release switch, door lock connector and wiper/washer switch. See **Figure 8** and **Figure 9**.

6. Remove the remote control plate and courtesy lamp.

7. Remove the upper molding and air outlet.

8. Installation is the reverse of removal.

Door Window
Removal/Installation

Refer to **Figure 10** for this procedure.

1. Remove the trim panel as described in this chapter.

2. Carefully remove the water deflector with a putty knife.

3. Mark the location of the 2 anti-rattle pads, then loosen the pads and move as required for glass removal.

4. Position the window glass as required to access glass nut holes in the inner mounting plate.

5. Mark the position and remove the stabilizing guide and glass top.

6. Remove the 3 nuts holding the glass to the regulator.

7. Remove the glass with studs and stop through the slot at the top of the door.

8. Installation is the reverse of removal.

SEATS

The bucket seats are secured to adjuster track assemblies. The track assembly is fastened to the floorpan of the vehicle. If removing both bucket seats, perform the procedure on each seat.

12

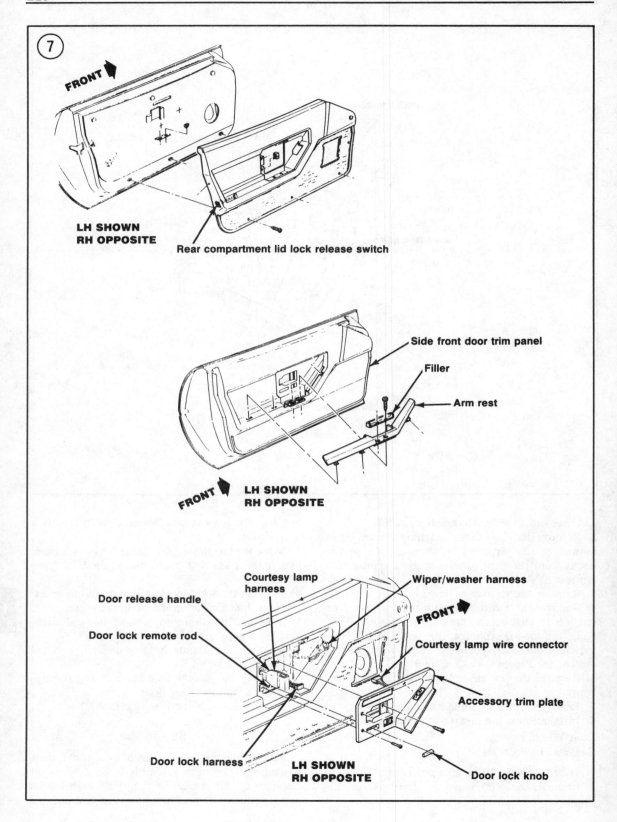

⑦

FRONT ►

LH SHOWN
RH OPPOSITE

Rear compartment lid lock release switch

Side front door trim panel

Filler

Arm rest

FRONT ►   LH SHOWN
RH OPPOSITE

Courtesy lamp
harness

Door release handle

Door lock remote rod

Wiper/washer harness

FRONT ►

Courtesy lamp wire connector

Accessory trim plate

Door lock harness

LH SHOWN
RH OPPOSITE

Door lock knob

Removal/Installation

Refer to **Figure 11** for this procedure.

1. Move the seat to its full forward position. Pull seat back forward to uncover rear support bracket bolts. Remove the nuts.

2. Reposition the seat back and move the seat assembly to its full rearward position. Remove the trim cover over the front support bolts. Remove the nuts.

3. Driver's seat—Reach under the seat and disconnect the motor-to-switch and switch harness-to-body harness connectors. See **Figure 12**.

4. Remove the seat and track assembly from the vehicle.

5. To separate the track assembly from the seat, invert the seat on a clean workbench.

6. Remove the track-to-seat bolts. Separate the track from the seat.

7. Installation is the reverse of removal.

INSTRUMENT PANEL TRIM PADS

Upper Trim Pad
Removal/Installation

Refer to **Figure 13** for this procedure.
1. Disconnect the negative battery cable.

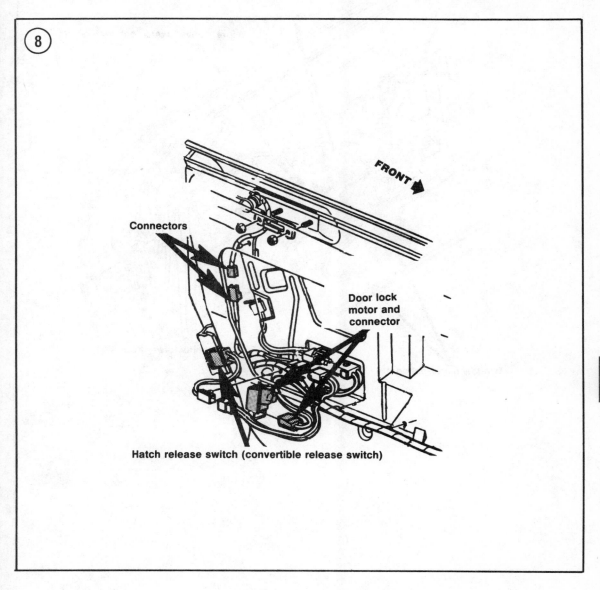

⑧

FRONT

Connectors

Door lock motor and connector

Hatch release switch (convertible release switch)

12

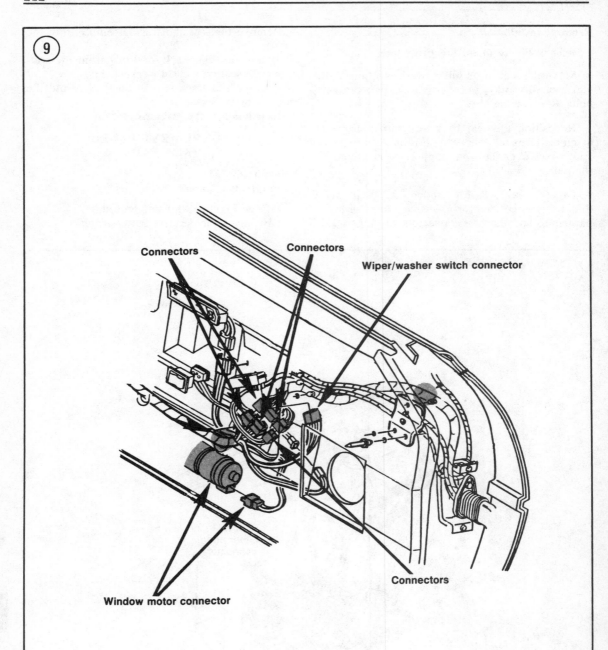

⑨

Connectors

Connectors

Wiper/washer switch connector

Connectors

Window motor connector

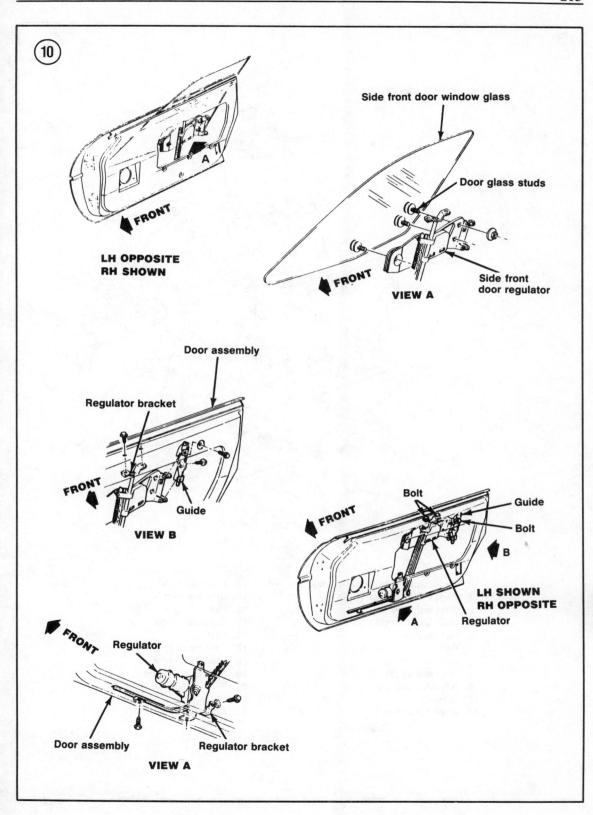

10

**LH OPPOSITE
RH SHOWN**

FRONT

Side front door window glass

Door glass studs

Side front
door regulator

FRONT

VIEW A

Door assembly

Regulator bracket

FRONT

Guide

VIEW B

Bolt

Guide

Bolt

FRONT

B

**LH SHOWN
RH OPPOSITE**

A

Regulator

12

FRONT

Regulator

Door assembly

Regulator bracket

VIEW A

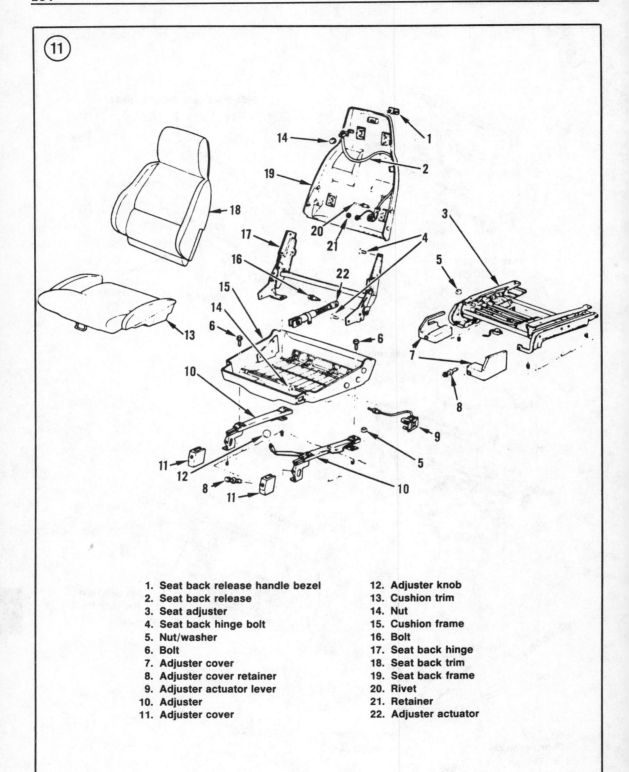

1. Seat back release handle bezel
2. Seat back release
3. Seat adjuster
4. Seat back hinge bolt
5. Nut/washer
6. Bolt
7. Adjuster cover
8. Adjuster cover retainer
9. Adjuster actuator lever
10. Adjuster
11. Adjuster cover
12. Adjuster knob
13. Cushion trim
14. Nut
15. Cushion frame
16. Bolt
17. Seat back hinge
18. Seat back trim
19. Seat back frame
20. Rivet
21. Retainer
22. Adjuster actuator

2. Remove the instrument panel cluster bezel (**Figure 14**).

3. Remove the steering column tilt lever.

4. Remove the 5 screws holding the instrument panel pad to the carrier.

5. Remove the 2 defroster duct screws.

6. Carefully disengage the upper trim pad from the carrier. Reach under the pad and disconnect the radio speakers, then remove the pad from the vehicle.

7. Installation is the reverse of removal.

Lower Trim Pads
Removal/Installation

Refer to **Figures 15-17** for this procedure.

1. Disconnect the negative battery cable.

2. Remove the upper trim pad as described in this chapter.

3. Remove the right side close-out panel.

4. Remove the trim and fuse panel plate (right side).

5. Remove the right side flexible A/C hose and duct.

6. Remove the 2 carrier-to-side glass defroster hose screws.

7. Remove the right front trim pad.

8. Remove the right lower carpeted panel.

9. Remove the lower trim pads.

10. Installation is the reverse of removal.

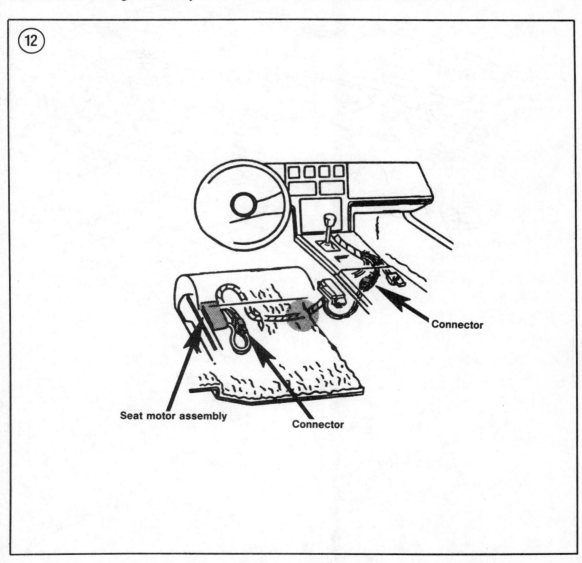

(12)

Connector

Seat motor assembly

Connector

12

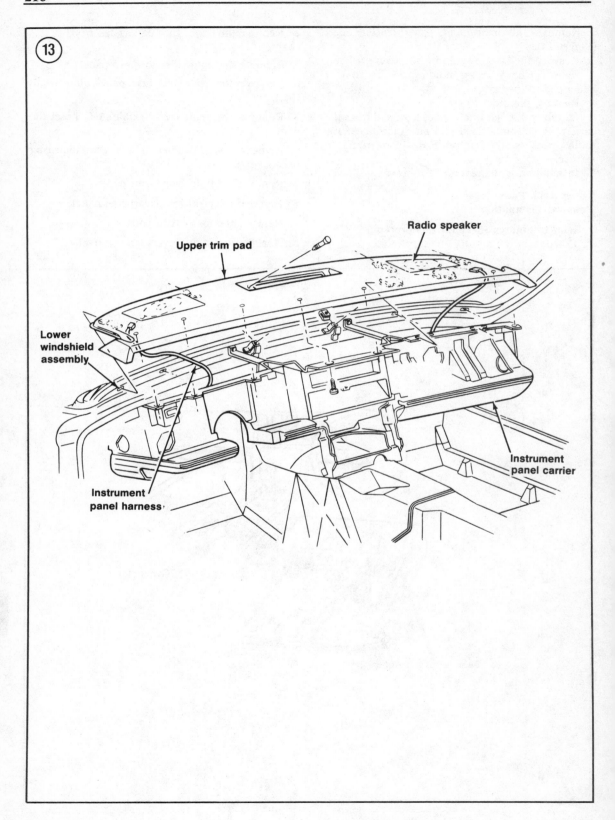

(13)

Upper trim pad

Radio speaker

Lower windshield assembly

Instrument panel harness

Instrument panel carrier

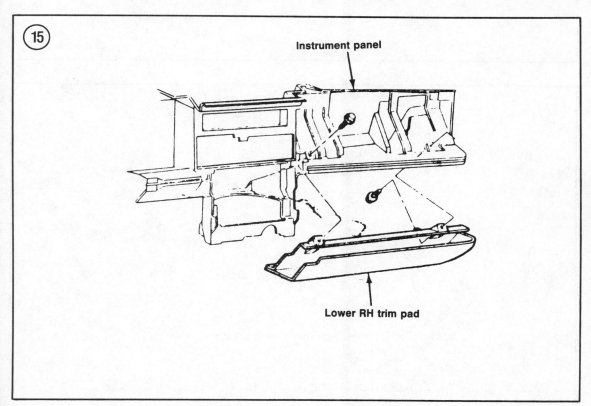

14

Instrument panel

A/C air side
outlet seal

Side window
defroster seal

Headlamp
switch knob

15

Instrument panel

Lower RH trim pad

12

CONSOLE

Trim Plate Removal/Installation

Refer to **Figure 18** for this procedure.

1. Disconnect the negative battery cable.

2. Remove the 2 screws from the lower part of the instrument panel bezel.

3. Remove the shift lever knob.

4. Remove the screws holding the console plate. Lift the plate enough to disconnect the bulb connectors, then remove the plate.

**Console Compartment and
Side Trim Panel
Removal/Installation**

Figures 19-22 show details of accessory trim plate, side trim panel and console compartment removal/installation. **Figure 23** and **Figure 24** show electrical connections underneath the console.

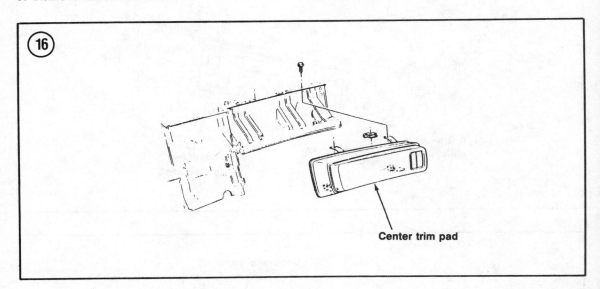

(16)

Center trim pad

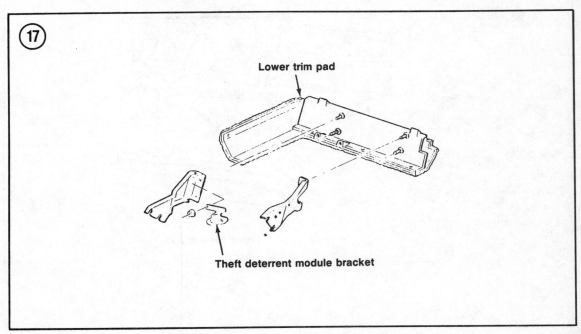

(17)

Lower trim pad

Theft deterrent module bracket

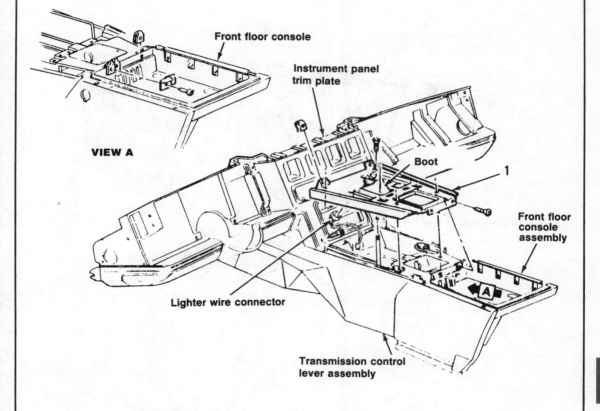

1. Trim plate assembly — front floor console

Front floor console

Instrument panel
trim plate

VIEW A

Boot

1

Front floor
console
assembly

Lighter wire connector

A

Transmission control
lever assembly

12

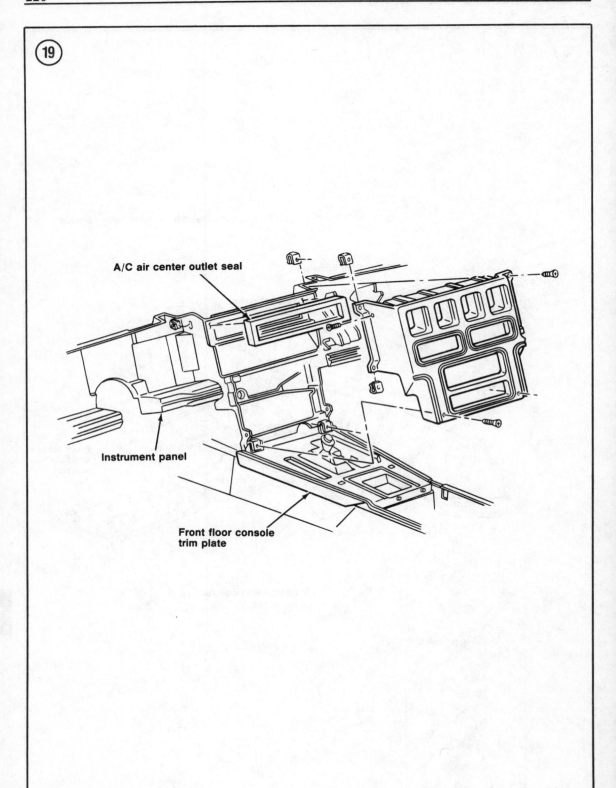

A/C air center outlet seal

Instrument panel

Front floor console
trim plate

(20)

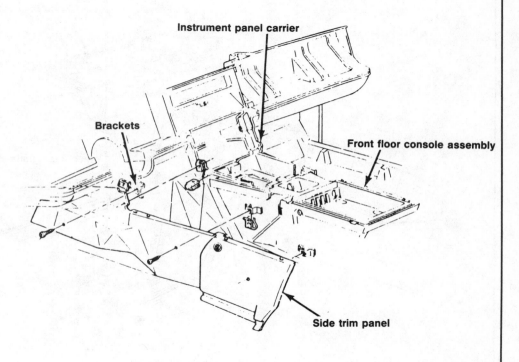

Instrument panel carrier

Brackets

Front floor console assembly

Side trim panel

12

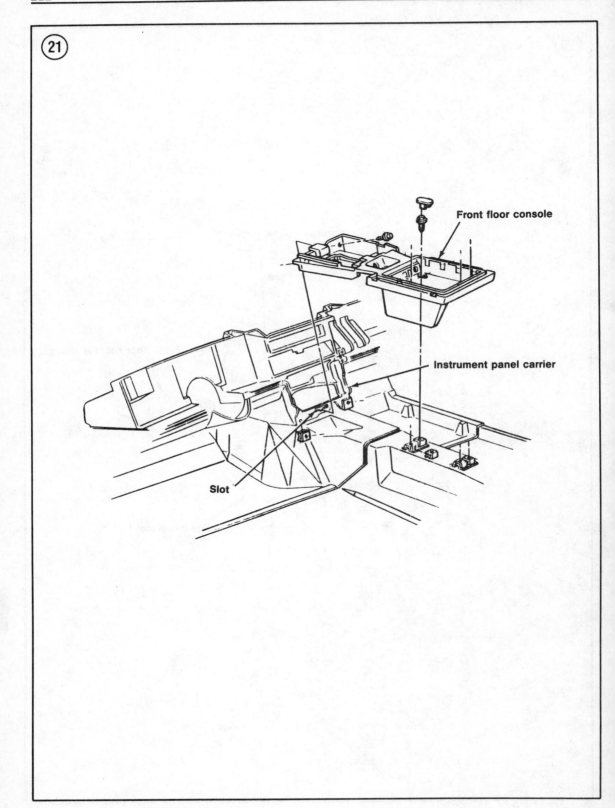

Front floor console

Instrument panel carrier

Slot

㉒

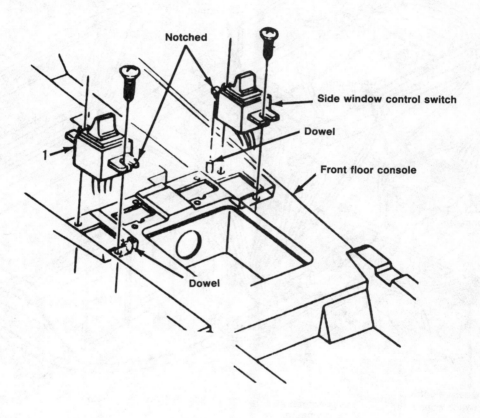

Notched

Side window control switch

Dowel

Front floor console

1

Dowel

12

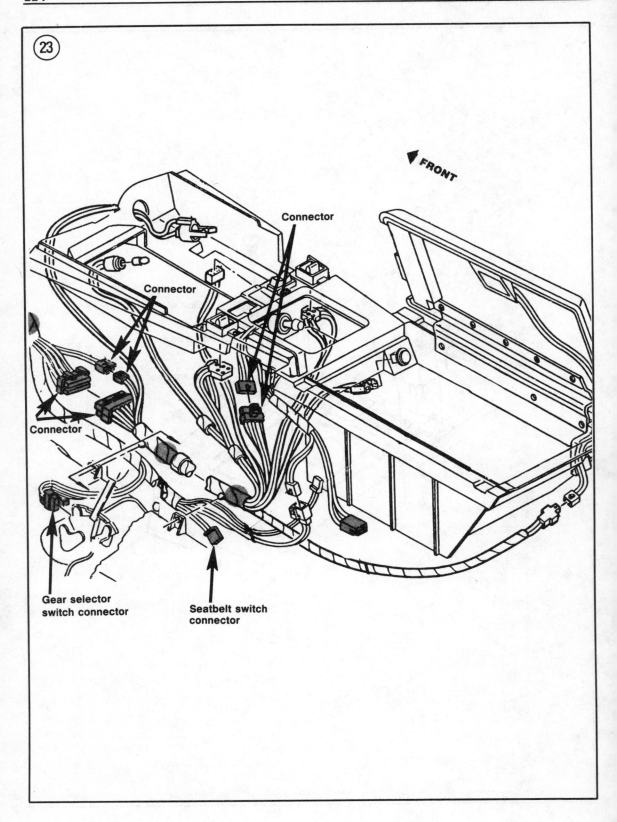

㉓

FRONT

Connector

Connector

Connector

Gear selector
switch connector

Seatbelt switch
connector

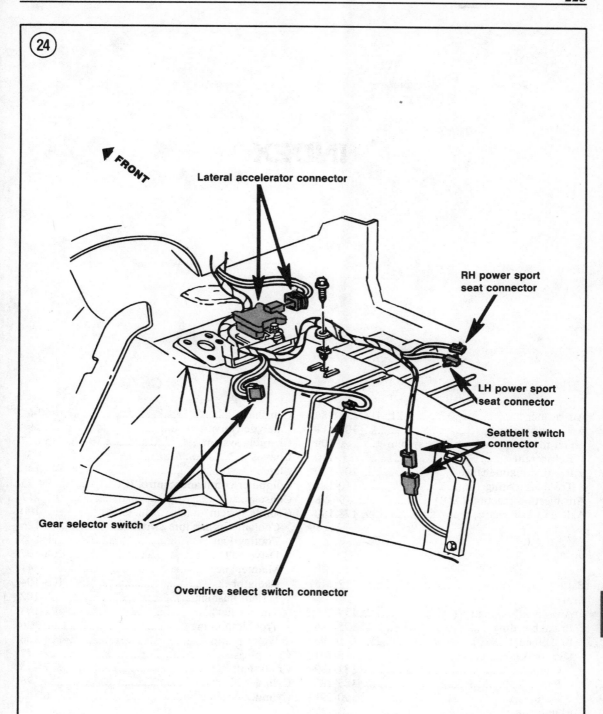

24

FRONT

Lateral accelerator connector

RH power sport
seat connector

LH power sport
seat connector

Seatbelt switch
connector

Gear selector switch

Overdrive select switch connector

12

INDEX

13

13

SKILL LEVEL AND TIME ESTIMATING GUIDE

The time estimates and skill level data that follow were prepared in conjunction with Mitchell Information Services, the leader in providing this material to professional mechanics, garages and fleet operators.

This section will tell you 2 vital things about 126 different jobs on the Chevrolet Corvette:

How long the job takes.

How complicated the job is.

1. How long the job takes: This is the same time figure used by dealers and independent shops to estimate labor charges. Times are shown in tenths of an hour (6-minute intervals). For example, a labor time of 0.3 is 3 tenths of an hour or 18 minutes.

These times are estimates which generally reflect the needs of an average trained auto mechanic using factory recommended tools and following factory recommended procedures. They include allowances for repair preparation, normal cleanup associated with repair, road testing, mechanic personal needs, preventive measures and any other service that would normally accompany an individual operation.

Times do not include allowances for diagnosis, machine operations or obtaining substitutes for factory recommended special tools.

Estimated labor time can be used in 2 ways:

a. If you decide to have a job done professionally, you can compare the time specified in this chart with the shop's labor estimate for the same work.

b. If you decide to do a job yourself, you can use the estimated time, together with the job's skill level, to estimate how long it will take you.

WARNING
Unless you are a professional mechanic with a fully equipped shop, you should expect a job to take you longer than the estimated time. Since the skills and equipment possessed by home mechanics vary widely, it is impossible to estimate how long a job should take a home mechanic. Use the estimated labor times as a rough guide only. Never hurry a job, trying to finish within the estimated time. You may damage the vehicle or injure yourself.

2. How complicated the job is: Each job is placed in one of 4 skill levels:

A. HIGHLY SKILLED—Requires the use of precision measuring tools and highly specialized measuring equipment. Also requires thorough knowledge of complicated systems and strong diagnostic ability. Some jobs in this category can be done by home mechanics. Often, money can be saved by removing and installing a part yourself and having a shop do only the part of a job which requires special training and equipment. The manual will tell which of these jobs can be done by home mechanics.

B. SKILLED—Requires the use of basic tools and simple measuring devices. Accurate diagnosis is required using special test equipment. Must have basic knowledge of complex systems. Many skilled jobs can be done by a beginner using the Clymer manual. Often it is faster and more economical to have the job done by a shop, and the manual will point out such instances.

C. SEMI-SKILLED—Diagnosis is limited to a single possible cause of a problem. Must have basic knowledge of component or system operation. Can be done by a beginner using the Clymer manual.

D. LOW SKILLED—Repair consists of part replacement only. Can be done by a beginner using the Clymer manual.

The letter indicating skill level follows each job description.

Model Identification

Vehicles in this list are identified by model year, model code and date of manufacture. To identify your vehicle's model year and model code, refer to the vehicle identification plate in the engine compartment. Date of manufacture is usually listed on a plate on the driver's doorjamb.

Abbreviations

Several abbreviations are used in this guide. They are:

a. R&R: Remove and replace. Includes removal of part or assembly from vehicle, transfer of attached parts to new part or assembly and installation of new part of assembly on vehicle. Includes any alignment necessary to reposition new part or assembly.

b. R&I: Remove and install. Includes removal of part of assembly from vehicle and installation of same part or assembly on vehicle. Includes any alignment necessary to reposition part or assembly.

14

SKILL LEVEL AND TIME ESTIMATING GUIDE

1. Accelerator cable R&R (C)
Labor time 0.6

2. Air conditioning belt replacement (D)
Labor time 0.7

3. Air filter element R&I (D)
Labor time 0.3

4. Air pump belt replacement (C)
Labor time 0.4

5. Alternator belt replacement (D)
Labor time 0.3

6. Alternator R&R (B)
Labor time 1.3

7. Automatic choke overhaul
Labor time 0.6

8. Automatic transmission O/H (A)
Includes: R&I transmission assembly, inspect and replace necessary differential parts and road test.
Labor time 7.3

9. Automatic transmission throttle linkage adjustment (C)
Labor time 0.3

10. Automatic transmission neutral safety switch R&R (C)
Labor time 0.5

11. Battery test (C)
Labor time 0.8

12. Battery R&R (C)
Includes: Test
Labor time 0.8

13. Brake booster R&R (C)
Does not include bleed system.
Labor time
Hydraulic (diesel) 0.8
Vacuum 0.7

14. Breaker point R&R (C)
Not applicable.

15. Camshaft R&R (B)
Includes: Replace lifters, adjust ignition timing and valves.
Labor time
1984 .... 8.3
1985 .... 9.6
1986-1987 .... 12.3

16. Carburetor O/H (B)
Not applicable.

17. Carburetor and/or gasket R&R (B)
Not applicable.

18. Charging system test (B)
Includes: Check battery, regulator and alternator output.
Labor time 0.6

19. Clutch plate or disc R&R (C)
Does not include resurface flywheel.
Labor time 3.6

ABBREVIATIONS
For full explanation of abbreviations, see the first page of this section.
Skill levels:
  A. Highly skilled
  B. Skilled
  C. Semi-skilled
  D. Low skilled
R&R: Remove and replace
R&I: Remove and install

20. Clutch pedal adjustment (C)
Labor time 0.5

21. Clutch bleeding (C)
Labor time 0.7

22. Clutch release bearing R&R (C)
Labor time 3.3

23. Clutch master cylinder R&R (C)
Includes: Bleed system.
Labor time 1.8

24. Clutch slave cylinder R&R (C)
Includes: Bleed system.
Labor time 0.8

25. Compression test (C)
Labor time 1.0

26. Connecting rod R&I (piston and rod assembly R&I) (A)
Includes: Remove carbon and cylinder ridge, replace rod bearings, adjust idle speed and timing.
Labor time
1984
  One
    Right side 9.0
    Left 8.2
  One each side 11.8
  All 16.6
1985-1987
  One
    Right side 10.5
    Left 9.3
  One each side 13.8
  All 18.3

27. Connecting rod bearing R&R (B)
Labor time
  One 2.2
  All 4.8
Additional time
  Where cruise control interferes, add: 0.2

27. Connecting rod bearing R&R (B) (cont.)
Additional time (cont.)
  Where electronic engine system interferes, add: 0.5

28. Cooling system flushing (D)
Labor time
  Flush 0.7
  Reverse flush 1.0
  Clean and flush [1] 2.0
(1) Includes: R&R hoses and thermostat.

29. Crankshaft R&R (A)
Includes: R&I engine, replace bearings and oil seals, adjust idle speed and ignition timing.
Labor time 12.6
Additional time
  Where cruise control interferes, add: 0.2
  Where electronic engine system interferes, add: 0.5
Combination times—Piston and rod assembly R&I
  Includes: R&I cylinder heads, remove carbon and cylinder ridge.
  One 3.4
  One each side 5.0
  Each additional 0.3

30. Crankshaft pulley R&R (C)
Labor time 0.8

31. Crankshaft rear seal R&R (B)
Includes: Pack and add only for upper rope seal. If necessary to replace upper rope seal, use crankshaft R&R.
Labor time
1984 .... 2.0
1985-1987
  Std trans 3.8
  Auto trans 3.0

32. Cylinder head R&I (A)
Labor time
1984
  Right side 9.8
  Left 10.2
  Both 14.4
1985
  Right side 11.3
  Left 10.2
  Both 15.4
1986-1987
  Right side 12.4
  Left 10.7
  Both 16.9

SKILL LEVEL AND TIME ESTIMATING GUIDE (continued)

32. Cylinder head R&I (A) (cont.)
Additional time
Where air cond. interferes,
  add: 0.5
Where air pump interferes,
  add: 0.5
Where cruise control inter-
  feres, add: 0.2
Where electronic engine system
  interferes, add: 0.5

33. Differential O/H (A)
Includes: R&I transaxle assembly, inspect and replace necessary differential parts and road
test.
  Labor time 7.3

34. Differential R&R (C)
  Labor time 3.8

35. Distributor cap R&R (C)
  Labor time 0.6

36. Distributor R&R (C)
Includes: Adjust ignition timing.
  Labor time 0.8

37. Drag link R&R (4WD)
Not applicable

38. Drive plate R&I
See Flywheel, Auto Trans

39. Drive shaft R&R (C)
  Labor time 1.5

40. Drive shaft center bearing R&R (C)
  Labor time 0.7

41. EGR valve (C)
  Labor time
  1984-1985 .... 2.3
  1986-1987 .... 2.6

42. Engine mount R&R (C)
  Labor time
  Right side 1.0
  Left 0.8

43. Engine oil and filter change (gasoline) (D)
  Labor time 0.3

44. Engine oil and filter change (diesel) (D)
Not applicable.

45. Engine O/H (A)
Includes: Replace rings, main
and rod bearings, crankshaft
and camshaft. Remove cylinder
ridge, hone cylinders, grind
valves and adjust idle speed
and timing.
Does not include rebore or pin
  fit align.
  Labor time 32.1

46. Engine R&I (A)
Includes: R&I only those components necessary for the
removal of the complete engine
assembly.

---

46. Engine R&I (A) (cont.)
Does not include transfer parts
or tune-up.
  Labor time 7.5

47. Engine short block R&R (A)
Consists of cylinder block
fitted with pistons, rings,
connecting rods, camshaft and
all bearings, timing chain or
belt (except O.H.C. engines)
and sprockets.
Includes: Grind valves, clean
and transfer cylinder head,
fuel and electrical assemblies,
engine mounts, manifolds,
valve covers, oil pan and pump,
timing cover, water pump,
clutch assembly and flywheel.
Adjust fuel mixture, idle
speed, timing and valves where
applicable.
  Labor time 19.8

48. Evaporative emission canister R&R (C)
  Labor time 0.3

49. Flywheel R&R (C)
  Labor time
  Std trans 3.6
  Auto trans 3.7

50. Float adjustment level (B)
Not applicable.

51. Fuel filter R&R (D)
  Labor time 0.5

52. Fuel pump R&R (B)
  Labor time 1.5

53. Front shock absorber R&R (C)
  Labor time
  1984-1985
  One side 0.5
  Both 0.8
  1986-1987
  One side 0.8
  Both 1.3

---

54. Front spring R&R (C)
Not available.

55. Front hub R&R (B)
  Labor time
  One side 0.8
  Both 1.2

56. Front wheel bearing R&R (C)
Includes: Replace inner and
outer bearings, cups, seals
and repack.
  Labor time
  One side 0.8
  Both 1.2

57. Front axle R&R (4WD)
Not applicable.

58. Free wheel hub O/H (4WD)
Not applicable.

59. Free wheel hub R&I
Not applicable.

60. Front brake pad R&R (C)
Includes: Repack front wheel
bearings on drum brakes only,
bleed system and adjust brakes
where necessary.
  Labor time
  One 0.8
  Both 1.6

61. Front brake caliper R&R (C)
Includes: Bleed system and re-
place pads if necessary.
  Labor time
  One side 0.9
  Both 1.5

62. Front caliper O/H (C)
  Labor time
  One side 1.7
  Both 2.9

63. Fuel pump test (B)
Includes: Check capacity.
  Labor time 0.5

64. Headlight replacement (D)
Does not include adjust head-
lamps.
  Labor time
  One side 0.3
  Both 0.5

65. Headlight switch R&R (B)
  Labor time
  1984 .... 0.5
  1985-1987 .... 0.9

66. Heater hose replacement (D)
  Labor time
  w/ air cond 0.7
  w/o air cond 0.6

67. Heater core R&R (A)
  Labor time
  w/ air cond 3.5
  w/o air cond ...... Not available.

14

SKILL LEVEL AND TIME ESTIMATING GUIDE (continued)

68. Horn R&R (D)
Note: Does not include diagnostic time.
Labor time
One 0.3
Two 0.5

69. Idle mixture adjustment
Not available.

70. Idle speed adjustment (B)
Labor time 0.3

71. Igniter R&R (pulse generator)
Not applicable.

72. Ignition coil R&R (C)
Includes: Test.
Labor time 0.7

73. Ignition switch R&R (B)
Labor time
1984 .... 0.7
1985-1987 .... 0.9

74. Ignition timing and adjustment (B)
Includes: Check and adjust dwell angle.
Labor time 0.5

75. Load sensing valve
Not applicable.

76. Lower ball joint R&R (B)
Does not include align.
Labor time
One side 1.1
Both 2.0

77. Lower suspension arm R&R (B)
Does not include alignment.
Labor time 0.9

78. Lower suspension arm shaft R&R (B)
Does not include alignment.
Labor time 1.0

79. Manifold R&I (B)
Labor time
Intake
1984-1986 .... 4.1
1987 .... Not available.
Exhaust
1984
Right side 2.7
Left 1.5
1985
Right side 3.8
Left 1.5
1986-1987
Right side 3.8
Left 1.4

80. Master cylinder R&R (C)
Labor time
1984-1985 .... 0.8
1986-1987 .... 1.1

81. Master cylinder O/H (B)
Includes: Bleed system.
Labor time
1984-1985 .... 2.0
1986-1987 .... 2.3

ABBREVIATIONS

For full explanation of abbreviations, see the first page of this section.
Skill levels:
A. Highly skilled
B. Skilled
C. Semi-skilled
D. Low skilled
R&R: Remove and replace
R&I: Remove and install

---

82. Oil pan R&I (C)
Labor time 1.5

83. Oil pump R&R (C)
Labor time 1.6

84. Power steering belt replacement (C)
Labor time 0.5

85. Piston and rod assembly R&I (each) (A)
Includes: Remove carbon and cylinder ridges, replace rod bearings, adjust idle and timing speed.
Labor time
1984
One
Right side 9.0
Left 8.2
One each side 11.8
All 18.3
Additional time
Where air conditioning interferes, add: 0.3
Where cruise control interferes, add: 0.2
Where electronic ignition interferes, add: 0.5
Where pwr strg interferes, add: 0.3

86. PCV valve R&R
Not available.

87. Pitman arm R&R (B)
Does not include alignment.
Labor time
1984 .... 0.7
1985-1987 .... 0.5

88. Power steering pump R&R (C)
Labor time 0.6

89. Power steering pump O/H (C)
Labor time 1.3

90. Radiator R&R (D)
Labor time
1984-1985 .... 1.3
1986-1987 .... 1.5
Additional time
w/ auto trans, add: 0.2
w/ fuel injection, add: 0.2

---

91. Radiator hose R&R (D)
Labor time 0.8

92. Rear axle housing R&R (A)
Not available.

93. Rear axle shaft R&R (C)
Includes: R&R bearing, oil seal and flange studs.
Labor time
One side 1.5
Both 2.3

94. Rear wheel bearing R&R (C)
Labor time
One side 0.9
Both 1.4

95. Rear brake drum R&R
Not available.

96. Rear brake shoe R&R (C)
Includes: Repack front wheel bearings on drum brakes only, bleed system and adjust brakes where necessary.
Labor time 0.8

97. Rear caliper R&R (C)
Includes: Bleed system and replace pads if necessary.
Labor time
One side 0.9
Both 1.3

98. Rear caliper O/H (B)
Labor time
1984-86
One side 1.4
Both 2.3

99. Regulator R&R (C)
Includes: Test.
Labor time 1.0

100. Ring job (A)
See job #85

101. Rocker arm assembly R&I (B)
Labor time
1984-1985
Right side 0.8
Left 1.0
Both 1.8
1986-1987
Right side 4.0
Left 1.0
Both 4.7

102. Shock absorber, rear R&R (D)
Not available

103. Spark plugs R&R (C)
Labor time 0.8

104. Spring R&R, rear
Labor time (leaf spring) 1.0

105. Stabilizer bar R&R (C)
Labor time
One side 0.6
Both 0.9

106. Starter R&R (D)
Labor time 1.1

107. Starter test (B)
Labor time 0.5

SKILL LEVEL AND TIME ESTIMATING GUIDE (continued)

108. Steering Damper R&R
Not available.

109. Steering gear R&R (B)
Includes: Rack and pinion gear.
Labor time 1.9

110. Steering knuckle R&R (B)
Not available.

111. Tension Strut R&R
Not applicable.

112. Thermostat R&R (D)
Labor time 0.8

113. Tie rod R&R (B)
Includes: Adjust toe-in only.
Note: Deduct 0.4 if alignment
is also performed.
Labor time
One side
Inner [1] 2.0
Outer 0.8
Inner and outer [1] 2.1
Both
Inner [1] 2.2
Outer 1.0
Inner and outer [1] 2.4
(1) Includes: R&I steering
gear assembly

114. Timing chain R&I (B)
Includes: R&I camshaft sprocket
and adjust timing.
Labor time 3.2

115. Toe-in adjustment (B)
Includes: Adjust to steering
gear high point and center
steering wheel.
Labor time 0.6

116. Torsion bar R&R
Not available.

ABBREVIATIONS
For full explanation of
abbreviations, see the first page of
this section.
Skill levels:
A. Highly skilled
B. Skilled
C. Semi-skilled
D. Low skilled
R&R: Remove and replace
R&I: Remove and install

---

117. Transfer case O/H
Not applicable.

118. Transfer case R&I
Not applicable.

119. Transmission mount R&R (C)
Labor time 0.6

120. Transmission (standard) O/H (A)
Includes: R&I transmission assembly, inspect and replace
necessary parts and road test.
Labor time 10.3

121. Tune-up (B)
Includes: Check compression,
clean or replace air cleaner,
spark plugs. Inspect and or
replace distributor cap and
rotor. Inspect ignition
cables. Adjust ignition timing
and idle speed.
Does not include distributor R&I.
Labor time 1.8
Additional time
Where air conditioning inter-
feres, add: 0.3

---

122. Universal joint R&R (C)
Labor time
One (inner or outer) 1.9
Both (one side) 2.3

123. Upper ball-joint R&R (C)
Does not include alignment.
Labor time
One side 0.8
Both 1.3

124. Upper suspension arm R&R (C)
Does not include alignment.
Labor time 1.0

125. Upper suspension armshaft R&R (C)
Labor time
Right side 1.6
Left 1.3

126. Valve job (A)
Includes: Remove carbon,
clean valve guides and
tune engine.
Labor time
1984
Right side 9.8
Left 10.2
Both 14.4
1985
Right side 11.3
Left 10.2
Both 15.4
1986
Right side 12.4
Left 10.7
Both 16.9

14

NOTES

NOTES

NOTES

NOTES

NOTES

NOTES

NOTES

NOTES